POACHERS WERE MY PREY

# POACHERS WERE MY PREY

## Eighteen Years as an Undercover Wildlife Officer

## R. T. STEWART

As told to W. H. "Chip" Gross

Black Squirrel Books™

KENT, OHIO

© 2012 by The Kent State University Press, Kent, Ohio 44242

All rights reserved
ISBN 978-1-60635-137-6
Manufactured in the United States of America

In certain cases, names of individuals have been changed for purposes of confidentiality.

🐿™ BLACK SQUIRREL BOOKS™
Frisky, industrious black squirrels are a familiar sight on the Kent State University
campus and the inspiration for Black Squirrel Books™, a trade imprint of The Kent State
University Press
www.KentStateUniversityPress.com

Cataloging information for this title is available at the Library of Congress.

16  15  14  13  12      5  4  3  2  1

For my two kids,

Clint and Bobbie Jo,

who I never saw enough of

during my undercover career.

# CONTENTS

# FOREWORD

*Kevin O'Dell, Supervisor (retired), Covert Wildlife Law Enforcement Unit, Division of Wildlife, Ohio Department of Natural Resources*

Why was R. T. Stewart such an exceptional undercover wildlife law enforcement officer? What made him so good at what he did? As R.T.'s supervisor for several years, I speak from experience when I say that he was a true chameleon, someone who could blend in with almost any group of people in any situation. He could "walk the walk and talk the talk" of a hard-core poacher, and throughout his long career, even if the bad guys suspected him of being someone other than he seemed, which several poachers did, none of them ever managed to break his cover or unveil his true identity as an officer.

Stewart had a talent for connecting and communicating with people. While he wasn't particularly gifted at putting words on paper—I know, as I had to read his many investigation reports—he was amazingly good at communicating face to face. If he could talk directly to someone, he could "read" that person instantly and charm him into a real liking for him in a matter of minutes. He often told me how poachers would tell him things about their lives they had rarely told anyone else, and would make these confidences just a few days after meeting him.

Stewart understood how people work. He realized early in his career that people liked to be praised. If he could convince people that he admired them—if he could put a person on a pedestal, at least in his or her mind—it stroked that person's ego. Stewart was often able to use this quirk of human nature to his advantage. He also learned never to compete with poachers. He always wanted them thinking they were better than he was at most everything, although that was seldom the case.

Stewart himself wondered, at times, why he was able to do the things he did so easily and proficiently. I believe his success was partly a result of his life experiences and partly a result of the natural gifts he was born with. Stewart grew up relatively poor and had a range of experiences before being hired by the Division of Wildlife. He worked in coal mines, took part in strikes, suffered through periods of unemployment, and witnessed the illegal use of drugs and alcohol. He also earned a college degree and taught college for several years. In short, before becoming a wildlife officer in Ohio at the age of thirty-five, he'd done it all and in the process had met and interacted with many different kinds of people. And all the while, either consciously or subconsciously, he was learning what made people tick, especially poachers. This meant he brought to the job a level of maturity lacking in many younger officers.

Stewart is also a man of common sense, something that seems in short supply these days. This he combined with his street sense and woods sense. He's also self-reliant. If something breaks, he can fix it or knows how to improvise if he can't, and that ability is a huge asset for an officer working far afield and often alone. But I believe the essential characteristic that made him successful was his work ethic: Stewart worked hard, and he worked long hours. Successfully completing an undercover wildlife law enforcement investigation often requires months and sometimes years, but this hard reality did not discourage Stewart. It was always about getting the job done. If he had to work twenty-four hours a day to finally get the bad guys behind bars, Stewart did it. Of course, the fact that R.T. is a serious night owl—he hates getting up early—no doubt helped too, as most really serious illegal activity takes place late at night, the time of day when R.T. was most alert.

Finally, Stewart and the Division of Wildlife in Ohio's Department of Natural Resources came together at just the right time. The two were a natural fit. Just when that state agency was ready to begin long-term undercover wildlife investigations, Stewart was ready to begin his undercover career. Ultimately, it was a marriage that many wildlife poachers wished had never happened.

I congratulate R. T. Stewart on his extensive and very successful career in undercover wildlife law enforcement, a career much longer than most undercover officers can sustain. It was a pleasure working with and supervising him, and although we had our differences at times, I'm honored to call him my friend.

I know you'll enjoy reading his book. I had a sneak peak at the manuscript, and it's all here and all true: the good and the bad of professional undercover wildlife law enforcement work. It's often said that the best poachers make the best game wardens. In other words, it takes one to catch one. I'm just glad Stewart was on our side . . .

# INTRODUCTION

*W. H. "Chip" Gross*

I first met R. T. Stewart in the late 1980s when we were both young wildlife officers working for the Ohio Department of Natural Resources (ODNR), Division of Wildlife. We would see each other occasionally at the district office or at meetings, but after a few years I eventually noticed that R.T. was not around as often as before. When I asked my law enforcement supervisor about him, I was told that Stewart was on "special assignment." I later learned that meant undercover wildlife law enforcement work, something the Division of Wildlife had only dabbled in up to that time. If the agency was getting serious about undercover work by placing its first undercover officer in the field full time, however, it couldn't have made a better choice than R. T. Stewart.

Few people in this world are as perfectly suited for the job they do on a day-to-day basis as Stewart was for work in undercover wildlife law enforcement. His temperament and his mental and physical skills were great advantages and, allied with his in-depth knowledge of hunting, fishing, and the ways of the out-of-doors, as well as of human nature, these qualities allowed Stewart to "walk the walk and talk the talk" of a wildlife poacher—a secretive role he played for eighteen years. It is said by those of us who know him best that he could definitely "live the lie."

Stewart and I continued to bump into each other occasionally throughout our careers with the Division of Wildlife, but as the years passed he looked less and less like the uniformed officer he once had been. His once-short brown hair was now shoulder length; he sometimes sported a partial or full beard; and instead of a crisp tan and green Division of Wildlife uniform, he wore tattered, stained blue jeans, usually a shirt with sleeves cut off raggedly at the shoulders, and always his signature white cowboy hat.

During those years he could tell me little about the cases he was investigating, and I understood. As uniformed officers, we were informed about undercover investigations only on a need-to-know basis. This policy was for the protection of the undercover officers, as you never knew who might let slip a careless word to the wrong person, which in turn might blow an officer's cover, getting him hurt or possibly killed. For that reason, the less said the better to everyone concerned.

We uniformed officers were also instructed that, should we ever inadvertently run across and recognize an undercover officer while in the field, we were not to acknowledge him in any way. We were simply to pretend we didn't know him, treat him as we would any other member of the public, then get away from him and the people he was with as quickly as possible.

Ironically, I almost helped blow Stewart's cover once myself, without realizing it until years later. You'll read about the incident in chapter 2. At the time, I was editor of the Division of Wildlife's quarterly magazine, *Wild Ohio,* and had written an article about undercover wildlife law enforcement officers. I had the okay from the Division's Law Enforcement Section to do the article, and the story did not name any of the undercover officers discussed. But R.T. was deep into an undercover investigation at the time—Operation Redbud—and the bad guys in the poaching ring he was infiltrating somehow got a copy of the magazine and read the story.

The poachers showed R.T. the article and kidded him about being an undercover officer. He was, thankfully, able to bluff his way out of the sticky situation, leaving the poachers none the wiser, but R.T. later told me that he would have wrung my neck had he been able to get his hands on me. Fortunately for me, I was working in a comfortable, air-conditioned office at the division's state headquarter in Columbus, Ohio, at the time. R.T., on the other hand, was living in a vermin-infested house trailer with the bad guys.

As R.T.'s undercover career progressed and he learned of my growing interest in writing, he one day sidled up to me at a meeting and said in his slow, southern-Ohio drawl, "Hey, someday when all of this is over, I'd like you to write my book . . . you okay with that?"

"Sure," I said. "I'd love to, R.T. When you thinkin' . . . ?"

"Don't know for sure," he said, "but when I decide to pull the pin, I'll be back in touch."

It was years later when R. T. Stewart finally decided to "pull the pin." He contacted me and simply said, "Well, I'm on my last undercover investigation. You can start shopping the book idea around." I did just that, and the result is what you now hold in your hands, *Poachers Were My Prey: Eighteen Years as an Undercover Wildlife Officer*. Both R.T. and I are grateful to Kent State University Press and its excellent editors and staff for publishing this book.

I consider it a privilege to present R.T.'s story, and I am honored that he chose me to write it. I regard him as a friend, and I have the greatest respect for him and the professional undercover work he did for nearly two decades. Since Stewart's story is a memoir recalled after the fact, detailing events many years in the past, its dialogue necessarily is not exact—being an approximate re-creation rather than an exact transcription of the conversations that occurred. Readers also should be aware that the names of most of the people discussed—fellow officers and bystanders as well as suspects—have been changed to preserve their privacy.

If I were a poacher, I would not want R.T. Stewart on my case. Like a blue-tick hound on the fresh scent of a raccoon on a damp night, Stewart was relentless in his pursuit of wildlife poachers. The following pages are an inside look into his life as an undercover wildlife officer—a window on a world few people even know exists. Come along with me now as we enter the dangerous, dark world of undercover wildlife law enforcement, as seen through the eyes of R. T. Stewart.

Come along and look over his shoulder as he "lives the lie."

# 1

# OPERATION CLANBAKE

"You ain't no damn game warden, are ya?" the poacher snarled.

I looked him straight in the eye and lied. "Game warden? I ain't no game warden!"

The poacher paused, mulling over my answer, then added quietly, "Then why you askin' so many questions?"

It was early in my eighteen-year career as an undercover wildlife law enforcement officer, and I was learning things every day—the hard way. One of those things was knowing when to push for information and when to sit back and listen. Obviously, I'd asked one question too many and too quickly for this particular poacher.

Poaching, the illegal taking of wildlife, goes on every day in the United States and throughout the world. Many millions of dollars change hands annually from the illegal sale or trade of antlers, hides, horns, meat, feathers, fur, teeth, claws, gallbladders, and other wild-animal parts. As a result, wildlife populations—including those of some endangered and threatened species—suffer, and legitimate, law-abiding sport hunters get a black eye.

My very first undercover investigation was Operation Clanbake—so named because one of the two groups of poachers targeted in the case called themselves "The Clan." Begun in the spring of 1992, it was intended to identify and arrest those responsible for the illegal killing and sale of white-tailed deer in southeast Ohio, as well as the illegal snagging and sale of walleyes from the Maumee River, a major Lake Erie tributary in Ohio. The impetus for the investigation was a series of complaints received the previous year about two families of known poachers living near Laurelville. These complaints spurred a discussion among

Division of Wildlife law enforcement supervisors, who decided to respond by trying an undercover investigation in the southeast section of the state.

When Operation Clanbake began, I was a uniformed wildlife officer working in central Ohio. However, two previous jobs gave me experience that helped prepare me for undercover work: before joining the Division of Wildlife, I had served as a natural resources instructor at Hocking College in Nelsonville, Ohio, while also working undercover, in my spare time, for the state Department of Liquor Control and the local county sheriff's office.

When I proposed working undercover to my supervisor, I learned that some Division of Wildlife officers in the northwest part of the state were already considering an undercover project: a confidential informant had contacted one of the officers, Don Carter, offering to provide information about a group of poachers living in Toledo, a large city located on the western shore of Lake Erie in northern Ohio. Such an idea was new, however. The Division of Wildlife had never before had a covert wildlife law enforcement unit, and had never conducted an in-depth undercover investigation. Everything we were considering was new and untried, and, as we would all eventually learn, this undercover project was definitely going to be on-the-job training.

The initial months of the operation took place in Hocking, Fairfield, and Ross counties in southern Ohio, and at the beginning, my cover was anything but watertight. I was issued a leased, unmarked pickup truck. However, a law enforcement check of its registration led back to the name of the truck's leasing company, not to me. In undercover work that's not good, and I'll explain why later. In addition, I had no covert identification—no driver's license issued under an alias, no false social security number, no fictitious documents at all, in fact—papers we soon learned I absolutely needed. To get me these false credentials, I suggested that my supervisors contact the Ohio Department of Liquor Control, the agency for which I'd previously worked undercover. I knew they had extensive experience equipping their covert officers with these credentials and would know what I needed. But all of that took time, so it wasn't until we were well into this investigation that my partner and I had proper false identification.

After reading the intelligence reports about the suspected poachers and being briefed by my supervisors, I headed for southeast Ohio. I was expecting a limited investigation into the illegal taking of white-tailed deer and wild turkeys. I had no idea how large the investigation would eventually become, nor that it would involve much more than just violations of wildlife law.

I took several days to scout the area, even driving by the suspected poachers' houses a few times. And in addition to scouting, I was also looking for a house or cabin to rent. I wanted to establish a base of operation close to the bad guys. I made my initial contact in the case by going to yard sales and just casually talking to people, asking about hunters in the area. Eventually, I found a yard sale being held by someone who knew the suspects we were targeting. I've never been accused of being shy, so once I learned the name of the guy holding the yard sale, I simply drove to the house of one of the main targets and knocked on the front door.

The suspect, Steve Sullivan, opened the door himself, and, using my alias, I introduced myself as Bob Thomas. I told Sullivan I was from the Columbus-Marysville area and was looking for a place to hunt, adding that his neighbor, the guy holding the yard sale, had suggested I talk to him.

Sullivan immediately began to relax. "Oh, yeah, I know him," he said.

That broke the ice. Soon we were deep in hunting talk, with Sullivan telling me about the many white-tailed deer in the area. Although Sullivan naturally did not mention anything about his poaching activities, it was a productive first meeting. We stood outside and talked for about an hour. Since I knew from intelligence reports that Sullivan liked beer, I had cans of beer on ice in a cooler in my truck. I offered him one, and he accepted it.

It was a warm spring afternoon, and to get out of the sun we sat just inside his open garage on folding lawn chairs, drinking beer and talking. At this very first meeting, Sullivan invited me to go hunting with him that fall. When I left, I told him I would stop back sometime later that spring. Getting into my truck, I also told him I was looking for a hunting camp to rent in the area. Could he let me know if he heard of anything available? He said he would.

Even that first day, we hinted to each other about poaching, although neither of us came right out and said we would kill wildlife illegally. Nevertheless, the implication was clear. As I was leaving I remember saying something like, "Well, if all else fails, I've got my tree stand sitting out there. . . ." Grinning, I pointed to my truck. Sullivan got the point immediately and nodded in agreement. "Yeah," he said, "that's the only way we hunt, too," meaning by vehicle and from the road.

Sullivan's agreement partially showed his hand, although fuller exposure would come only later in the investigation. He also mentioned the names of some of the people who hunted with him, and since I already knew those names from the intelligence reports, his comments confirmed that I was on the right track. Again, it had been a very good first contact.

In the days that followed, I began searching more seriously for a hunting camp to rent. The Sullivan family lived on Stump Run Road. Eventually I found a vacant house trailer on Long Run Road, about two miles away. To say the trailer was a dump is an understatement. It had electricity, but that was about it. It lacked running water and an indoor toilet, and it was overrun with field mice, wasps' nests, and cockroaches. There were even a few snake skins inside, where snakes had crawled into the trailer and shed their papery skins before slithering back out. Most of the windows had cracked or broken glass, and a few stood completely open, the glass having been smashed by vandals.

Despite the trailer's deplorable condition, its location was right, so I did some digging and found the owner, whom I'll call George Karns. He lived about a hundred miles away in Columbus, Ohio, just across the street, ironically, from the state headquarters of the Ohio Department of Natural Resources, Division of Wildlife. My straightforward approach had worked for my initial meeting with Steve Sullivan, so I decided to try it again with Karns. I drove to Columbus and knocked on his door, and when he answered I told him I was a hunter looking for a camp to rent in southeast Ohio and had seen his trailer. Would he be interested in renting it to me?

"If you clean it up, you can use it for free," Karns said. I guess he was just pleased that someone would be on the property from time to time, keeping an eye on the place. The price was definitely right for our undercover investigation because, basically, we had no budget. This initial project was all being done on a very thin shoestring.

Over the following weeks, I spent a few days cleaning up the trailer, enough to make it minimally livable. While in the area, I stayed in contact with Sullivan, dropping by his house to let him know I had a hunting camp close by. He was pleased to hear that, and we drank a few beers to celebrate.

I furnished the trailer by buying used furniture for a few bucks at yard sales. I also bought what eventually came to be known as the infamous "John Deere" fan. It was so named because one of the fins was bent just enough that every time the fan rotated it would contact the fan guard and make a clicking sound. At high speed, this sounded just like a John Deere tractor motor. Since the trailer had no running water, I kept the bathroom door closed. When at night I would hear mice or other critters scurrying around in the bathroom or under the trailer, I'd turn on the John Deere fan to drown out the sounds so I could sleep. That's how rough this place was.

As I laid the groundwork for the investigation, my supervisors were working to obtain a different pickup truck for me to drive, one that would be registered to me under my alias rather than to the leasing company I mentioned earlier. When I got a call to report to the district office, I thought I was meeting my supervisors to update them on the progress of the investigation and to pick up my new truck. But when I walked into the office there sat two wildlife officers from northwestern Ohio, Terry Sunderhaus, the district law supervisor, and Officer Don Carter.

Through conversations with his fellow supervisors, Sunderhaus had heard that I'd rented a house trailer in southeastern Ohio. This was a stroke of luck, since Officer Carter had learned, from an informant in northwestern Ohio, whom I'll call Larry Cotts, that the poachers from Toledo hunted in the same general area I was investigating. It was a lengthy, enlightening meeting, and after several hours all the officers and supervisors agreed that we should combine the two undercover projects into one. We would try to take down both groups of poachers—the group from Toledo and the group from Laurelville—at the same time. We would kill two birds with one stone. Thus Operation Clanbake was born.

To accomplish this double objective, my first task was to introduce the two groups of poachers and get them together. As a green, untested undercover officer, I found that a tall order, but at least I now had a partner; my supervisors informed me that Officer Don Carter and I would be working together on the case. I was very pleased. I liked Don, and joining forces would make our work safer; we could watch one another's back. I'd also learned, during my short time undercover, that covert law enforcement work can be very lonely at times. It would be nice to have Don to bounce ideas off. In addition, he was older than I, and I was happy to be able to draw on his experience. His maturity and years of expertise as a wildlife officer would be assets in resolving this case.

Don informed me that the poachers living near Toledo were involved not only in deer poaching—supposedly illegally killing more than one hundred deer annually—but also in the sale of walleyes, a fish highly prized by sport anglers on Lake Erie. The poachers were illegally snagging large female walleyes with eggs as they swam up the Maumee River in the spring of the year to spawn. Both snagging the walleyes and selling them are wildlife law violations in Ohio. Don said his informant, Cotts, had given him information about the group of poachers on more than one occasion.

This being my first undercover investigation, I was leery about working with an informant because I realized that one false move by such an informant could get me, Don, or both of us hurt or killed. In law enforcement work, there are two types of informants. A *witting* or *knowing informant* is someone who knows who the bad guys are as well as the identity of the good guys—that is, the undercover officers. This situation is dangerous for an undercover officer because you don't know the informant's motive. At any time, he or she could turn on you, revealing your true identity to the poachers. An *unwitting informant* is someone who gives a third person information about the bad guys but does not know who the undercover officer is, or even that one exists.

Since it is much safer, I prefer to work with the latter kind of informant, and later in my career I did just that. During this first investigation, though, I had little choice; Don and I both worked Don's knowing informant, Cotts. I discussed my apprehensions with Don but told him it was ultimately his call. If he had confidence in Cotts, I'd go along with his decision. But before he introduced me to the guy, we had another conversation, tinged with a bit of gallows humor. If Cotts should rat on us and we survived it, I asked, who would get to shoot him? It was a joke, but serious too: it was starting to dawn on me just how dangerous a situation we were getting ourselves into.

As an undercover officer you are constantly acting, constantly pretending to be someone you're not. Acting tough is part of this; you probably won't follow through on your threats to people, but an informant has to believe you will.

When Don first introduced me to Cotts, therefore, he had already told the informant that I was close to crazy, and warned him that I would kill Cotts if things went bad. We met the informant at a restaurant in Circleville, Ohio, and I did my best to look the part of a half-crazed undercover officer/poacher. I'd let my hair grow to shoulder length and was wearing a full beard. This seedy appearance, together with the fact that I was six feet two inches tall and weighed about two hundred pounds at the time, helped me get into the role. I talked somewhat politely to Cotts while we were inside the restaurant, eating, but when we went out to the parking lot, I immediately got in his face.

I backed him up against the side of his car and said with a scowl, "Now that you know who I am, you need to know something. I don't like you. And I am going to tell you something else, right up front. If you get me or my partner hurt during this investigation, you ain't gonna live to tell about it . . . 'cause I'll kill ya. You understand that?"

Cotts's eyes opened wide, and he nodded quickly several times. Don and I had planned this confrontation to scare the guy as best we could. We weren't serious, but we had to make Cotts believe we were. For our safety, our informant needed to be convinced that I actually would kill him if anything he did caused the operation to go wrong.

In retrospect, Larry Cotts was one of the best informants I ever worked with during my nearly two decades undercover. He had involved himself out of a desire for revenge: one of the poachers had made advances toward his girlfriend, and he was looking for a way to pay him back. I learned through the years that many informants are motivated by revenge.

Cotts played his role with the poachers to the hilt—so well, in fact, that eventually we had to work him out of the investigation so that we could deal directly with the poachers themselves rather than through him. We also eased Cotts out so he would not have to testify in court following the investigation. We were trying to protect his identity from the poachers; once they were arrested, they would try to figure out who had ratted on them, and if they succeeded, the informant's life could very well be in danger.

One benefit of a good informant is that he or she can cut in half the time it takes an officer to conduct an undercover investigation, simply by getting you inside the group of bad guys much sooner than you could on your own. Moreover, since time is money, this decreases the cost of an undercover investigation as well. I estimate that the confidential informant in this case eliminated at least six months of legwork for us.

Ohio's spring hunting season for wild turkey opened in late April that year, and Cotts told the group of Toledo poachers that he had two buddies (Don and me) who had rented a hunting camp in southern Ohio. The bad guys wanted to come see the "camp"—our trailer—and we wanted to buy some illegal walleyes from them, so we had Cotts, our informant, tell the poachers to bring walleyes with them when they came to hunt.

The first of the Clanbake group that we met through Larry Cotts was Doug Andrews, the ringleader of the Toledo poachers. Andrews was an intimidating character, unstable and violent. Of all the poachers I have known over the years, Andrews was the only one I really feared. We later learned he had shot and killed a man just a few months before we met him, and when Andrews told us the story of the killing, he seemed completely unfazed at having taken a human life.

Andrews was also boastful about his poaching. At our very first meeting, we bought seventy-seven pounds of walleye fillets from him, and he bragged about consistently overbagging walleyes—that is, taking more than the daily limit of fish allowed by law. After talking and drinking beer for a few hours, we drove with Andrews to Sullivan's house, where we introduced the two poachers. They hit it off right away and soon, without any prodding from us, were talking openly with each other about their illegal hunting and fishing activities.

Their boasting was great news for Don and me, for it meant that they were "predisposing" themselves. In legal terms, *predisposition* is when a suspect does or says something that leads an undercover officer to determine that he or she has broken the law before the officer ever becomes involved with the suspect. A person with a past wildlife law violation or other criminal history, or who has been the subject of previous complaints of such crimes, has predisposed himself. The suspect's own testimony or an eyewitness account of illegal acts also counts as predisposition. Finally, if a wildlife officer witnesses "fruits of a crime," even if he or she has not directly witnessed the crime itself, the suspect is deemed to have predisposed himself. In the case of poaching, such fruits of the crime can include dead animals, or pieces or parts of dead animals, such as meat, antlers, or feathers. Such a determination denies to the suspect the defense of entrapment. Legally, the term *entrapment* refers to actions by the undercover officer. In claiming entrapment, a suspect asserts that the undercover officer has placed the thought of illegal action into his or her mind, a thought the suspect might never have had on his own.

By exchanging tales of their poaching exploits with no coaching or hints from us, Andrews and Sullivan had predisposed themselves. Don and I just sat back and listened, trying to remember the details of their conversation long enough to be able to write it all down for our eventual court testimony. Moreover, since the poachers had raised the subject themselves, the defense of entrapment had been taken off the table and Don and I were now free to join in the talk about poaching. Up until that time, we'd had to be careful about what we said concerning poaching, but now the suspects were themselves fair game.

The two poachers, Andrews and Sullivan, took such a liking to one another during that first meeting that we all went out after dark that night and illegally shot three deer together. Driving the rural roads and playing the light of a flashlight from the window over the woods and fields on either side, we looked for deer. Once we spotted one, we shot it in the head or neck from the vehicle with a .22 magnum caliber rifle equipped with a telescopic sight.

That night was my first up-close encounter with men who appeared to have no conscience about killing wildlife illegally, and it shocked me. Two aspects of the expedition especially bothered me. First, all three of the deer we killed were does (females) carrying unborn fawns. White-tailed deer in good habitat normally give birth to twins each spring, sometimes even to triplets or quadruplets. It bothered me that we killed not only does, but pregnant does with unborn young in their wombs. Second, when one of the three deer we shot did not die immediately, a poacher jumped out of the truck and beat it in the head with a tire iron to kill it. I could hear the doe bawling in the road ditch as he continued beating her until she died.

The casual cruelty of Andrews and Sullivan sickened me. I realized they were hardcore poachers who didn't care at all. To them, each deer was just another carcass with a dollar sign on its head. I wanted to see them arrested and convicted in the worst way. I vowed to myself that I would do whatever it took to eventually put these guys behind bars. And I was willing to place my life on the line to make it happen.

After that night, however, we didn't see much of the Toledo group for a time. We went wild turkey hunting a few times that spring with the southern Ohio group of poachers, but since the Toledo poachers did not hunt turkeys, they didn't return to the trailer that spring. Over the summer, though, that changed. Sometimes both groups of poachers would gather at the trailer to hang out. These occasions allowed Don and me to continue building a rapport with both groups of poachers and to encourage them to get to know one another. Since these get-togethers required us to stay at the trailer three or four days per week, we worked to clean it up and mow the yard from time to time. We even planted a vegetable garden, hoping to make it look like we were planning to stay in the area for a while.

At one of our weekend cookouts with the bad guys, we learned from Steve Sullivan that two deputies from the local county sheriff's office were giving him road-kill deer slips in exchange for pickup-truckloads of firewood. A road-kill slip is a document issued in Ohio by law enforcement officers to a motorist who accidentally hits and kills a deer with a vehicle. The slip proves to any inquiring law enforcement officer or deer processor that the motorist has acquired the deer legally. Sullivan and his relatives were using the road-kill slips to cover the deer they had poached—and the deputies knew it.

Operation Clanbake was conducted before cell phones were in widespread use, so if Don or I wanted to make a telephone call to our supervisors or call our wives at home, we had to drive to the nearby town of South Perry and use a pay phone, located outside a small grocery store. Since we had no running water at the trailer, the grocery was also where we filled up plastic milk jugs with our drinking water.

During the summer, we bought more illegal walleyes from the Toledo poachers when they came to visit. At the invitation of the Sullivan family, members of the Johnson family also started attending our summer cookouts. One weekend, even George Karns, the owner of our trailer, showed up. We soon discovered he used illegal drugs. He particularly favored marijuana, often lighting up a marijuana cigarette that he would pass around the group, but there was also evidence that he may have been involved with other drugs. There always seemed to be a lot of five-gallon propane tanks sitting around the outside of the trailer. At the time, neither Don nor I had any idea as to what so much propane could be used for, but I later learned propane is often used in the manufacture of methamphetamines. Karns may not actually have been making meth—we never found out for sure whether he was or wasn't—but it was possible. All we knew was that whenever he came to visit, he always left a propane tank or two behind. He occasionally used the empty tanks for target practice, as he liked to see them explode when he shot them.

Often during an undercover investigation, unexpected events can blow an officer's cover, potentially getting him injured or killed. One such incident happened later that summer at a biker bar we frequented with the poachers in a small town near the trailer. The bar was a rough place, but it had a large kitchen, and we talked the owners into allowing us the use of it to fry up some of the walleye fillets we'd bought from Andrews. One day, Don and I were in the kitchen cooking walleye and everyone in the bar was eating the fish, drinking, and enjoying themselves.

Unbeknownst to us, an employee of the Ohio Division of Wildlife just happened to drop by the bar that evening for a drink. Since Don and I were in the kitchen frying fish, we never saw him and he never saw us. As far as we know, he never knew we were even there. But the next day, the employee went back to Division of Wildlife headquarters and told Dick Scott, head of the wildlife law enforcement section, about this walleye fry at the bar, commenting that so much fish was being handed out for free that the place should be investigated. The visit by the wildlife division employee was coincidental, but it was a close call for Don and me. I've often wondered what might have happened had the employee seen and recognized us. Thankfully, that never happened.

By early fall, we'd established a solid rapport with both the Sullivans and the Johnsons, the two main southern Ohio families targeted by our investigation. Our relationship with them was so good, in fact, that in October we got a visit from two of the younger members of the families. They turned up at the trailer after dark one evening and said, "Come on, let's go huntin' tonight. It's time to start killing some deer." So Don and I jumped in our truck and drove off with them. We "shined" (spotted with flashlights) and shot a couple deer that night. As we drove, we learned that Billy Sullivan already had a couple of illegal deer hanging in an outbuilding on his property. We offered to buy the deer from him, and he agreed. The purchase price for those animals was anywhere from twenty to eighty dollars per deer, depending on its size; generally during this investigation, we paid between forty and sixty dollars each for the illegal deer we bought from these poachers.

That night, we made the mistake of shooting a deer too close to a local farmhouse. The farmer recognized our vehicle, and the next day, he stopped by our trailer and chewed us out for poaching, threatening to call the local game warden if we didn't stop. We didn't take his threats seriously and just kind of blew him off. But the incident worked in our favor in one way, by showing that we were becoming known as poachers in the community. Along with our associating with the Sullivans and Johnsons, this helped build our cover.

A few days later Doug Andrews called from Toledo, saying he wanted to come to the trailer and shoot more deer. The routine previously followed by his group of poachers was to drive all the way from Toledo to southern Ohio, about a three-hour trip, shoot deer all night, and then drive straight back to Toledo, where they'd process the deer and sell the meat. Now that we had our trailer camp, though, Andrews and his group could stay overnight and avoid making the long round trip in a single day. This pleased the Toledo poachers immensely, and they saw it as a bonus that they were staying with two other poachers just like them.

Members of the Toledo group would drive to the trailer and stay with us for a day or two; we'd shoot deer each night; and then they'd drive home, taking the venison with them back to Toledo. Our trailer became a sort of staging area for the poaching, a place where we would not only eat and sleep but also clean and process the illegal deer, often canning the venison for the trip to Toledo. The group even had buyers placing special requests for illegal game that the poachers would fill to order.

Once Andrews came to the trailer when I was there by myself; for some reason Don Carter was not available for a few days. When we went poaching that night, something happened that changed my entire way of thinking about how I conducted undercover work.

Following our usual shine-and-shoot method, we shot a deer from Andrews's Chevy Blazer. Usually, if the deer didn't fall immediately upon being shot, we just kept driving. We wouldn't even bother to come back later to look for the deer. We would generally shoot does instead of bucks, since they were easier to kill. A buck we shot with our .22 magnum rarely fell immediately. Most bucks were just too big and strong for such a small bullet, unless you made a perfect head shot.

This particular night, Andrews was driving and I was sitting in the front passenger seat of the vehicle, holding the rifle. Andrews had the flashlight, shining its beam from the driver's side window into the woods and fields as we drove past. He eventually spotted a deer, stopped the vehicle, and took the gun from me, pointing it out the window. Andrews was just about to pull the trigger when we saw vehicle lights approaching from behind. They appeared to be flashing lights, meaning law enforcement.

We took off fast, and Andrews threw the flashlight out of the driver's side window. Handing me the rifle, he yelled, "Throw it out! Throw it out!" I launched the gun out the passenger window into the darkness, and when it hit the ground, it went off with a boom, a bullet zinging off in who knows what direction. As I heard the gun go off, I could already read the newspaper headline in my mind: Game Warden Killed in Undercover Investigation, Shot by Own Gun.

The vehicle behind was coming up on us fast, so Andrews tromped the accelerator and we began flying down the road, going around curves so fast my butthole was puckering. I'm thinking, "This is ridiculous! This vehicle is going to crash and we're both going to be killed, and all because of a stupid deer!"

We eventually outran the other vehicle, and to this day, I don't know who was chasing us. It could have been a law enforcement officer or just a local landowner. I was badly shaken by the incident, to say the least, but I didn't want to show it. Eventually, we circled back and collected the flashlight and rifle we had tossed. Andrews had yelled, "Mark it!" when he'd handed me the gun to throw out the window. I had marked the spot in my mind, and we returned there and cast about, looking for it. It had hit a dirt bank beside the road, gone off, and bounced back, and we found the gun lying beside the blacktop, so close to the side of the road that anyone driving by could have easily spotted it.

I was so shaken by the incident that all I wanted to do was go back to the trailer and call it a night, but not Andrews: he wanted to continue poaching, so we did, killing three more deer that night. Andrews was a hardcore poacher. That high-speed chase had scared me shitless, but it hadn't fazed him in the least.

The car chase was a real wake-up call. We got back to the trailer early the next morning, but when I finally fell into bed, I couldn't sleep. All I could think of was that car chase. I could have been severely injured, if not killed. The part that scared me the most was knowing that my life had been in Andrews's hands—he was in control, not me. I realized then and there that I had to change my game and work smarter if I was going to survive as an undercover wildlife officer.

The primary lesson I learned from that incident was that, in the future, I should get and retain as much control as possible when working with poachers. From then on, I always drove when we went shooting deer at night. That way, I could control how fast the vehicle was going and, for the most part, where we went. However, the car chase also had another effect. It caused me to doubt myself. Did I really have what it took to work undercover?

———

The woods of southern Ohio were glowing with their brilliant fall colors, but although Doug Andrews had told us a lot about the other members of the Toledo poaching ring—Ron Kendrick and the Hymore brothers (Rick and Gary)—Don and I had still not met them. Within a few weeks, however, Cotts, our informant, brought Kendrick to the trailer for his first meeting with us. He sold us some walleyes, then said he wanted to go shoot some deer. So that night we went out and shot deer, only this time I drove. Kendrick and Cotts stayed with us a few days, then returned to Toledo.

I hadn't been home—my real home—in about four days, and I was tired. Also, since the trailer lacked running water, I'd not had a shower during that time either. I not only looked bad, I smelled pretty bad, too. I was wearing a camouflaged hunting shirt with the sleeves cut off, a pair of ragged camo pants, and old, scuffed, blood-stained boots. I looked and smelled like a real "varmint." When Kendrick and Cotts finally left, I decided to drive home and take a break from the investigation for a few days. At the time I lived in Plain City, Ohio, about a two-hour drive northwest from the rented trailer.

I took a different route home each time I went, just to make sure none of the bad guys could pattern my movements should they follow. The beater pickup truck I was driving while undercover had a dented, mismatched cap covering the truck bed, and I had spray-painted the words "farm use" on both doors of the truck. At the time, many people in southern Ohio did that with their old farm trucks to save money on their annual vehicle registration. Soon I was driving through the town of Hilliard, a suburb of Columbus, a town that doesn't see too many vehicles marked "farm use." Unfortunately, with my mind on the investigation, I wasn't paying much attention to my driving. As a police car pulled in behind me and turned on its flashing lights, I realized I was driving ten miles per hour over the speed limit in a school zone. "Oh, shit," I thought, "this is not good."

There was no place to stop, so I continued down the road about a hundred yards before finding a place to safely pull over. A female officer exited the police car, walked up to the driver's door of my truck, and told me I should have stopped immediately, as soon as she turned on her flashing lights.

"But there was no place to pull off . . . ," I tried to explain, but she was not having any of it. She then told me she stopped me because I was doing thirty miles per hour in a twenty-mile-per-hour school zone, and asked to see my driver's license. I knew my driver's license was in my alias name, Bob Thomas, but I also knew that if she ran the truck registration, it would come back to her as not in file.

"Is the truck yours?" she asked me.

"Yes."

"Well, if the truck is yours, Mr. Thomas," she said, "the license number comes back as not in file."

"Well, you see, Ma'am, I just bought the truck a few days ago," I lied, stalling for time. "Maybe the registration isn't in the system yet."

She then asked to see the truck's registration. I knew it wasn't in the glove box, but I told her I thought it was—trying to bullshit her—and started to reach for the glove box. "Don't move!" she said, and I froze.

"Mr. Thomas, do you have any guns in your truck?" Her right hand was now on the grip of her sidearm. She probably knew that I did have at least one gun with me, as I had several rounds of loose ammunition lying around inside the cab. I did that on purpose to make my truck look as much like a poaching wagon as possible. My mind was racing now, trying to think of what to say, whether or not I should tell her the truth about who I was. Finally I admitted, "Yeah, I got a gun."

"Put your hands on the steering wheel, Mr. Thomas," she said sternly, "and don't move." I did so, and she asked, "Is your gun loaded?"

"Yep," I replied.

The officer reached for the radio microphone on her shoulder, called for backup, and within seconds I could hear sirens coming from two different directions. Within a few minutes a second city cop car pulled up, followed by a sheriff's cruiser. The three officers pulled me out of the truck's cab—none too gently, I might add—and spread-eagled me over the hood. All traffic on the street was now stopped, the drivers gawking at the hillbilly being patted down by the local gendarmes.

The officers searched me and then the deputy sheriff, a male officer, said, "I hear you have a loaded gun in your truck, Mr. Thomas."

"Yeah," I said. "It's under the seat."

He asked what kind of gun, and I told him it was a .45 caliber handgun.

"Is that the only one you have?"

"No, I got a .380 pistol in my duffel bag."

"Is it loaded?" the deputy asked.

"Yeah, it's loaded."

"Is that all the guns you have, Mr. Thomas?"

"Nope, there's also a shotgun behind the seat."

"Is it loaded?"

"No, but the .22 magnum rifle is. . . ."

All told, I had four guns in my truck, two handguns and two long guns. I also had a pair of hawk talons hanging from the rearview mirror with some pheasant feathers attached to them. It is illegal in Ohio, as in most states, to possess parts of nongame birds.

"Are those hawk talons, Mr. Thomas?" the deputy asked, pointing toward the rearview mirror.

"Nah, they're pheasant feet. Can't you tell by the pheasant feathers?" The officer looked doubtful but said no more about it.

The three officers then handcuffed me and put me in the back seat of one of the police cars. They then began searching the cab of my truck, certain they were going to find illegal drugs. By the appearance of my truck and the way I was dressed, I no doubt perfectly fit the profile of a "druggie."

Sitting in the back of the cruiser, I could hear radio traffic coming over the police radio. The officers had run the Vehicle Identification Number (VIN) number of my truck, and I heard the dispatcher's voice saying the truck belonged to the Ohio Department of Natural Resources. That was bad, but it would have been catastrophic had one of the poachers been sitting in the cruiser with me and heard it. The woman officer then radioed her supervisor, telling him the situation and asking what she should do. He told her to impound the truck, arrest me, and bring me in.

Up to that point, I was still playing the good ol' boy, but now I was starting to think that I might have to tell these officers who I really was to get myself out of this jam. Within minutes, the female officer's police supervisor showed up, leaned into the cruiser window and asked, "Anything you want to tell us, Mr. Thomas?" He probably hoped I would confess to stealing the truck. Instead, I gave him a shock when I said, "I'm an undercover officer for the Ohio Division of Wildlife . . . and I'm on my way home."

Looking doubtful, he asked me if I had any identification that would corroborate my story. I told him I didn't. "Then do you have anyone we can call to verify what you're saying?" he asked. I gave him my supervisor's phone number, and the officer made the call. I then saw him talking to the other officers. After a few minutes, the woman officer returned to the cruiser, opened the back door, took off my handcuffs, and handed me back my driver's license.

"You need to contact your supervisor as soon as possible, Mr. Thomas," she said disgustedly. "If that's your real name. Have a nice day." And that was that.

The encounter ended on a humorous note, though. As the deputy sheriff was leaving—the officer who had noticed the hawk talons—he leaned out the window of his cruiser and asked, "Hey, Thomas, I gotta know . . . are those really pheasant feet hanging from your mirror?"

"Nah," I said. "They're really hawk talons. You were right."

"I knew it!" he said, laughing. He slapped the side of his car and drove away.

An interesting sidelight to the incident is that the three officers were so focused on finding illegal drugs in the cab of my truck that they never discovered the three illegal dead deer I had hidden under a tarp in the bed of the truck.

When I got home, I was so filthy that my wife would not let me into the house with my clothes on. She made me strip on the back porch, then head directly to the shower. I had told her that the trailer I was occupying had cockroaches, and she was taking no chances that any of those critters might hitch a ride home in my clothing or other gear.

———

Throughout the fall, both Andrews and Kendrick came to the trailer from time to time, and we continued poaching deer. We always hunted at night, never during the day, and we approached our illegal hunting much like a job, keeping to a schedule. We'd go to bed about 7:00 P.M., then get up about 2:00 A.M. and go shoot deer until dawn. When we began seeing vehicles on the road in the early morning, people driving to work, we'd quit for the night and head back to the trailer.

To try to minimize the number of deer we were killing, Don and I would often make intentional mistakes when poaching with the bad guys. When we first saw a deer, for example, we might make too much noise inside the vehicle as we approached, or I'd stop the vehicle too close, attempting to make the deer run. Sometimes we'd shine the flashlight into the scope of the rifle so the guy holding the gun would be temporarily blinded and unable to see the deer.

This inept behavior generally irritated the poachers, making them think we didn't know what we were doing. However, that was a good thing, since a poacher who thinks he is better at this poaching game than you are will be less likely to suspect you of being an undercover officer. You just don't want to make your subtle sabotage and bumbling seem too obvious.

At this point in the case, it was not uncommon for Andrews and Kendrick to stay at the trailer with Don and me for three or four days in a row, killing deer every night. They were clever in their hunting tactics. They never knowingly drove down a dead-end road to shoot deer, fearing they might be trapped by another vehicle pulling in behind them and blocking their escape route. Also, they often cruised the main highways for deer, even four-lane highways, a smart strategy both because most law enforcement officers didn't expect poaching on main highways and because it yielded easy shots. Surprisingly, we shot many deer on such highways. Often, the deer would be standing right in the median, presenting an easy shot, since you didn't need a light to see them.

Most poachers choose little-used back roads to do their dirty deeds, but not these guys; they knew what they were doing. They knew our uniformed officers' mode of operation, and were not stupid or careless about what they did or where they did it. They avoided the areas where wildlife officers typically sit and watch for poaching. Occasionally they even got so bold as to shoot deer standing in people's rural front yards. They got away with it for two reasons. First, they didn't have to use a flashlight to see the deer; the deer were illuminated by the outdoor security lights most people had shining from dusk to dawn. Second, they only took such shots in the wee hours of the morning. By the time a householder heard the shot and woke up enough to get to a window to see what was going on, we were already gone, usually within a minute or less.

———

We were now eight months into Operation Clanbake, and things seemed to be moving along well. We were poaching deer regularly and buying deer carcasses from both sets of poachers, and the two groups were getting to know one another and interacting well. One night we shot a deer near Tar Hollow State Park. I specifically remember the incident, because the deer, illuminated by a security light, was eating an apple beneath an apple tree in the front yard of a house. We shot the deer, it fell, and two of us ran into the yard and dragged it back to the truck. As we sped away after shooting this particular deer, I heard the deer begin kicking in the back of the van. Apparently it wasn't yet dead, as we'd thought. Don Carter, who was in the back of the van with the deer, yelled, "This deer is coming back alive!" The commotion grew, with deer hooves hitting the sides of the van and the deer's head bouncing off the roof.

"Open the damn door!" yelled Don. "Get back here and open the door! This deer's killin' me!" In such a confined space, the deer was beating Don up pretty good. Keep in mind that the van door could only be opened from the outside.

I stopped the van as fast as I could, jumped out, and ran toward the rear to open the door for Don. I thought I'd put the van's gearshift lever into park, but in all the excitement I must have put it in neutral instead, because the vehicle started rolling down the road on its own. I chased the van down, jammed the gearshift into park, then ran around to the back door and threw it open. As I did, the deer came bounding out just like a steer out of a rodeo chute. And, just like a cowboy, the poacher sitting in the front passenger seat of the van jumped out and ran the deer down, grabbing it around the neck and bulldogging it just like a steer wrestler. Down over the road bank the two of them went into the black of the night.

The poacher had been carrying a rifle when he exited the van, and within a few seconds we heard the rifle fire once, bam! "Got 'em!" the guy yelled from the dark. We left that deer where he'd shot it, kept going, and shot several more deer that night, returning just before daylight to pick up the first one. All told, we killed a total of six deer that night. Don has never forgiven me for allowing the van to roll down the road by itself as he fought the wounded deer in hand-to-hand combat. I told him to quit whining and pointed out that technically it had not been hand-to-hand combat, but hand-to-hoof.

———

Ron Kendrick was also a waterfowl poacher, and the Lake Erie marshes near Toledo offer some of the best duck hunting in North America. Knowing that, and suspecting that his group probably poached ducks and other waterfowl as well as walleyes, I kept telling Kendrick that I wanted to go duck hunting with him sometime. The only problem with this plan was that I had never been on Lake Erie before. In fact, I was scared to death of it. The most southern of the five Great Lakes, Erie is serious big water and must be respected. I knew that fishermen, as well as the occasional duck hunter, drown on Lake Erie every year. But duck hunting would give me a chance to meet the rest of the Toledo poachers, so I knew I had to go.

As I've already said, I never trusted Doug Andrews, and here's why. He owned a house in Toledo with a second-story apartment that he rented to a man and woman. One day, the couple got into a domestic dispute, and Andrews, living on the ground floor of the house, heard the woman upstairs screaming. He grabbed a handgun, stepped outside to see what was happening, and saw the woman come running down the steps, her upper body covered with blood. Within seconds, her partner appeared at the top of the stairs holding a knife and began chasing her down the steps. At that point, Andrews raised his handgun, took aim, and shot the guy, hitting him in the neck. The man collapsed, rolled to the bottom of the stairs, and died at Andrews's feet.

When Andrews recounted the story, he said coldly, "Blood was a-spirtin' out of his neck, and I just stood there and watched him die." The incident proved to me that Andrews was just the kind of guy I thought he was, a hard man who had little remorse, if any, for much of anything he did. For Andrews, shooting that guy was just like shooting a deer; it didn't faze him at all. Andrews was not indicted for this shooting. In fact, not only did a grand jury believe the story of self-defense he and the woman told but the local newspaper even depicted him as a hero for saving the woman's life. But more about that story later.

When I drove up to Toledo to go duck hunting, Andrews took me to Kendrick's house, where they showed me their trophies: mounted heads with large antlers from deer they'd poached, as well as a freezer full of walleyes and other illegal game. When we left to go duck hunting, well before dawn the next morning, I met the Hymore brothers, Gary and Rick, for the first time. I eventually learned that the Hymores were not only poachers but, like many bad guys, were also thieves and into illegal drugs as well. The more I learned, the more I questioned my sanity for getting involved with this group.

Even that first morning I wasn't too happy. As we set out at 4:00 A.M., it was black-dark. I was going duck hunting on a huge, dangerous lake that I'd never been on before, with a bunch of real bad guys I barely knew. The thought crossed my mind that if they were taking me out into the middle of the lake to push me overboard and drown me, there was nothing I could do about it: I'd be done. And to top it all off, I glanced around the boat and saw no life jackets or any other safety equipment. I had no idea where I was or where we were going, and I was as much afraid of the lake as I was of the poachers.

To my relief, the sun eventually came up that morning and we had a good duck hunt, meaning we shot more than our allowable limit of waterfowl. And when the duck shooting wasn't fast enough to suit the poachers, they'd shoot an occasional seagull as it flew by. Gulls, like other nongame birds, are protected by law, but that meant nothing to these poachers. They simply shot the gulls for fun, leaving them lying on the water to float away on the waves.

During that hunt, the poachers got to talking about eating prime rib for supper that night, prime rib that Kendrick regularly stole from the restaurant kitchen at Maumee Bay State Park, where he worked. Sure enough, that evening we literally stuffed ourselves on succulent prime rib. After dark, a police cruiser from Oregon, Ohio (a suburb of Toledo), containing two officers, pulled into the driveway of Kendrick's house, where we were having supper. But instead of the poachers getting nervous about the presence of the police car, Kendrick grinned, went to his freezer, and got out a big slab of frozen prime rib that he carried out to the officer's cruiser. He loaded the prime rib in the trunk of the cruiser, along with all the ducks we'd killed that morning, and smiled as the officers waved and drove away.

Inwardly, I was shaking my head. The longer this investigation went on, the more it mushroomed, revealing more and more suspects. Not only were sheriff's deputies trading with poachers in the southern part of the state, but now city police officers were involved up north. I was not able to get the officers' badge numbers, but I did commit to memory the unit number on the side of their cruiser. It would be easy enough later to track down the names of the officers assigned to that car on that particular night.

We continued duck hunting over the next few days, and during that time the poachers told me that the outboard motors on the boats we were using were stolen. They had stolen the motors from local boat storage facilities and marinas, anywhere people stored watercraft over the winter. That night, to show me how easy such theft was, the Hymores stole yet another motor. They had already located the outboard they wanted, so we simply drove to the boat storage area, and I stayed in the truck while they got out and took the outboard.

The storage facility was surrounded by a locked, chain-link fence, so I don't know how they got in. They may have cut the fence or picked the lock, but either way they were gone only a few minutes. The poachers didn't normally sell the motors they stole; they simply used them for their own hunting and fishing trips. And if a motor developed a mechanical problem, they'd just junk it and go steal another one. My impression of the evening was that stealing outboards was not an uncommon event for these guys, nor was it difficult for them.

Remember, this was my first experience with working deep undercover in wildlife law enforcement, and I was starting to think that I was way out of my league. After all, I hadn't signed up to handle serious crimes such as theft or dealing illegal drugs. I thought I'd just be dealing with people who poached wild animals. By now, though, I was committed to seeing this case through to its end, wherever it took me, so I had to continue playing the game as long as possible. And while doing so I had to try to remember all the names, places, times, and dates of the crimes I was witnessing and record all that information on paper, as soon as I had a chance to get away from the bad guys.

Here's an example of what I mean. One of the Hymore brothers worked at a local sporting goods store and would steal merchandise by way of what the group called a "sleeping bag sale." Members of the poaching ring would go into the sporting goods store, decide what merchandise they wanted, then tell Hymore. When he went to work the next day, he'd take the items the group wanted off the display shelves and carry them to a storage area in the back of the store. He'd then stuff the items into a new sleeping bag. He'd put the sleeping bag back into its original box and reseal it. When he left the store later that day at the end of his shift, he'd pay for the sleeping bag—paying maybe twenty or thirty dollars with his employee discount—and walk out of the store with not only the sleeping bag but also the hundreds of dollars' worth of stolen merchandise stuffed inside, mainly hunting and fishing equipment.

Another member of the group worked at a local farm-supply store and would do the same thing there. Needless to say, the poachers were well supplied with whatever equipment they thought they needed for their illegal hunting and fishing trips.

A few times during the several days I stayed at Andrews's house, he left me alone. When he did, I tried looking around for more evidence of criminal activity. I wasn't too worried about Andrews detecting my snooping, since at that time video surveillance cameras in homes were in their infancy. While I knew Andrews might have hidden cameras and might be testing me, I believed it was unlikely. I discreetly took pictures of the inside of the house and drew a rough diagram of the rooms to help in obtaining search warrants when we finally took down these poachers. One thing I came across was a pellet gun. Andrews used it to silently (and illegally) shoot squirrels in his yard and off the surrounding utility wires. He'd clean the squirrels, freeze them, and then sell the meat, just like he would deer.

———

A few days after my visit to Toledo, Don and I had an appointment to meet with our supervisors. We were also meeting Andy Pierce, a federal law enforcement agent with the U.S. Fish and Wildlife Service. Since, by law, waterfowl are considered migratory game birds, we now had hard evidence—thanks to my duck-hunting trips—that the poachers had broken federal wildlife laws as well as state laws. This meant we could now bring the Feds in on the case.

By that point in the investigation I had become a very light sleeper, no doubt from stress. But I didn't realize just how tightly I was wound until the day of the meeting.

In an undercover investigation you never know what will happen next, day or night. And an officer on an undercover investigation is most vulnerable when he's asleep. During those hours you're basically defenseless. Knowing that, I had begun to sleep with a handgun under my pillow, sometimes even falling asleep with it in my hand. I knew I had to be ready for anything and everything at all times.

The day of the meeting with the federal officer and my supervisors, I had been taking a nap and Don and another guy came into the bedroom to wake me up. Groggy, I forgot where I was for a few seconds, and, fearing that it was the bad guys coming through the bedroom door to get me, I instantly sat up in bed with the pistol in my hand, pointing it at the two officers. Don and the other man immediately threw up their hands and backed away, startled and disturbed. That's when I started thinking I was too deeply immersed in this investigation, and that maybe undercover work was not for me. Nevertheless, I was determined to see at least this investigation through to its end. I wasn't going to quit.

Ohio's season for hunting deer by gun was scheduled to open, as it always does, the Monday following Thanksgiving, and for the next step in our investigation, Don and I had arranged for all the Toledo and southern Ohio poachers to meet at the trailer camp for an entire week of hunting. But just three days before everyone was due to gather at the trailer, I got a shocking phone call from my supervisor, Dick Scott.

"Your undercover project is shut down," Scott said. "Abort the investigation. Immediately."

"What?" I said, incredulously, "Why?"

"I can't tell you any more right now," Scott said. "But whatever you do, don't go back to that trailer. I don't care if you have personal items there or not; don't go back. That's a direct order. You understand me?"

I tried to protest, but Scott wouldn't budge. "Look, R.T., if you go back to that trailer, you'll likely be killed. The bad guys have discovered who you and Don are. I know that for a fact. Your lives have been threatened, and the investigation has been compromised. Don't go back there. This project is officially shut down."

Don and I were devastated by the news. After working on this case for nine months, we were finally ready to get all the poachers together in one place for the very first time and get the last few pieces of evidence we needed before taking them all down. And now the investigation was called off. I kept pressing my boss for an explanation, and all he would say was that there were other law enforcement agencies involved and that we, meaning the Division of Wildlife, weren't the highest authority. To this day, I've not been back to that trailer. I've driven by it a time or two, but I have never stopped, let alone gone inside.

What we eventually learned is that the pay phone we used outside the grocery store in South Perry had been wiretapped. Unbeknownst to us, the FBI also had been working an undercover project in the area, suspecting the Hocking County sheriff of selling illegal drugs, among other shady activities. An undercover FBI agent working within the sheriff's office learned that the sheriff had discovered Don and I were undercover wildlife officers. The sheriff had told his deputies, who had told the Sullivans and the Johnsons, and the two poaching families were so mad they swore they'd kill us. The undercover FBI agent had contacted the Ohio Attorney General's Office with his information, and the Attorney General's Office had contacted our supervisor, Dick Scott, who immediately called off our investigation. To make a long story short, the Hocking County sheriff was indicted several years later on various charges, including corruption in office. Unfortunately, the Sullivan and Johnson families were never prosecuted for their many violations of wildlife laws.

Don and I were very disappointed, to say the least, but we worked to salvage as much of what was left of the investigation as possible. We believed—although we did not know—that the southern Ohio poachers had not revealed our identity to the Toledo poachers. We may have been naïve, but we were willing to take that chance. If we were still to have any chance of arresting the Toledo poachers, however, we had to find some excuse for calling off the scheduled weeklong deer hunt without raising their suspicions. As luck would have it, The Clan, as they called themselves, had already given us what we needed.

Before the opening of gun deer-hunting season, Andrews and Kendrick had come to the trailer for a few days and we all went out and shot some deer. We went back to the trailer that night about midnight to take a break, but when it came time to go back out Don and I begged off. We were too tired, we told Andrews and Kendrick, and just wanted to go to bed. We urged them to go hunting without us. The poachers shrugged and left, but about 4:00 A.M. a taxi cab pulled up in front of the trailer and Andrews and Kendrick stepped out. This was very unusual, because we were a good ten miles from any town having a taxi.

"What's going on?" Don asked sleepily from his bed as I looked out the bedroom window of the trailer.

"Looks like our boys got busted," I said. "They're getting out of a taxi cab."

"A taxi cab . . . ?" Don said, sitting straight up in bed.

Sure enough, a deputy sheriff had caught the pair poaching and arrested them. They were charged not only with mishandling a firearm in a motor vehicle but with carrying a concealed weapon; this was in the days before carrying a concealed weapon in Ohio was legal with the proper permit. The officer had also impounded their vehicle, which explained why the pair had returned in a taxi. As it turned out, it was fortunate Don and I hadn't gone back out with the poachers that night, as we surely would have been arrested, too.

We thought it was funny that they'd been caught, but the incident taught us a valuable lesson. From that day forward, neither Don nor I carried a handgun when we went poaching. That way, if we ever were stopped by law enforcement, we would at least avoid the charge of carrying a concealed weapon. We realized that such a charge would only create additional problems for us as undercover officers. Instead, all we took along was the .22 magnum caliber rifle we'd been poaching with, since carrying that kind of gun in a pickup truck was common in rural Ohio.

Luckily, the event we dubbed "the taxi cab incident" gave us a perfect excuse to call off the weeklong hunt with the Toledo poachers. Since Andrews and Kendrick had been arrested, we told them, the local wildlife officer was watching us closely, even stopping by our trailer and wanting to search it. That was not true, but it got us off the hook with no one the wiser.

––––

Ohio's season for hunting deer with primitive weapons (when hunters are allowed to hunt deer for a few days with muzzle-loading rifles) was scheduled for January. We figured this was our last chance to nab the Toledo group during the 1992–93 hunting season, so we contacted our supervisor, Dick Scott, and begged him to let us give the Toledo poachers one more try. We told him we didn't think the Sullivan and Johnson families had told them about our true identities as wildlife officers, although we admitted that there was always a possibility someone from one of those two families had tipped off the Toledo poachers. Either way, after spending nearly a year on building our case, we were willing to take that chance. It took some convincing, but Scott finally agreed to let us give it one last try. But, he warned us, "if the least little thing doesn't look or smell right, you guys get your asses out of there! Understand?"

We called the Toledo poachers and told them we'd like to hunt with them during the muzzle-loader season, and they invited us to stay with them at a cheap motel in Gallipolis, Ohio. This was dicey, since I grew up near that area, and I was afraid one of the locals might recognize me. Even though I'd changed my appearance quite a bit since living in the area, there was still a chance I might be identified—what undercover officers call "being made."

The motel where we met the poachers provided accommodations only a little better than our trailer camp, the main difference being that the motel at least had running water. The rooms had holes in the walls, the place was filthy, and the water pipe coming out of the wall in the shower didn't even have a shower head attached to it. The water ran out of the pipe at an angle, hitting the wall of the shower stall, and you had to shower from the spray bouncing off the wall. Our room was immediately beside the poachers' room and there was only one bed per room, so Don and I had to sleep together.

Don was beginning to have chest pains about that time during the investigation, and later, after the investigation was over, it was determined that he had a mild heart attack. I remember that we passed a hospital on our way to the motel, and I asked him if he wanted to stop so a doctor could check him out. Don shook his head no.

"Okay, but it's your last chance," I said. "And if you go down I ain't giving you mouth-to-mouth!" I was kidding him, of course; I was concerned both for my partner's health and for my own. Remember, Don was my only backup.

"I don't know how much help I can be to you the next few days, R.T.," considering how rough I'm feeling," Don replied, "but I'm in this investigation to the end. Let's go." We drove past the hospital and headed for the motel.

That first day of the muzzle-loader season, the Toledo poachers and I went hunting while Don, still suffering from chest pain, stayed at the motel. We hunted on a local farm and killed a couple of deer and a wild turkey. The turkey was out of season, and we didn't even bother to field tag our deer or check them at an official check station, both of which were required by law.

The first time during undercover work that I seriously thought I was going to be shot and killed occurred at the motel later that day. We had returned to the motel after hunting and dropped off some of the guys. Then Kendrick and I drove down the street to get a sandwich at a nearby fast-food restaurant. While there, I recognized two high school friends who knew what I did for a living. They saw me, and I began to panic, fearing they might come over and begin talking to me in front of Kendrick. Luckily, they didn't. I later learned that the pair, Mike Wolford and Todd Snowden, had been briefed by one of my brothers that if they ever saw me out in public they were never to approach me or the people I was with unless I spoke to them first. Thankfully, they remembered my brother's advice and ignored me. But that incident was fresh in my mind as Kendrick and I drove back to the motel.

I pulled up in front of the door to the poachers' room, but Kendrick and I remained in my truck, eating our sandwiches and talking. Don had been lying down alone in our room when we left, with all the bad guys in the adjacent room. Now I saw the door to the poachers' room slowly begin to swing open. I continued watching the door and all of a sudden the muzzle of a twelve-gauge shotgun protruded from it, pointing directly at me from less than twenty feet away!

The first thought racing through my mind was that the bad guys had set us up: that they had separated Don and me, killed him, and now were going to kill me. Remember, after having to call off the other half of this investigation, we didn't know for sure if these poachers knew our true identities or not. I dropped the sandwich I was eating into my lap and started to reach for the pistol in my coat before realizing I didn't carry one anymore. About that time the guy pointing the shotgun at me broke up laughing—it had all been a joke!

It may have been a joke to the poachers, but it scared the hell out of me. I had been terrified, convinced I was a dead man. Jumping out of the truck, I started cussing the poachers, who were all laughing their heads off. I tried to hide my real feelings by acting tough, but in reality I was just glad to be alive.

"I'll guaran-damn-tee you one thing, you sons o' bitches," I hollered at them. "I'll have the last laugh over this!"

I was thinking ahead to the day we'd finally take down these scumbags and I'd see them all in jail, but of course they had no idea what I meant. They just continued to laugh and hee-haw. Later that night I told Don what had happened, and he laughed, too.

Because Don was still having chest pains, I hung out in the poachers' motel room most evenings that week, allowing Don to have our room to himself so he could rest. That's when the poachers would pull out their stash of marijuana, roll a joint, and pass it around. And there I sat, wanting to act like one of the boys but reluctant to smoke dope with them.

So when the cigarette would come to me I would pretend I was taking a toke. Continuing playing my role, I'd kid the guy holding the joint, saying something like, "Hey, pass that weed on around here, will ya? . . . It's supposed to be puff, puff, pass; not puff, puff, hold." After more smoking and drinking one evening, the group decided it was time to go kill some serious numbers of deer, and we did. During the next three nights, we shot and killed a total of twenty-four deer, all illegally.

Don bought all twenty-four deer from the bad guys, paying them in cash. The deer carcasses were piled one on top of another in the bed of our truck and covered with a locked truck cap. One at a time we'd take a deer out of the truck, carry it into the motel room, and skin and process it in the bathtub. We gutted the deer outside first, in the back of the poachers' pickup, and threw the entrails in the motel dumpster. This motel was so filthy that the owners couldn't have cared less about what we were doing, just as long as they got their room rent money. Needless to say, no one ever came to clean the rooms, so no one knew what we were doing in there. Even if they had known, they probably wouldn't have cared, or said anything about it.

When Don was making the buy of the deer from the poachers in the parking lot, I was in our room watching, trying to photograph the cash transaction through the window. I turned off all the lights in the room, locked the door, and pulled the curtains to where I could see out only through a small hole, just enough for the camera's lens to poke through. As I was doing this, I was also smoking a cigar. So as to have both hands free to take the photos, I took the lit cigar from my mouth and laid it on the edge of a counter.

All of a sudden, as I was taking the pictures, two of the poachers walked directly in front of the camera lens and tried to open the door to my room. I hid the camera as fast as I could, grabbed the cigar off the counter, and stuck it in my mouth. The only problem was that in my haste I put the lit end of the cigar into my mouth, burning my lip. I played up the incident, using it as an excuse as to why it had taken me so long to open the door. Thankfully, the poachers had no suspicion that I'd been taking their photo.

After several more days at the motel, Don and I felt we finally had enough evidence to indict every individual in the poaching ring. It was time to begin winding down the investigation. The two Hymore brothers were the ones who did all of the shooting that final week, and until then we had not gathered much evidence on them except for their Lake Erie waterfowl hunting violations, which were minor. Now we had them: killing twenty-four deer in three nights makes for a pretty strong poaching case.

———

All told, Don Carter and I had spent fifteen months undercover on Operation Clanbake, logging countless hours of investigative work and spending many, many days and nights away from our homes and families. In the takedown of undercover wildlife cases, the prosecutors in the counties involved are notified, along with the uniformed state wildlife officers assigned to that area. Other law enforcement agencies may be notified as well, but only on a need-to-know basis.

Many of the prosecutors, wildlife officers, and other law enforcement officers and agencies we notified were stunned to learn that this investigation had been going on for so long in their area and that they knew nothing of it. But they all were glad to hear about it, as our hard work would finally put to rest many of the complaints they had been receiving about these poachers for years.

During the final phase of a covert investigation, the undercover officer stays in contact with the bad guys but tries to see less and less of them. This tactic is intended to protect the undercover officer, since as more and more people become aware of an investigation, the more dangerous it becomes for him. In rural counties especially, the grapevine works very well, and you never know who might work in the courthouse or in a law enforcement position—someone who might know the bad guys or their families and tip them off about the pending takedown. Someone may even slip up unintentionally, putting the undercover officer at risk. As a rule, you have to be very cautious and stay on your guard just before a takedown. In other words, you run through the tape.

In this case, to reduce the risk to us, we obtained sealed search warrants. That meant that, other than the judges and prosecutors, no one knew who was going to be served with the warrants until the actual day of the takedown. Don and I had to testify in front of a judge in order for him to issue and sign the sealed warrants. Usually, such testimony is given by the undercover officer(s) in the judge's chambers, but sometimes a judge will come to another location, if necessary, to keep an officer's identity secret.

Arrest warrants and search warrants were issued in three Ohio towns: Chillicothe, Gallipolis, and Toledo. Ironically, when we met the judge in his chambers and he read that Doug Andrews was one of the people to be arrested, he commented that the name sounded familiar. The prosecutor reminded him that Andrews was the same guy who had shot and killed the knife-wielding man chasing the woman down the steps several months earlier. "Isn't that interesting," the judge said. "A few months ago he was a hero, and tomorrow he's going to jail."

The court decided it needed some additional personal information about the poachers for the arrest and search warrants, and it was up to Don and me to get it. Using our heads, we came up with what we thought was an ingenious plan. We told the poachers that we were both now working temporary jobs in Indiana and could get them all good-paying jobs there, too, if they were interested. All they had to do was fill out the job application form we'd supply them; then we'd submit it to our boss in Indianapolis. We created a false job application and gave copies to the poachers, who filled them out in record time, no questions asked. The bogus applications gave us all the personal information about the poachers the courts needed: full name, address, date of birth, social security number, everything.

Finally, the Division of Wildlife takedown teams were assigned, assembled, and briefed. The takedown took place at first light, on the morning of February 10, 1993. All the suspects were arrested without incident and transported to Chillicothe and Gallipolis for incarceration. Clan members and others, a total of twenty people, were charged with 256 wildlife law violations. Once convicted, they were assessed fines in excess of $24,000 and were ordered to pay restitution in excess of $14,000 to the state of Ohio for the loss of wild animals. They also had their hunting privileges in Ohio revoked for a combined total of eighty-eight years and forfeited one vehicle and four guns to the state. In addition, Clan members were sentenced to a total of eighty-six days in jail (with thirty years' probation) and were ordered to do community service work within nineteen different programs.

I was very apprehensive on the day of the takedown, concerned for the safety of the uniformed officers making the various arrests and serving the nine search warrants. As it turned out, though, the takedown could not have gone more smoothly. All the bad guys were taken completely unawares and arrested without incident. Doug Andrews, for example, was taking a bath when the wildlife officers arrived at his house. Of the nine Clan members arrested, eight were incarcerated and one was released on his own recognizance.

After it was all over and I was driving home that night, I felt very proud to be a part of the Ohio Department of Natural Resources, Division of Wildlife. I was elated at what we as a state wildlife agency had accomplished. As an undercover officer, you sometimes feel isolated from your fellow officers because you work alone so much. But now that the investigation was finished, I finally got to see and joke once again with my fellow officers, many of whom were close friends I hadn't seen in more than a year. That was a very rewarding feeling. And when I saw the men arriving in their dress uniforms for the investigation's final take-down, looking sharp and ready to kick butt, it made me feel good. Real good.

I will never forget the emotions I experienced that night. When I finally got home and realized that everything was over, that Operation Clanbake had been successfully completed, I cried like a baby. No doubt that emotional letdown signaled my release from the mental stress I had been living under for nearly a year and a half.

Operation Clanbake was the first undercover investigation the Division of Wildlife had ever attempted in the agency's more than century-long history. It had ended well, and we'd learned many things. Some things we could improve on in future investigations, but for the most part we had done many things right the first time. The bottom line was that Don and I were both alive and unhurt, and the bad guys were in jail, no longer poaching Ohio's wildlife. Following the case, both Don and I received death threats from the poachers, but nothing ever came of them. And after some well-deserved rest, we were both ready to tackle our second undercover assignment, Operation Redbud.

# 2

# OPERATION REDBUD

Operation Redbud, the second undercover investigation I was involved in, mainly targeted the poaching of wild turkeys, although, like Operation Clanbake, it uncovered other crimes. We dubbed it Redbud because spring is the time of year when redbud trees bloom in Ohio, and it is also the time of year for hunting spring gobblers.

It began early in 1995, when our supervisor, Dick Scott, head of the Law Enforcement Section of the Division of Wildlife in the Ohio Department of Natural Resources, contacted me and my partner, Officer Don Carter, about plans for an undercover investigation in southeastern Ohio. The suspected poachers, he told us, supposedly operated from a bar, the WW Tavern, in the small town of McConnelsville, located in Morgan County.

The primary targets of the investigation were Donald "Lee" Lilly Jr. and Claude Maxwell, but Scott encouraged us to try to identify other poachers as well; any additional evidence we could gather would be considered gravy. We knew going into the investigation that Claude Maxwell was the manager and bartender at the WW Tavern. Based on that information, I began hanging around McConnelsville, trying to lay some groundwork in the case, learn a little about the area, and become familiar with the bar and the two prime poaching suspects.

I had been in the area about two weeks, living out of my van in a public campground, when I heard on a local radio station that a guy in the area had some used farm equipment for sale. I gave the guy a call, found out what equipment he had, and asked to stop by and see it. I told him I was from Marysville, Ohio, a town about one hundred miles away, and said that I was in the area scouting places to hunt wild turkeys when the season began later that spring. He told me today was not a good day for him, but urged me to give him a call if I wanted to view the equipment later that week. I gave him my fictitious name for this undercover operation, Bob Thomas, and hung up the phone.

When I was first working myself into a particular geographical area undercover, I liked to stop at yard sales or other modest local events and just visit with people. Eventually, I'd guide the conversation around to hunting and fishing and if someone seemed interested and knowledgeable, I'd try to get his or her name. I'd then use that name as an introduction to someone else in the neighborhood, saying something like, "Hey, I was just down the road at John Smith's yard sale, and we got to talking, and he says you're quite a hunter. . . ." and before you knew it we'd be in a conversation.

I can't count the number of times I've used that technique to wangle an invitation into a guy's home during my very first conversation with him. Such people didn't know me from Adam, but soon I'd be sitting in their houses while they filled me in on their entire neighborhood. Another technique I've used to get information is to pick up hitchhikers in an area I was interested in. The hitchhiker would give me a name or two that I would then mention to locals on first meeting them. They would recognize the name, which would allay their wariness of me as a stranger. Soon they'd be telling me all about their community.

After speaking with the man selling farm equipment, I drove to McConnelsville later the same day to make my first visit to the WW Tavern. As an undercover officer, you quickly learn that when locals go into a bar they enter through a certain door. People who have not been to the bar before usually enter by another door. Since an outsider doesn't know which door is which, you take your chances during your first visit, but if you go through the wrong door, you stand out to the locals as an outsider. The WW Tavern had only two entry doors, so I figured I had a fifty-fifty shot at picking the right door. I pulled on a beat-up ball cap and walked in—through the wrong door, I later learned.

What saved me from being labeled as too much of an outsider was the particular ball cap I was wearing. Knowing that Claude Maxwell was an avid turkey hunter, I had worn a cap embroidered with a wild turkey on the front. I had a physical description of Maxwell from intelligence reports, but not a very complete one. About all I knew of him for sure was his name.

I walked in, sat down at the end of the bar, and ordered a beer. And when the bartender set my drink in front of me and saw my hat, he asked, "You a turkey hunter?" I was soon to learn that the man behind the bar was none other than Operation Redbud's number two target, Claude Maxwell.

"Oh, yeah," I said. "I been turkey huntin' a long time. Practically all my life. . . ."

Maxwell asked where I was from, and I told him Marysville, adding that I was in the area doing some scouting for the spring turkey-hunting season, sleeping in my van. He must have liked something about me, because one thing led to another and before long he started telling me stories about how many turkeys he'd shot and killed through the years. He wasn't talking about poaching, but in legal terms Maxwell was predisposing himself the very first day I met him.

As I explained in chapter one, *predisposition* is a legal term describing how a suspect incriminates himself through words or actions before an undercover officer becomes involved with that suspect. A suspect who has predisposed himself early in an investigation cannot then claim entrapment as a legal defense, since an officer cannot have planted the idea of committing a crime into the mind of someone who has already considered or acted on such an idea.

Maxwell and I continued talking in the bar, discussing hunting in depth for several hours. Three or four other people joined the conversation, and soon we were all drinking, talking, and laughing, having a great time together.

Shortly after 5:00 P.M., a young man walked into the bar—the evening bartender, it turned out—sat down, and began listening to our conversation. He looked at me intently and finally said, "I know you . . ." As soon as I had seen the young man walk in, I had known him too. Before becoming an officer with the Division of Wildlife, I had been a natural resources instructor at Hocking College in Nelsonville, Ohio, and the young man, Tim Eaton, had been a student at the school. You never know who you might run into during an undercover investigation. It's just one of the chances you take, especially working undercover in your home state.

I had hoped Eaton wouldn't recognize me, but he had. Now I pretended not to know him.

"You're R. T. Stewart, aren't you?" Eaton asked.

"I hate to disappoint you," I said, "but that ain't my name. I'm Bob Thomas."

"Man, you sure look like Stewart," he responded, shaking his head. "And he was a big-time turkey hunter, too. Hunted with a bow and arrow, as I remember."

"No, I don't know him," I said. Making light of the situation, I joked, "Is this Stewart good lookin'? Does he have a lot of money? Cause if he does, I might be him then. . . ."

I've always had a certain amount of luck when it comes to undercover work, and something happened right then that no one would believe if it were in a novel. The guy sitting beside me at the bar asked, "What did you say your name was?"

"Bob Thomas," I answered.

"Hell, I talked to a guy on the phone today named Bob Thomas who said he was from Marysville . . . was that you?"

"If you have farm equipment for sale, that sure was me," I said. "And you told me I couldn't come see you today because you had things to do, and here you are drunk in a bar!"

So when this guy sitting beside me at the bar—and yes, he was drunk—started vouching for me, saying that I really was Bob Thomas, not R. T. Stewart, it diverted the conversation away from my true identity. It was just one of those timely, extremely fortunate coincidences that have saved me time and again during undercover work. I can't explain it. Maybe God was looking out for me at that moment. I just know it happened.

Ironically, when Operation Redbud was over and through the courts, one of the main suspects told various people that Eaton had tried to tell the poachers several times who I really was, but none of them had believed him. Eaton had grown up in the McConnelsville area and the locals had known him all his life, but the poachers still believed me over him. I just must have had enough believability—some say the gift of bullshit—to convince them that I really was Bob Thomas, not R. T. Stewart.

———

That first meeting with Claude Maxwell at the WW Tavern broke the ice, and he invited me to go groundhog hunting with him. During those first few hunts together, he began talking more and more about turkey hunting. That's when I showed him some turkey tails, feet, and beards I had stashed under the seat of my van for just such a purpose. My first objective in the case was to build credibility with Maxwell by proving to him I was a serious turkey hunter.

"Sounds like we have a lot in common," I said, showing off my trophies. I hoped Maxwell thought so, too.

To make a long story short, he bought my ruse. Looking at me one day across the bar, Maxwell finally asked, "Would you like to go turkey huntin' with me some mornin'?"

"Sure!" I said. "When we goin'?"

Maxwell invited me in March, well before the Ohio turkey-hunting season opened in late April. A few days later I showed up at his house about daylight, as he had instructed me, and we headed for the woods. Unfortunately, it started raining, so we changed our plans. Rather than heading into the woods, we drove the rural roads in his pickup truck, looking for turkeys.

As Maxwell and I drove around, with me in the passenger seat of the pickup, we spotted a small flock of wild turkeys on the left side of the road. But before Maxwell could stick his gun out the driver's-side window and shoot, the turkeys crossed in front of us and were now on my side of the road. Quickly handing me his shotgun, Maxwell hissed, "Shoot! Shoot em!" I took the gun, rolled down the window, aimed, and fired.

There were about eight birds in the flock, and I shot to the right, intentionally trying to miss. Unfortunately, some of the pellets from the overspray of the shot hit a hen turkey on the edge of the flock and knocked her down. I was surprised to see the bird fall, especially since I had not been aiming at her, but I didn't hesitate. Jumping from the truck, I ran to the flopping turkey, grabbed it by the neck, ran back to the pickup, and threw it into the truck bed. I hadn't intended to kill that turkey, but the incident may have worked in my favor, building my credibility with Maxwell and convincing him that I was a poacher, just like him. Who knows? Maybe he was testing me that first morning. If he was, I had passed the first test.

We took the hen turkey back to his house, skinned it, and cleaned it, and somewhere during the morning we forged the beginnings of a friendship, a certain bond. He saw that I was a turkey hunter, had some woods sense about me, and believed he could start to trust me.

During our later hunts together, Maxwell kept referring to Lee Lilly—the number one target of this investigation—as a frequent hunting buddy. But even though I continued to hunt with Maxwell throughout the spring, killing turkeys both in and out of season, I never did get a chance to meet Lilly. At that point, however, it didn't matter. I had already gathered enough information and evidence to justify a full-scale undercover investigation of this group of poachers.

———

The first stage of any undercover wildlife investigation generally consists of a two- to three-month fact-finding period to determine if violations of wildlife law are occurring. The evidence and information collected are then evaluated by a team and a decision is made as to whether or not a full-scale undercover investigation is justified. Each preliminary undercover investigation has a list of goals and objectives. One is to determine if wildlife law violations are indeed happening, and if so, to what extent. A second goal is to determine who's committing the violations and what type of equipment is being used. If the violations are significant, an undercover operation is initiated. If not, the information is turned over to the local, uniformed wildlife officers assigned to that area, who are expected to follow up. Based on what I had found thus far, the Division of Wildlife determined to continue with Operation Redbud.

The next step was to rent a house in the area where my partner Don and I could live. The location of an undercover residence, known as a "safe house," is important; it must be close to where the bad guys live, but not too close. You must live near enough that your targets see you as a familiar part of their environment, but far enough away to give yourself a little freedom from the constant pressure and stress of undercover work—a little mental and physical space.

You don't want your targets dropping by every day or stopping by unannounced, both to preserve that precious down time and to safeguard your identity. An undercover officer must document the evidence he has gathered and complete other paperwork. If you have bad guys stopping by daily, especially unannounced, it will be difficult and dangerous to carry out these tasks. The ideal location for an undercover house is on a route the bad guys will not be traveling daily. You want them to have to make an effort, go out of their way, to get to where you live.

For Operation Redbud, Don and I wanted a house located outside the town of McConnelsville, a run-down dwelling that would fit our image as outlaw poachers, and one with enough privacy that we could skin and process poached game animals where people driving by couldn't see what we were doing from the road.

We found our undercover house about fifteen miles from McConnelsville, near the small town of Bartlett, Ohio. It was an old house trailer, and a pretty rough one at that—maybe not as run-down as the trailer we'd used in Operation Clanbake, but close. This particular trailer smelled bad, had rat holes chewed in it, and one interior wall had completely rotted away. In addition, the roof leaked. We rented the trailer for one $120 per month. Our budget for rent was $150 per month, so we thought we were doing well to find something for less. Actually, we didn't have a formal budget for the investigation. Like Operation Clanbake, this investigation was being done on the cheap. When we did get a little extra money from our supervisor, Don and I thought renting a few videos for our weekend's entertainment was a big splurge.

The fact that we now had moved to the area bolstered our credibility with Maxwell and other members of the poaching ring. Moreover, after selecting our safe house and moving in, we discovered an extra advantage of its location: it was just two miles from the home of Claude Maxwell's in-laws. That was a stroke of luck, because Claude didn't like his in-laws and would come visit us when his wife went to visit her parents.

During that summer, we focused on setting up and establishing our undercover residence so that it would be ready for fall, the time when most poachers begin getting serious about killing deer illegally. We mostly hung out at the WW Tavern, getting to know the regulars. Don and I got to be such bar flies that we eventually started tending bar and even doing a little of the cooking for the patrons, grilling sandwiches and that sort of thing.

One evening we sat in the bar talking to two locals, Danny Miller and Cliff Tanner. They told us that they had shot a deer the night before—well before the start of the legal deer-hunting season—and that they had just picked up the meat from a buddy who had butchered the deer for them. We acted skeptical, so they offered to show us the meat. They took us out to the parking lot and, sure enough, there was the packaged deer meat in the back of their pickup truck. Little did Miller and Tanner realize what they were doing, but by showing us the venison they had just predisposed themselves, revealing the fruits of a crime.

I memorized the license plate number of their truck and ran the registration the next day, just to confirm that Miller and Tanner were who they said they were. It checked out, so the next step was to find out who was processing the deer for them. Such leads show how, as time went on, our suspect list grew from our various contacts at the bar. Even as the investigation mushroomed, though, we continued to focus on our two main targets, Lee Lilly and Claude Maxwell.

The next night, Miller and Tanner were back at the bar and soon talking about going to poach another deer. Don and I felt we had built up enough of a relationship with them to invite ourselves along, so we said, "Hey, let's go! We'll drive, and you shoot." They took the bait, and out the door we went.

One thing I'd learned during Operation Clanbake was to retain as much control as possible when poaching with suspects. You have to do this subtly, so the bad guys don't suspect they are being manipulated, but it can be done. Poaching can be as much a social event as it is about killing animals. Most poachers like to shoot and kill wildlife with multiple people along. It's difficult to explain, but it's almost like the atmosphere in a college frat house. In some poachers' minds, the more people tagging along for the illegal kill, the more fun. In order to accommodate as many people as possible in a vehicle, therefore, I incorporated a beat-up panel van into my undercover equipment.

Since I owned a van, the poachers always wanted me to drive. This literally put me in the driver's seat, exactly where I wanted to be. As the driver, I could control not only the speed of the vehicle but where we went and, therefore, in what direction the poachers would shoot. For example, if I didn't want them shooting at a deer with a house or other building in the background, I'd position the van so that couldn't happen. Unbeknownst to the poachers, I could also control the surveillance video equipment hidden in the van.

In addition, I'd never drink before driving. I told the poachers that I didn't want to get busted for DUI if we got stopped by law enforcement. They seemed to agree with my logic and never questioned my refusal to drink. Don't think that Don and I never drank during this investigation, though. There were nights when both of us were so tipsy when leaving the WW Tavern that we'd argue about which one was sober enough to drive the two of us home.

Returning to my story about Miller and Tanner, though, they agreed that we could come hunting with them, and we left the bar with them that night. Then suddenly they realized they didn't have a gun with them. Claude Maxwell offered to lend us one of his guns if he could go along, but we first had to drive to his nearby hunting cabin to pick up one of his high-powered rifles. When he got back into the van with the gun, Maxwell informed us that he could find only one cartridge for the rifle. "But that don't matter," he said. "We can kill a deer with just one shot."

We drove out on a rural road away from town, and, slowing to a crawl, we rolled down a window and began shining the beam from a powerful spotlight into the woods and fields, looking for deer. White-tailed deer, being nocturnal as much as diurnal, have eyes that glow white when struck by a beam of light—the typical deer-in-the-headlights look. It wasn't long before we located some does and their fawns feeding in a picked corn field.

Unbeknownst to most of the poachers, I had a .22 magnum rifle in the van, a common poaching gun. In case someone took it from us unexpectedly, though, Don and I had rigged the rifle so that only we could fire it. That way, at least we knew the poachers couldn't shoot us using our own gun.

What happened next was one of the more humorous incidents of Operation Redbud. Danny Miller picked his target, got ready to shoot from the window of the van, aimed the rifle, pulled the trigger—and nothing happened. All you could hear was the firing pin snap, then Danny beginning to cuss.

"What's wrong?" I asked.

"I lost the bullet."

"What do you mean you lost the bullet?" I said. "We only got one bullet, and you lost it?"

"I told you, I lost the damn bullet," he said. "I must have forgot to load the rifle and dropped the bullet on the floor of the van."

By this time all of us except Miller were laughing so hard our sides hurt. Eventually, one of the guys located the lone cartridge lying on the van's running board and handed it to Danny. He loaded his rifle and fired. Then we heard him say, under his breath, "Damn. . . ."

"You mean to tell me that we only had one bullet and you missed?" I said. Once again, everyone in the van was dying laughing except, of course, Danny Miller.

"Give me the other gun," he growled, knowing that Carter and I kept the .22 magnum rifle in the van, so I handed him the .22. Don, watching the doe from the van's back seat, said, "At this distance, aim about two inches high, Danny."

Even though Miller's first shot had missed, the deer still stood, staring at the spotlight beam, but it was almost a football field length away. Our .22 magnum had no telescopic sight, just open sights, so we figured Miller would surely miss the deer at such a long range. It was a very difficult shot, literally a shot in the dark, and it didn't help that we were all razzing him as he took aim. Miller took careful aim for his second shot and squeezed the trigger; the rifle bucked and roared, and the doe dropped stone dead from a head shot. It didn't even quiver.

Miller never hesitated. Jumping from the van, he took off, running through the field toward the downed deer. Keep in mind it was pitch dark and he had no flashlight with him, only a knife for gutting the deer. In the meantime, the other guys and I drove up the road, turned around, and drove back to where we had let Miller out. By that time—a total of only about eight minutes by my watch—Miller had field dressed the deer and dragged it back to the road. And, again, he had done all of this in the dark, without the aid of a flashlight.

That's how proficient Danny Miller and some of the others in the group were at poaching. During the court trial, Miller's defense attorney tried to suggest to the jury that this was the first time his client had ever done such a thing. But Don and I testified that there was no way Miller could have performed as he did that night in the dark had he been a novice poacher; his skill and speed showed that he had killed many deer previously in precisely that same manner. The jury believed us, not Miller's attorney.

After killing the deer, we returned home, where we skinned and butchered the animal. The next night, we were right back at the WW Tavern, ready to party with the boys again. But when we arrived we found the poachers angry and upset. They had found out that someone had run the license plate number of Miller and Tanner's pickup truck through law enforcement channels and were trying to figure out who had done so.

They started quizzing us about anything we might know, figuring we were the only other people who knew of the deer they'd killed two nights previously. Thinking quickly and trying to shift their suspicion away from Don and me, I asked them if they had been spotlighting anywhere before they came to the bar two nights ago. They eventually admitted that they had shone their spotlight around a few fields before showing up at the WW Tavern.

"Well, there's your answer," I said. "Someone saw your truck, got your license number, and turned you in."

Meanwhile, we were wondering how they had found out that their license plate had been checked. Eventually, we learned that the poachers had a friend who worked for the Ohio Department of Transportation (ODOT); through the state's two-way radio system, he had overheard that the Ohio Department of Natural Resources was running the license plate number of the poachers' pickup truck. Looking into how he could have overheard our request, we discovered that the state radio rooms for ODOT and ODNR were located across the hall from one another in Columbus, the state capital, allowing Miller and Tanner's ODOT friend to hear the radio call from ODNR and alert them that they were under suspicion. It had been a close call and had the bad guys figured out it was us who had run their vehicle registration, such a mistake could have blown our cover. Luckily, though, we survived it. We also learned from it. From that point on, all checks on vehicle license number registrations during the investigation were run over the phone and behind closed doors, not over the radio, just to make certain no one was listening who shouldn't be.

———

During the remainder of that winter, as the poachers illegally killed more and more deer, Don and I continued to compile and log more and more evidence against them. They weren't selling the venison, so there were no commercialization laws being broken, but the group killed a lot of deer. If I had to guess, I'd say they killed one hundred or more over the course of our investigation. They would either eat the venison themselves or give it away to family and friends.

Don and I continued to go poaching with the gang throughout the winter. The group got so bold that one night they shot a deer and gutted it in the road ditch in front of an occupied residence. Just as we were finishing up, a car came down the road and we all tried to pile into my van at once to get away. Everyone made it in but Maxwell; he slipped and fell, and I almost ran him over on our way out of there.

The person in the approaching car called the local sheriff's office on us. The poachers knew who had turned us in and were not happy about it. Returning to our undercover house, Don and I went inside, but two of the poachers remained outside, near the van, taking a leak. What they didn't know was that we had a hidden video camera in the van, which taped their conversation as they pissed.

When Don and I played back the tape later that night, we were shocked to hear that the poachers were actually plotting to kill the man who had turned us in to the authorities—not just beat him up to teach him a lesson, mind you, but kill him. This knowledge put Don and me in quite a fix. We had information that an innocent person might be killed, but we had obtained the information through an illegal wire tap.

Why was our tape of the conversation illegal? The only way an officer can legally record a conversation in Ohio is if at least one participant in the conversation knows it is being recorded. The two poachers didn't know they were being recorded. We did, but we were inside the house and not part of the conversation.

Once the poachers left for the night, we finally decided to call our supervisor. We phoned him about 2:00 A.M., getting him out of bed, and told him what we'd heard. He told us he'd call us back once he ran the situation up the chain of command. The answer came back down to do nothing, just let the situation ride for now and see what happened. It was ultimately the right decision. Thankfully, nothing happened. The threat, it turned out, was just drunk talk.

The season for hunting deer by gun in Ohio opened at the end of November, and the group of poachers operating out of the WW Tavern had a field day. They would act the part of legal hunters during the daytime, while in fact they were shooting as many deer as possible and hiding them in the field. Then at night, they would return under cover of darkness to drag the illegal carcasses out to the road. At our house trailer, we had two poles that we called the hanging pole and the poaching pole. We hung our legal deer from the hanging pole, properly tagged in case any game wardens showed up. We hung our illegal deer from our poaching pole until we could butcher them. Naturally, our poaching pole was well hidden, located several hundred yards behind the house, deep in the woods, where no one could see it from the road. The poaching pole wasn't in a building; it was just a wooden frame erected in heavy brush. It might possibly have been spotted from the air, but not easily.

An interesting side note here is that we'd skin our deer, both legal and illegal, with the aid of a four-wheeled, all-terrain vehicle (ATV). We'd begin by slitting the deer's skin with a knife. Then, using a stout rope, we would tie a fold of the deer hide over a billiard ball. Finally we'd attach the other end of the rope to the ATV, put the vehicle in gear, and drive forward. The deer hide would peel off the carcass in seconds, as slick as pulling a sweater over your head.

———

During the week of Ohio's deer gun-hunting season, some twenty-five to thirty guys were hunting out of our place, each doing about as many illegal things as legal. This allowed us to continue to build our overall case, while the number of bad guys involved continued to mushroom. So many illegal activities were going on that week of the deer gun season that we could barely keep track of all the violations.

Although, unfortunately, this is no longer the law in Ohio, at that time hunters were required to wear their hunting license tag in the middle of their backs on their outer layer of clothing. That helped us figure out the names of some of the violators. We'd write down each hunting license number, then later match the numbers with names. To help remember these hunting license numbers, especially if I didn't have a pencil and paper handy, I'd write the numbers in the dust on the dashboard of my van or maybe in the mud alongside a road.

We used the same technique for recording the serial numbers of firearms. If I got a chance to look closely at a guy's gun, I'd always try to memorize the serial number, although if the poacher was watching, I wouldn't make it obvious. Then I'd write down the number the first chance I got. Sometimes we'd use pocket-sized tape recorders to record names, numbers, and other evidence.

Another piece of equipment we would use for gathering evidence was a video camera. The camera itself was hidden in the rear of my van, while most of the controls were located up front, under the dashboard, where I could access them. At the time, though, VCRs were still in their infancy, so before recording, Don or I had to go to the back of the van, remove the panel cover hiding the VCR, turn on the power and the microphone, and add a blank tape. Even a fresh tape gave us no more than an hour of recording time. There were many times while out poaching that someone would shoot a deer, and all the guys would pile out of the van. I would then drive down the road, jump out, put a new tape in the VCR, and then drive back and pick up the bad guys. Since this took several minutes, some of the guys started questioning me as to why I was gone so long.

"Where the hell you been?" they'd ask.

"I had to take a leak," I'd respond—or some such excuse.

Yet as primitive as the video equipment was, it was still effective. The bad guys never suspected their conversations and illegal actions were being recorded.

One time there were no less than a dozen people in my van—I told you poaching could be a social event—and some of the poachers were literally sitting right on top of the hidden tape compartment. Don and I were both worried that their combined weight might break the panel cover, exposing the VCR. I therefore had a contingency plan worked out. If they did fall through and discover the VCR, I was going to grab the closest gun I could find, bail out of the van, and draw down on the poachers. Such a move would blow our cover and end the investigation, but at least Don and I would survive. Don joked that if we were ever discovered he would pull a gun on me and yell, "He's an undercover game warden! Get him!" Thankfully, neither one of our escape plans ever had to be implemented.

———

Claude Maxwell and his wife lived in an apartment above the WW Tavern, and Don and I worked to develop a strong friendship with him. Before too long, this friendship had extended to his wife and children, to the point his kids were calling me Uncle Bob and Don (since he was older), Grandpa. Claude's wife would even ask us for personal help at times. Once she asked us what gifts we thought Claude might like for Christmas, and a couple of times she even asked me to speak to Claude about issues they were having as a couple.

Don tried to warn me one night about Claude's wife. "Watch out," he said. "She's getting sweet on you." I might be slow about that kind of thing, but I couldn't see it. The next time we were in the bar, however, she had her hands all over me, and the following day she called me on the phone, saying in no uncertain terms that she wanted to make love to me. Since I was married at the time, I had no interest in her offer, so I made sure from then on that I was never alone with her.

I had deliberately cultivated a close friendship with the Maxwell family, and being a young and still somewhat inexperienced undercover officer, I didn't realize that I might be getting too close psychologically. Neither Don nor I recognized that our emotions were engaged, or realized how the friendship might affect us, and the investigation, at a later time.

Over time, however, our friendship with the family began to undermine our objectivity as wildlife officers. I remember several nights when Don and I talked about calling Claude and warning him about the investigation. That may seem unbelievable after all the time and effort we had put into this investigation, but that's how close we had grown to Maxwell and his family. We knew that when the takedown finally came, it would break his heart to learn who we really were and realize how we had deceived him and his family. The prospect broke our hearts, too. We knew we had a job to do, but an undercover officer still has feelings. The bottom line is that a law enforcement officer is still a human being.

Claude and I became so close, in fact, that we enjoyed just hanging out together. We'd go drinking together, attend truck pulls, fish, and hunt. The only difference between us was that he was on one side of the law and I was on the other. Despite that divide, we became almost like brothers. What drew me so close to Claude and his family was the fact that he was genuinely a very nice person. He would do almost anything for you. Also, he was good company—fun to do things with and comical to be around. In short, I liked him. I liked him a lot. And he liked me.

It's hard to explain and possibly hard to believe for those who have not worked undercover, but it happens. Sometimes you develop real feelings of friendship for the people you are trying to arrest. Even so, Claude Maxwell is one of only a handful of poachers with whom I developed a genuine friendship during my undercover career. Most of the poachers I targeted were hard men that I deeply disliked. Some I think I may even have hated. With such types, I just faked friendships, and I was glad when the investigation was over and I knew they were going to jail. I developed no bond with them and had no regrets.

Does all of this pretending to be someone you're not weigh on an undercover officer's mind over time? I'd have to say yes, it does, especially in cases targeting suspects with children. Most of the poachers I came to know were rotten parents. Some poachers would rather get drunk every night than spend any money on their kids, even for the basic necessities of life. I've seen kids sleeping in bedrooms so cockroach-infested that they had roach bites all over their bodies. And many would let special events like Christmas or birthdays come and go with no gifts for their wives or kids. The families of many poachers literally had nothing. It was pitiful.

As much as I enjoyed being around Claude Maxwell, I despised Lee Lilly, the main target of Operation Redbud. Don, my undercover partner, didn't like Lilly either, but we had to befriend him if we were going to get the evidence we needed. However, our relationship with Lee Lilly was nothing like the friendship we built with Claude Maxwell. The difference was like night and day. One of the few compliments I could pay Lee Lilly was to admit that he was an excellent woodsman. He could call wild turkeys like he was one himself; he had good woods sense, and he knew how to kill game. There was no doubt about it: he was truly a poacher's poacher.

———

By this point, I was so deeply immersed in Operation Redbud that three or four months might pass between my visits home to see my own family. I was also reluctant to make such visits because I was working this case less than one hundred miles from my home, and I was afraid of blowing my cover. Finally, I had reached a point where I really didn't want to go home. Going home meant facing reality: family problems, bills, and kids. In my undercover persona, by contrast, I could pretty much do what I wanted when I wanted to do it. And I could get away with nearly anything. I could go drinking, run around at all hours of the day and night, poach. Knowing you can do almost anything and get away with it can be a heady, addicting experience.

I want to make it clear, however, that during all of my years undercover I never cheated on my wife sexually. Given all the time I spent away from home and all the freedom I had, some people may find that hard to believe, but I never did. I had a few close calls, where I thought I might be forced into sex to preserve my cover, but ultimately I stayed true to my spouse. I even developed a cover story to explain my disinterest in women.

I always told poachers that I was single so that I didn't eventually have to produce a wife. The downside of that cover story, however, was that once the poachers got to know and like me, they kept trying to fix me up with their sisters or other single, female relatives. Part of my cover story was that I didn't work because I'd been injured in the West Virginia coal mines and was receiving disability payments. But the bad guys didn't know how I'd been injured. So one day, when several of us were together, I lowered my voice and asked, "Boys, can you keep a secret . . . just between us? I hope you don't tell no one else, because what I'm about to tell you is embarrassing. But once I do tell you, you'll understand why I'm not interested in women."

The room got real quiet, and I started my lie. "Remember I told you that I got hurt working in the coal mines?" They all nodded. "Well, I got one kidney bruised bad in the accident and almost lost it, and had my hip broke. But the most embarrassing thing is that I had both my testicles crushed. . . . I can't have sex."

I saw the group of men visibly wince, so I paused for effect, then continued. "Not many people know that about me, and I hope you don't tell no one. I still flirt occasionally to keep up my manhood, but please don't try and hook me up with women no more." The beauty of that story is that no guy is ever going to question it, and none of the poachers ever did.

Don Carter went home more often than I did during the investigation, at times not returning for several weeks. He was older than I, and as the investigation progressed, the stress started to wear on him, taking both a physical and mental toll. Since I was younger, the stress affected me less; I was full of vim and vigor for undercover work. After all, Operation Redbud was only my second undercover case, and I was truly enjoying the job. I ate, slept, and breathed undercover work, so much so that I didn't even want to go home.

As a result, I was almost always there, at our undercover house trailer, when Maxwell would telephone, sometimes in the middle of the night. Remember, this was in the days before widespread cell phone use, so landlines were the main means of communication. The fact that I had moved to the area and was usually at the safe house, unless I was at the WW Tavern, continued to build my credibility with the poachers.

––––––

After eleven months working this case, Don and I still had not met Lee Lilly, the primary target of our investigation. It seemed odd to me that as much as Claude talked about Lee he had never offered to introduce me to him, but I thought it best not to push the issue. I suspected my meeting Lilly was just a matter of time. We knew he primarily poached wild turkeys, mainly during late winter and early spring, and that time of year was fast approaching.

In February, Claude once again began talking about Lilly, and I finally said, "Some day you need to introduce me to him."

"Well, how about today?" Claude responded.

That very evening, Claude drove me to Lee Lilly's house, which stood only about two miles from the WW Tavern. I later learned that Lilly seldom came to the bar because he'd lost his driver's license through a DUI conviction.

During that first meeting with Lee Lilly, Claude vouched for me and bragged about all the turkeys, deer, and other game he and I had poached together. This immediately started building my credibility with Lilly, helping to convince him that I was a fellow poacher and could be trusted. Apparently convinced, Lilly proceeded to boast of his prowess as a poacher, showing me photos and trophies—such as turkey beards and fanned and mounted turkey tails—of some of the bigger birds he'd killed and telling me when and where he'd killed them. Most of the turkeys had been killed out of season, and some were even killed in other states, such as West Virginia. By telling me this, Lilly, like the other members of the ring, was legally predisposing himself.

Near the end of that first meeting with Lilly, I finally heard what I'd hoped to hear. "If you wanna go hunting with me someday," Lilly said, "we'll go."

"Just let me know when and where, and I'll be there," I answered enthusiastically. Lilly could tell I was anxious to hunt with him, but he had no idea of my real reason why.

It was only about two days later that Lilly called. "Hey, I talked to Claude, and he says you're cool"—a statement I took to mean that I could be trusted. "If you wanna go turkey huntin' with me, be here tomorrow morning about daylight."

Lee Lilly and I hunted together for the first time that next day and killed two jakes (year-old male turkeys). It seemed ironic that I had failed to connect with Lee Lilly for the first eleven months of this investigation, and yet was invited to go poaching with him only two days after finally meeting him. Actually, though, the fact that I was now in the woods with the main target of the investigation was not just dumb luck; it was the payoff for the eleven months of effort I had put into building a friendship with Claude Maxwell.

I continued hunting with Lilly throughout late winter and spring, and eventually Don started hunting with us, too. We hunted as often as three or four times per week from February until late April, when the legal turkey-hunting season began. Then we never hunted together again. "I like havin' the woods to myself," Lilly said. "There's too many other hunters in the woods during legal season."

Most serious poachers are good woodsmen, and Claude Maxwell and Lee Lilly were top of the line. They didn't have to use spotlights and shoot from vehicles on the roads to kill animals; they did so for fun or, at times, just to kill something. They knew they were skilled, and, like most poachers, they thrived on the admiration of their buddies. The other guys in the poaching ring were awed by their skill, and looked up to up them, and this respect was a source of pride for Maxwell and Lilly.

To gather evidence of our illegal turkey hunting with Lilly, Don and I came up with the idea of hiding a small video camera inside my turkey-hunting vest. I still have the vest and the camera is still inside it. The crude camera had only limited capabilities, so at some point every morning during a hunt I'd say that I had to go take a crap. I would then use that time away from the others to turn on the camera's microphone and recorder and connect a small battery.

One morning, Maxwell and Lilly almost caught me rigging the camera. Circling around through the woods, they came upon me actually taking a crap: I really was doing what I said I was doing when out of their sight. Had they come just a few moments later, they would have found me fiddling with the hidden camera. Their timing was just another of those lucky breaks that I experienced over my undercover career.

The hidden camera in my hunting vest allowed me to videotape several illegal turkey hunts with Lee Lilly. The date that appeared in the camera's viewfinder, and was imprinted on the final tape, verified that the hunts were out of season, but to be sure I would try to get verbal confirmation, talking openly about the hunts with the camera rolling. I'd say something like, "Man, Lee, we're out here in the middle of February. Isn't this great! I can't believe this." So I had sound recorded, too.

Eventually, Don and I got to the point where we openly carried a video camera on our hunts, and the poachers accepted it. Don would videotape me and I'd videotape Don. Then we'd say something to the poachers like, "Hey, guys, we're making a tape for ourselves, but if you don't want to be in it we won't show you." When they said, "We don't care," we would go ahead and tape them—clear evidence collected before their very eyes. We even captured Lilly on camera saying, "The turkey hunting was good today, March first, but let's get outta here before a game warden shows up."

Surprisingly, during my eighteen years of undercover work, I was checked in the field by a uniformed wildlife officer only once or twice, and not until late in my career. This may have been because we were hunting in some pretty remote places or because the poachers knew where to hunt and where not to. Smart poachers are always very cautious when they first come out of the woods. When we neared a road, for instance, only one of us would go to the truck and that person didn't carry a gun or any game. The rest of us would stay in the woods, out of sight, until we heard the truck horn toot—our signal that it was safe to come out. And when we did finally emerge from the woods, it only took a matter of seconds to throw the guns and whatever animals we'd killed in the bed of the truck and take off. The only way a uniformed officer could have caught us would have been by staking out the truck and waiting for us to approach the road.

As I got to know Lilly, I discovered that he had a hunting cabin in West Virginia. Not surprisingly, he would kill turkeys illegally in that state, as well, and transport them back to Ohio. Claude had never been to Lee's cabin, so he didn't know its location, but after Lee and I became better acquainted, he invited both Claude and me to go to West Virginia to do some turkey hunting with him—before the legal hunting season, of course.

When I reported the out-of-state invitation to my supervisor, I admitted that I didn't know exactly where I was going. This made him nervous about the proposition, so I told him I would try to let him know where I'd be as soon as I found out myself. My supervisor was still doubtful about authorizing the trip, and told me to wait until I heard back from him, while he ran my request up the chain of command.

The answer came back down that I had permission to go, so I headed to West Virginia with Lilly and Maxwell, still without knowing where we'd be hunting. I didn't have so much as a clue. And to add to the danger, the West Virginia wildlife law enforcement agency didn't know I was going to be there.

Finally Lilly, Maxwell, and I arrived at Lilly's remote cabin in the Mountain State—a rundown shack really—and stayed several days. During our hunts we killed two turkeys. Claude killed one, Lee killed another, and I told them that I had shot at one but missed. In reality, I'd not even hunted all that hard and probably would not have shot a turkey out of season had the opportunity presented itself.

The incident I remember most clearly about the trip, however, took place one morning as I was sitting in the woods with Claude Maxwell. It was a beautiful, quiet mountain morning, and we were sitting, our backs against a tree, so close together that our shoulders touched. The hunting had been slow that morning, so we were taking a break, talking about family, friends, and life in general. Finally Claude said, "Bob, I'm glad you got to come on this hunt with us. You know why? Because, you've become one of my very best friends. . . ."

Taken by surprise, I didn't know what to say. I knew Claude was sincere, and I felt bad about lying to him, but finally I swallowed hard and said, "Yep, I believe I've found a true friend myself."

My supervisor had not heard from me for about a week, so as soon as possible after the trip I called him to report on where I'd been and what we'd done. I also told him that the poachers wanted to make a return trip and bring a fourth guy along. This time my supervisor refused permission to go, saying it was too dangerous. "What happens if you're found out while down there?" he asked. I protested, arguing that I had to go to maintain my cover, and he finally agreed. So I went back to West Virginia, and we killed two or three more turkeys out of season. This time we shot them from truck windows, and just about everything else we did on the hunt was also illegal. As a result, I accumulated more than enough evidence to bring significant charges against the poaching ring in West Virginia, as well as in Ohio.

———

One interesting sidelight that occurred during Operation Redbud took place shortly after our second trip to West Virginia. Several poachers and I were sitting outside one day, shooting the breeze, when one of the poachers, Danny Clemons, started talking about a story he'd read in *Wild Ohio* magazine concerning undercover wildlife officers. Claude asked for details, and Danny proceeded to describe how undercover officers sometimes infiltrate poaching rings to make arrests.

"Hell, the officers actually live with the poachers and everything . . . ," said Clemons.

"Yeah," Claude joked, "we thought Bob here was one of them game wardens at first, and we been teasin' him about it ever since. But he gets so pissed off, we don't even bring it up no more."

I couldn't believe what I was hearing. This conversation was hitting much too close to the truth. So to diffuse the situation, I started to jokingly cuss them all and took a large folding knife out of my pocket. As I ranted, I clicked open the knife. "Any of you call me a damn game warden again, and I'm gonna gut ya!" I roared. That conversation definitely made a certain part of my anatomy pucker. Ironically, the editor of that magazine and the author of the poaching story was Chip Gross, the coauthor of this book. Had I been able to get my hands on my friend at that time, I likely would have choked him!

———

After nearly a year and a half of undercover work on this investigation, I knew Operation Redbud was drawing to an end. Don and I had infiltrated the poaching ring, made contact with the two primary targets, and gathered solid evidence on them and many other people. But during a final trip to West Virginia, something happened that made me realize just how deep undercover I had gone.

I was standing on the porch of the poaching cabin in West Virginia, videotaping a rainbow just for the fun of it. No one else was at the cabin at the time, and I was narrating the scene for the camera. I told about the hunt we were on and how we had killed a few turkeys. But it was the way I ended the narration that shook me to my core. I simply said, "Signing off, Bob Thomas."

That incident made me stop and think—who was I really? I had to remind myself that I was not Bob Thomas, but rather R. T. Stewart. And with that I thought, "Man, I'm deep. Maybe too deep. So deep undercover that I'm not sure who I am anymore. Here I am living with these bad guys for a week in this remote cabin, no phone, no TV, no nothing, and they don't have a clue as to who I really am. And I'm starting to wonder if I know who I really am." In my mind, I'd almost become another person. Hearing myself say, "Signing off, Bob Thomas," made me realize that maybe I'd lost my real identity. Or at least I was close to losing it.

———

After that, Don and I began putting together the details of the case to eventually bring it to a close. We spent days filling out search warrants, arrest warrants, and completing stacks of other paperwork. I still have the bed I slept on during those many months undercover. I mention that because our two beds, mine and Don's, were only a couple feet apart in the tiny bedroom of the undercover house. Don and I placed boards from bed to bed and used that as a desk for our primitive Apple computer as we finished the paperwork on the case.

When the time comes for the actual takedown of an undercover operation, the arrests are usually made by uniformed wildlife officers, not the undercover officers who collected the evidence in the case. It is safer that way. If uniformed officers make the arrests, the bad guys are usually confused as to how they have been found out, and by the time they figure it out they're already in jail.

Before beginning the takedown of Operation Redbud, the Ohio Division of Wildlife first notified the state of West Virginia and informed its wildlife officers of what we had as evidence. Needless to say, they were very pleased and were eager to cooperate in any way they could. In Ohio, the search warrants had to be sealed, because in a small, rural community the news can get out too easily. In McConnelsville, a couple of poachers had connections with the Morgan County Sheriff's Department, as well as with people working at the local county courthouse. We had to make sure no information leaked out prematurely as to who was being arrested and what properties were to be searched—thus the need for the sealed warrants.

Don and I were transported to the local judge's house at night in the back seat of a vehicle with a blanket over our heads so that no one could identify us. We had to appear in person in front of the judge so that he could review and sign the various arrest warrants and search warrants we'd prepared and have them officially sealed. The next day, June 20, 1996, a group of some sixty uniformed law enforcement officers gathered for the final takedown of Operation Redbud, serving arrest warrants and search warrants simultaneously. Twenty-seven defendants—twenty-six men and one woman—were arrested and convicted of 225 charges and ultimately fined more than $38,000.

At the time, Operation Redbud was the largest undercover wildlife law enforcement investigation involving the poaching of wild turkeys anywhere in North America. As far as I know, it still is. We had Jay Langston, then editor of *Turkey Call* magazine—published by the National Wild Turkey Federation

(NWTF)—go with our uniformed officers when they served the arrest warrants and search warrants, to write a story about the investigation. We also arranged for other local, regional, and national media coverage about the case.

Start to finish, Operation Redbud lasted nearly a year and a half, and Don and I kept a video record of it all, starting from day one. In reviewing that video recently, I was surprised to see how spry and chipper Don and I were at the beginning of the investigation and how tired and stressed we both looked at the end. The video footage clearly showed how much I had changed during the investigation, both from the stress and the sheer length of the operation. I was slowly discovering that it's not easy living a lie.

As I thought would happen, Claude Maxwell's reaction to being arrested was one of emotional hurt and total disbelief. He just couldn't comprehend what was happening or believe that Don and I had been undercover officers. I was told by one of our uniformed officers who made the arrest that Claude simply dropped his head and made no attempt to resist. I have never talked directly to Claude Maxwell since, but he has sent word to me through our uniformed officers many times, and I have sent word back to him. He said he harbors no ill feelings toward me and Don, and that he still likes me. He said he understands that Don and I were just doing our jobs and that he had been in the wrong for poaching.

Maxwell was found guilty of seventy wildlife law violations, fined $11,000 plus court costs, and given a lifetime suspension of his hunting privileges in Ohio. He also forfeited to the state his four-wheel-drive pickup truck, an ATV, a crossbow, two twelve-gauge shotguns, and a high-powered rifle.

Today, Claude Maxwell owns a small bait and tackle shop near McConnelsville, and the uniformed state wildlife officer assigned to that county stops by the store occasionally. The officer tells me that Claude still asks about me every once in a while. I've even joked with Claude through our uniformed officers. "Tell Claude that if he's looking for someone to go hunting with him sometime, I'd be glad to."

Lee Lilly, on the other hand, reacted very negatively to being arrested. He did not resist, but he was extremely angry—in fact, "ready to tear someone's head off" would probably be a more accurate description. Basically, he wanted to kill Don and me once he found out who we really were. We received some anonymous death threats following the case, but, as in Operation Clanbake, nothing ever came of them. Obviously, I'm still around today to tell my story.

Lee Lilly was found guilty of fifty-two wildlife law violations, fined $10,000 plus court costs, and had his Ohio hunting privileges suspended for life. He also was sentenced to ninety days in jail and placed on six months probation and on house arrest for an additional six months. In addition, he forfeited a .22-caliber rifle and a twelve-gauge shotgun to the state.

Operation Redbud had been another success for Don and me, but it was the last undercover investigation Officer Don Carter ever worked. The accumulated stress of the Operations Redbud and Clanbake were just too much for him, and he soon retired. I, on the other hand, was energized by the success of this second undercover case. After a few months rest, I was ready to go under again, only this time in search of one particular poacher obsessed with large, trophy deer antlers.

# 3

# OPERATION EGO

The average person, especially a nonhunter, may find it difficult to believe how obsessed some poachers can get over large deer antlers—so crazed, in fact, that such poachers actually become addicted to poaching deer with trophy antlers. To these men, poaching for large antlers is as addictive as pornography is to others. Wildlife officers have even coined a clever term to describe this particular addiction: *hornography.*

The main target of my new investigation, Michael R. Barker, was just such a poacher. He did not poach for profit. Despite the value of the trophy antlers he acquired from the deer he poached—potentially worth tens of thousands of dollars—he did not sell them. Instead, he simply kept the antlers, mounting many of them in his home to swell his own ego and inflate his standing in the eyes of his hunting buddies. Hence the name of this particular undercover project: Operation Ego.

Although this case was one of my shorter ones, lasting only a month or two in 1994 and 1995, it has interest as the record of a case of extreme hornography. It targeted the taking of record-book white-tailed deer from two states, Ohio and West Virginia.

We undertook the case based on intelligence that several poachers, headed by Barker, were regularly driving into Ohio at night from West Virginia and using spotlights and high-powered rifles to shoot big bucks. If the poachers were in a hurry, they'd simply cut off the heads of the deer they killed, leaving the bodies to rot. If they had more time, they'd take the entire deer carcass back to West Virginia and check it at an official game check station, claiming the deer had been killed legally in the Mountain State with a bow and arrow. Barker already had several large bucks listed under his name in the West Virginia record book, but that wasn't enough for him. He always seemed to want just one more trophy deer, and it didn't matter to him how he killed it, legally or illegally.

The Ohio Division of Wildlife had received many complaints over a period of years about this particular group of poachers, and Barker himself had been arrested previously in both Ohio and West Virginia for illegally spotlighting deer while in possession of a firearm. The last straw in initiating this undercover investigation, however, was a videotape sent by an informant to the Ohio Division of Wildlife. The tape showed Barker's trophy room literally filled with trophy bucks, both heads and full-body mounts, in numbers that made it highly likely that they had been killed illegally. Astonishingly, the tape also recorded members of Barker's poaching ring in the act of killing many of those deer illegally and then bragging about it and explaining in detail the techniques and equipment they used. Apparently, the poachers had made the tape themselves as a memento. Barker had sent a copy of the tape to a friend of his in Buckhannon, West Virginia, and a third guy, a friend of the friend, had viewed the tape, made a copy, and sent it to the Ohio Division of Wildlife, Law Enforcement Section.

At the time, Michael Barker was a car salesman living near St. Albans, West Virginia—or so we thought. Keith Wood—we called him Woody—was the uniformed state wildlife officer assigned to Ohio's Meigs County, just across the Ohio River from West Virginia. Woody knew Barker well, not only because of the numerous complaints he'd received concerning him but because he had arrested Barker no less than five times previously. All told, Barker had already been arrested by Ohio and West Virginia wildlife officers an even dozen times. The charges? Always deer poaching and always trophy bucks. At the culmination of this investigation, this record would prompt a major confrontation between Woody and Barker.

I was first contacted about Operation Ego in the fall of 1994, when my supervisor, Dick Scott, asked me to travel to West Virginia to investigate. At the time, Scott was the head of wildlife law enforcement in Ohio, but, as he warned me, he had no authority to assign me to another state, so the investigation would be tricky. Was I willing to go secretly out of state?

Being young, gung-ho, and maybe a little too green or too stupid to say no, I agreed. "Good," said Scott. "But remember, you report to me and no one else, R.T. . . . In this particular case, the West Virginia DNR won't know you're coming. No one but me will know you're working out of state. You understand? So don't carry a gun or any identification." Then he added, "And if you get caught, just play your good ol' boy role, and I'll get you back home to Ohio somehow. It just may take awhile. . . ."

When I nodded, he began to fill me in on the intelligence concerning the case, concluding by saying, "Your primary objective in this investigation is to let me know when Barker is coming to Ohio so I can notify our uniformed wildlife officers. Hopefully, they will then be able to catch him in the field, actually poaching, and make an arrest. If you get anything else going while you're in West Virginia, we'll just consider that gravy. But your primary objective is to let me know when Barker is headed our way."

Scott paused, then warned me, "Whatever you do, R.T., don't get your cover blown while in West Virginia. Because if you do, this whole thing will be a political embarrassment that could cost me my job."

———

I drove to West Virginia a few days later. Once I arrived, my first stop was at the car dealership where Barker supposedly worked. He wasn't there. I stopped back several times thereafter, but never could find him at work. I had to find another way to make contact.

My next step was to make the rounds of the hunting and fishing stores in the area to see if anyone knew Barker. A few people had heard of him, but I couldn't get concrete information about where he might be found. I widened my search over the following month, knocking on many doors and talking to a lot of people, but to no avail. I simply could not locate Barker.

My usual methods for beginning an undercover investigation were not working. Finally, I just decided to go to the last address I had for Barker, knock on the door, and see what happened. I had no particular story prepared. If he or someone else answered the door, I'd make something up to explain my presence. After all, this was my third undercover investigation. I had enough confidence in myself by then to know I would come up with something believable. When I tried that approach, though, no one was at home. In fact, it looked as if no one had been living at that address for quite a while. It was downright discouraging.

Then a day or two later, Dick Scott called to give me new information. He'd received a recent report that Barker was now living near Ripley, West Virginia, up in the mountains in a hunting cabin. If that information was accurate, it explained why I'd not been able to locate him.

When I first drove past the hunting cabin near Ripley to look over the situation, I spotted Barker's vehicle in the driveway. The license plate was a match, so I knew I was finally on the right track. Now I could return to my standard tactic of seemingly meeting Barker by chance, through a local contact.

As in my first two undercover investigations, I tried to get the name of one of Barker's neighbors to help break the ice when I finally made direct contact with Barker. Stopping at the next house down the road, I knocked on the door. Unfortunately—again—no one was home. Frustrated, I finally decided just to drive back to Barker's cabin and knock on the door. If he answered, I'd tell him I was from Ohio, express an interest in hunting, and ask him if he knew of a good place to bow hunt.

I was tense when I rapped on the door of Barker's cabin. Making the initial contact with the main target in any undercover investigation is always nerve wracking, and I wanted this first meeting to go as well as possible. I knew this could be the break I'd been working toward for the past month, and didn't want to blow it.

Within a few moments Barker himself opened the door. I'd never seen him before, but knew it was Barker from an intelligence photo. Using the alias Bob Thomas, I introduced myself, and then told him, as planned, that I was from Ohio and was looking for a place to bow hunt. Did he know who owned the property just down the road?

He told me the name of his neighbor, and I asked if the neighbor ever allowed any hunting? "Well, they let me hunt. . . ." Barker replied.

"Do you think they'd let me hunt, too?" I asked.

"If you're hunting with me they will," he said, sizing me up.

That sounded positive and I felt I was making some progress, so I kept the conversation going by asking, "Do you know where Rutland and Salem Center are in Ohio?" Barker nodded. "Well, I live between those two towns," I told him.

I knew that was the area of Ohio in which Barker liked to poach, and his face brightened upon hearing that was my home turf. I figured that my apparent candor would appeal to him, and I hoped self-interest might kick in, too. I hoped he would figure that if he befriended me, he might be able to use my house in Ohio as a base for his poaching in the area—somewhere he could stay and shoot big deer at his leisure.

The conversation continued to go well, with Barker gradually warming up to me. Eventually, he invited me in, and the next thing I knew I was eating lunch with him, his wife, and their young child. We talked about hunting throughout the meal, and afterward he showed me snapshots of some monster bucks he'd killed. And I do mean monster bucks, lots of them.

Finally, Barker said the words I'd been waiting to hear, "You need to come back tomorrow and hunt with me." I grinned and nodded. "I can't take you along tonight," Barker continued, "because I've got two others guys going along with me, but you come back tomorrow, and we'll go hunting together."

Barker must have realized he'd just admitted that he hunted at night, but I didn't say anything, just remained quiet, letting the comment pass. We continued to talk, and about an hour later two men showed up at the cabin. That was my opportunity to leave, and I did so, but as I excused myself and headed out the door, I told Barker I'd be back first thing the next morning. "Looking forward to huntin' with ya," I said.

——————

As I drove away, I knew it had been a good first contact. After more than a month of hard trying I finally had my foot in the door with Barker and his gang of poachers.

Upon leaving the hunting cabin, I immediately phoned my supervisor, Dick Scott, to tell him I had finally made contact with Barker and had arranged to hunt with him the next morning. I also told Scott that I thought Barker was coming to Ohio that very night to poach deer, along with two other men.

"Are you sure?" Scott asked.

"No, I'm not sure, Dick. But he told me he couldn't hunt with me tonight because he had two other guys going along with him, and then they showed up at the cabin. It's only a guess, but I think they're headed for Ohio. Tonight."

There was silence on the other end of the phone for a few seconds. Then Scott said, "You contact Woody on your way home. Tell him you think Barker and two guys are headed his way. I'll call Woody myself just as soon as we hang up and tell him to expect your call."

In anticipation of hunting with Barker the next day, I immediately bought a West Virginia hunting license. After leaving the store I called Woody, told him I needed to meet with him ASAP, and drove to a spot near Pomeroy, Ohio, overlooking the Ohio River. When I told Woody not only that I had been working undercover in West Virginia for the past month but that I'd just had a meal with Barker and his family, he was shocked. This gave way to excitement when I added, "And I think he and two other guys are coming to Ohio tonight. Have our officers ready. . . ."

I drove home, got my hunting gear together for the next day's hunt with Barker, and went to bed late, but I didn't sleep very soundly. I guess I was apprehensive about what the next day might bring. About 3:00 A.M., the phone rang. It was Woody.

"We got him!" Woody said in an excited voice, nearly shouting into the phone. "We arrested Barker and two of his buddies tonight for spotlighting. Caught them right in the act!"

Just as I had suspected, Barker and his fellow poachers had crossed into Ohio earlier that evening, looking for deer. In the meantime, Woody had rounded up as many uniformed Ohio wildlife officers as possible and positioned them throughout Barker's suspected poaching area. The officers were waiting in patrol vehicles along back roads and the edges of picked cornfields, like cats anticipating a mouse leaving its hole. And, as luck would have it, other Ohio wildlife officers were working an airplane project that night just to the north.

An airplane project is when a fixed-wing aircraft is used for air-to-ground surveillance of possible illegal spotlighting activity. If an officer in the plane sees spotlighting after dark, he radios fellow officers on the ground and gives them the location coordinates so they can converge on the suspected poacher. Obviously, an airplane can patrol a much larger area much more quickly and easily than officers on the ground. Aircraft, both fixed-wing airplanes and helicopters, are wildlife officers' "eyes in the sky" and a valuable tool of modern-day wildlife law enforcement.

That night, the takedown began with Woody and Dana Aldridge, a special deputy with the Meigs County Sheriff's Office, sitting in the dark in Woody's patrol vehicle at the rear of a rural cemetery. The pair was watching the road in front of them for Barker or anyone else who might drive by, spotlighting. About 1:00 A.M., a car came slowly creeping along the road, and suddenly a spotlight from the car split the darkness in the field across from the cemetery, its beam searching back and forth for deer. Woody immediately pulled his vehicle onto the road so that the two vehicles were facing one another, then turned on his flashing lights and siren to stop the approaching car. The car, illuminated as it was by the beam of Woody's headlights, was recognizable as Barker's. But Barker ignored the officer's flashing vehicle lights and siren, hit the gas, and careened around Woody's vehicle. The chase was on. . . .

Woody radioed for backup and pursued Barker's vehicle over dark country roads at speeds of more than seventy miles per hour. But even at those dangerous speeds, Woody couldn't keep up with Barker. Fortunately, the Division of Wildlife airplane flying to the north had just completed its work there. When the pilot heard the radio traffic of the chase, he headed the plane south. Within a few minutes, the airplane had located Barker's speeding vehicle on the roads below. The pilot reported to converging officers that Barker was stopping and waiting at crossroads, trying to determine if anyone was still chasing him, and, if so, which way he should go. An added bit of drama here was that the airplane, after already flying most of the night, was now low on fuel. But the veteran pilot, John Clem, said over the radio, "If I run out of gas, I'll land this thing in a field if I have to . . . I'm not letting these guys get away!"

When the pilot finally determined for sure which way Barker was headed, he advised ground officers of the poacher's direction of travel and they set up a road block. But Barker blew through it at high speed, almost hitting one of the officers' vehicles. Ironically, not far past the roadblock, a pair of deer crossed in front of Barker's car and he swerved to miss them. As a result, he lost control and piled his vehicle into the road ditch. Barker jumped out and started running across an open field to escape, but the two men traveling with him stayed in the car.

Woody and the sheriff's deputy were the first on the scene. Locking up his brakes, Woody slid his vehicle to a stop beside Barker's, jumped out, and began chasing the poacher on foot. I'll let Woody tell the rest of the story from here, in his own words, just as he told it to me over the phone that night.

"I chased Barker about 150 yards, and he eventually fell down," said Woody. "And as he was getting to his feet, I tackled him. I kept yelling at him to stay down, that he was under arrest, even calling him by name, but he kept wrestling with me. He tore buttons off my uniform shirt and pulled off my clip-on tie. Then he made a grab for my gun.

"I could feel his right hand pulling up on the butt of my sidearm, and his left hand was on my holster. I yelled, 'No, Mike! No!' but he just kept trying to get my gun. I was able to hit him in the neck with my elbow and knock him away temporarily, but he came back and tried for my gun again. That's when Special Deputy Aldridge finally got there."

Officer Aldridge had been running parallel to Barker during the chase through the field, attempting to cut off his escape. He got to the scene of the fight between Woody and Barker as soon as he could, and quickly struck Barker across the back of the neck with a flashlight, knocking him unconscious. The two officers then handcuffed Barker and dragged him back to the road.

Nearly a dozen police vehicles were waiting there or just pulling up, their lights flashing and whirling and their sirens blaring. Handcuffed and lying face down beside the road were the two poachers who had stayed in the wrecked car. Their names were Warren Shirkey and Ricky Gobert, both residents of West Virginia.

While being interrogated, Shirkey and Gobert confessed to many violations of the wildlife laws, both in Ohio and West Virginia. As a result, search warrants were served on Barker's residence, and West Virginia wildlife officers discovered that most of the deer in Barker's trophy room—an unbelievable total of sixty-eight trophy heads and full-body deer mounts—had been shot in Ohio and checked illegally in West Virginia as bow-and-arrow kills.

Gobert even told of how he would drive his pickup truck from West Virginia to Ohio and leave it parked along a back road. When Barker's gang shot a deer from their car, they'd transport the carcass to the truck and offload it there, doing this several times per night. At the end of the night, Gobert would then drive his truck back to West Virginia, the poached deer hidden out of sight beneath the truck's cap. The car they used when actually shooting the deer was usually either one they rented or one from the car lot where Barker worked.

Gobert was found guilty on twelve charges of deer poaching in Ohio and ordered to pay $4,500 in fines and court costs. In addition, he paid $5,000 to the state of Ohio to buy back his pickup truck, the one used in transporting the illegal deer. His accomplice, Warren Shirkey, paid $540 in fines and courts costs on a single charge. Both men also lost their Ohio hunting privileges for life.

Barker appeared in Ohio's Meigs County Court facing a total of fifteen charges: fourteen deer poaching violations and one charge of assaulting a state wildlife officer. Found guilty on all counts, Barker was sentenced to eighteen months in a state penitentiary and ordered to pay $8,000 in fines and court costs. He also forfeited his vehicle, a two-year-old Chevy Lumina, his high-powered rifle, his spotlight, four mounted deer heads, and his Ohio hunting privileges for life. And that was just in Ohio; he faced similar charges in West Virginia.

Mike Barker had a long record of wildlife law violations before this investigation. Between 1975 and 1991, he had been arrested seven times for deer poaching in Ohio (five times by Officer Keith Wood), paying thousands of dollars in fines as a result. He also had forfeited two vehicles to the state of Ohio during those years. Ironically, it was his arrest in 1980 that led the Ohio Supreme Court to rule that the Ohio Division of Wildlife could indeed confiscate vehicles involved in wildlife law violations.

While in prison, Barker was nearly electrocuted. It seems he had made a few enemies in jail, and some of the other inmates were out to get him. They had rigged an electric floor-mopping machine to short-circuit when he turned it on, giving Barker a severe electric shock. Although he survived the incident, he lost the sight in one eye as a result. Prison was unkind to Barker in another way, as well. He developed testicular cancer during his incarceration. But he survived that, too, to serve his full sentence.

———

A side note to this operation is that it demonstrates the effectiveness of undercover wildlife investigation. During the fall of 1994, before I was sent in, uniformed wildlife officers in both Ohio and West Virginia had been working a coordinated enforcement project for months trying to catch Barker poaching. Officers had stationed themselves at both ends of three bridges crossing the Ohio River, ready to stop Barker as he returned from Ohio with illegal deer. But the officers failed to catch him crossing the river.

Once I was sent in, I was able to gather enough information about Barker to set up his arrest in little over a month. In saying this, I am not denigrating the importance of uniformed wildlife officers and the job they do. Nor am I implying that they are not skilled and hard-working. It's just that when wearing a uniform, officers are limited in certain ways that don't apply to undercover work. Posing as a hunter willing to break the law allowed me to get intelligence that uniformed officers had been unable to obtain after years of trying.

Officer Keith Wood made an interesting comment to me following this case. "It's hard to describe," he said, "what went through my mind during that fight and arrest of Barker. When Barker was grabbing for my gun, I thought he was going to kill me. It's an adrenaline rush like I've never experienced in my life . . . it was incredible, indescribable. I could hardly walk after the fight I was so wrung out. I just had to sit down for a while."

Woody continued, "And following the incident, I was emotionally drained. I thought of my family and of my own life, and how quickly it all could have ended. As a wildlife officer, you try not to think that something like that could ever happen to you, but I found out that it can. It was a real reality check."

When Barker was finally behind bars, I related my full story to Woody and the other Ohio wildlife officers involved in the case. I told how I had had a meal with Barker and his family just a few hours after meeting him for the first time. I kidded the officers that they had caught Barker way too quickly. "I was just getting started with him," I said, "and you guys spoiled all my fun!" We all laughed, but we also knew it was very satisfying to finally have this perennial deer poacher and his gang of no-goods out of the woods.

Woody's final comment about the case was telling, and seemed to sum it up well. "In all my years as an Ohio Wildlife officer, I never saw anyone with an obsession for large deer antlers like Mike Barker," he said. "To him, trophy antlers were an addiction just as powerful as drugs, alcohol, or gambling."

I told you some poachers can become addicted to hornography.

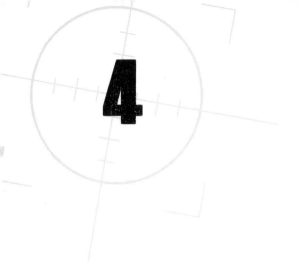

# OPERATION TAG

After the retirement of Don Carter (the wildlife officer who had partnered with me during my first two undercover investigations), some changes had taken place in the Division of Wildlife. The success of our past investigations had prompted the agency to form an official Covert Investigations Unit, and we even had an actual budget to work with. I had a new supervisor, Kevin O'Dell, who had paired me up with a new partner, an enthusiastic young officer whom I shall call Shaun.

Shaun was eager to learn undercover work, but like most young officers new to the job he was unsure of himself, lacking confidence. He had been given this investigation, Operation Tag, in 2000 to learn the ropes, but after several months, he found the case going nowhere. That's when I was called in to work with Shaun and help him get started. In undercover parlance, that's called "lining him out."

Operation Tag was so named because it concerned the improper use of deer tags. The Division of Wildlife had been receiving complaints that several deer check stations in eastern Ohio were checking deer that had been killed illegally. The check stations were handing out deer check slips to hunters like candy, allowing the hunters to tag their own deer without inspection. Not surprisingly, major abuses were occurring as a result.

Some hunters, for example, were shooting deer and checking them under other people's names, not their own. A hunter would claim his wife, girlfriend, cousin, uncle, or whoever had killed the deer, and then he would go and shoot more deer. All of this was highly illegal, since it allowed these hunters to take well over their legal bag limit of deer annually.

64

This investigation took place in and around the town of Richmond, in Ohio's extreme east-central region. At the time, I was living in Aberdeen, Ohio, just across the river from Maysville, Kentucky, and working a major undercover investigation along the Ohio River known as Operation River Sweep. Meanwhile, Shaun had found a safe house in Richmond, the general area of Operation Tag, and was trying to lay the groundwork for his first case.

Unfortunately, things weren't going well. Shaun kept telling our supervisor, O'Dell, that he couldn't locate anyone mentioned in the various complaints that had initiated this investigation. This was especially frustrating since O'Dell was still receiving intelligence about the suspected poachers, so we knew the poaching was still going on.

Shaun had been hanging out at a local hunting and fishing store, K & L Sports, one of the check stations supposedly checking deer illegally. He had gotten to know the store's owners and had prepared them for my arrival by telling them he had a buddy coming to visit. He also told them his buddy liked to 'coon hunt. When I arrived a few days later, I played up my role. I met the store owners and, with Shaun, hung around the store all that day. Remarking that I lived in West Virginia, I chatted casually with the store owners and the other guys who came and went. Finally, a group of guys came in that Shaun knew to be some of the suspected poachers. These guys were serious 'coon hunters, and I had purposely brought one of my 'coon dogs along with me as part of my cover. My dog proved a great ice-breaker. I soon got to talking with the group about 'coon hunting and 'coon dogs; one thing led to another; and that very day—at my first-ever meeting with these guys—they invited Shaun and me to go 'coon hunting with them that night.

That hunt was a turning point. In no time, these guys were predisposing themselves to me and Shaun, telling us about checking deer illegally at K & L Sports and other check stations in the area. They bragged that they could just walk in, get a deer tag from the store owner, fill it out in the name of anyone they wanted, and no one was the wiser.

———

The primary target in this investigation was a guy by the name of Kenneth L. Dorsey Jr., a suspected deer poacher who liked to shoot large-antlered deer. Shaun had been trying to meet him, but Dorsey had never come into the store while Shaun was there. One day, Dorsey finally showed up, explaining that he'd stayed away on purpose recently because of seeing Shaun's pickup truck in the parking lot. It seems Shaun's vehicle was painted the same dark-green color as the local game warden's truck, and Dorsey thought the game warden was hanging out at the store. In fact, the two trucks were similar in color because Shaun was driving an old, unmarked Division of Wildlife pickup truck. In retrospect, that wasn't a smart move on Shaun's part, as it might have caused the poachers to wonder why the two trucks were so similar, but fortunately it never did.

Dorsey was reportedly poaching monster bucks at night, spotlighting them from a vehicle and then shooting them with a high-powered rifle. Once Shaun and Dorsey had got acquainted, he began to talk me up, telling Dorsey that I liked to shoot big deer too and that I had a van with four-wheel-drive. Soon Shaun arranged for Dorsey and me to meet, and I drove the two hundred miles from Aberdeen to meet up with him and Shaun at the hunting and fishing store. We cooked some deer meat for supper that I'd brought along and did some drinking together. Over the next few months, we had several similar meetings, and soon Dorsey and the rest of the poachers were thinking of us as buddies.

When we'd meet the group, we would always bring a dead deer or two with us. Since they were not in season, naturally the poachers believed we'd killed them illegally, while in reality, the deer had been supplied to us by uniformed Ohio wildlife officers; the deer had been killed on farms or in orchards holding permits to shoot deer year round to prevent crop damage. After the hunting and fishing store closed for the day, we were often invited by Dorsey and his fellow poachers to go to a local bar with them. We'd go, of course, continuing to build a rapport with members of the group.

Besides poaching, Dorsey was also into snorting cocaine. We discovered he was involved with a local militia movement, too; every time we went to his house, he had a militia Web site displayed. This was a concern to us, because we didn't know how deeply he was involved in such activity or how it might affect our investigation. We simply hadn't run into anything like that before. Dorsey's involvement with the militia also raised the possibility that the Feds were watching him. This was just after Timothy McVeigh had bombed the Murrah Federal Building in Oklahoma City, so the FBI and other federal agencies were closely monitoring militias. At that time, in fact, every federal and state agency was on high alert for terrorist activities, both domestic and foreign.

One night, Dorsey finally said the words Shaun and I had been waiting to hear: "I wanna go shoot some deer. . . ." I told him I'd drive, and away the three of us went. Shaun and I had already hunted with Dorsey a time or two, but we hadn't shot anything. We just hadn't found a deer big enough to interest Dorsey on those nights.

One strange aspect of this case was that Dorsey always wanted to shine and shoot his deer within the city limits of Richmond, rather than on the rural back roads favored by most deer poachers. His reasoning was that all the big bucks in the area were living within the city limits, not in the country where legal hunters could get at them. I don't know to this day how we were able to shine and shoot within the town and not get caught. I expected to be arrested, so I never carried a handgun when we went poaching or did any drinking beforehand. As the vehicle driver, I didn't want to be arrested for DUI or for carrying a concealed weapon, as well as poaching.

Since Richmond was expanding into the surrounding farmland, its city limits encompassed many woods and fields; it wasn't like we were shining and shooting within a major metropolitan area. Nevertheless, people must have seen our spotlight late at night and heard the crack of the rifle. Yet, unbelievably, no one ever called the law on us that we knew of. One reason for our luck may have been Dorsey's family connections; his parents owned a large part of the town. In addition, he may have had some connections with local law enforcement—at least enough to know when certain law enforcement officers were working and when they weren't. Either way, we never got caught.

On this particular night, I was driving, Dorsey was sitting in the front passenger seat of my van, and Shaun was in the rear seat. We located a nice buck, and as I held the spotlight over the top of the van from the driver's window, Dorsey shot the buck from the passenger window. In case anyone had heard the shot or seen us, we drove down the road, turned around, and returned a few minutes later to the spot where the deer had fallen. Dorsey was a big, overweight guy who could hardly get around, and clearly, he wanted Shaun and me to do the dirty work, commenting, "That deer is quite a ways from the road . . . we're sure gonna have to drag him a long way back to the van."

I wasn't too eager to drag the deer a long way, either, so I responded, "Hold on, boys. We ain't draggin' no deer." Then I slipped the van into four-wheel drive and took off across the field, stopping right next to the dead deer. Shaun and I jumped out, loaded it into the back of the van within seconds, and away we sped, back to the road. Dorsey was not only pleased, he was also impressed. The incident confirmed his belief that Shaun and I were serious poachers, like him, and had done this type of thing many times before.

We continued our poaching that night with Dorsey, driving and shining within the city limits, and soon we saw another large buck standing on the left side of the road. I stopped the van and held the spotlight on the deer from the driver's window, thinking Dorsey would hand me the rifle so I could take the shot. Instead, he stuck the rifle across my chest with the muzzle pointed out the window. Just then the deer moved off to the left, and, thankfully, Dorsey didn't take the shot. Had he pulled the trigger with the gun so near my face, the muzzle blast could have injured me.

We drove up the road, turned around, and came back, and this time another large buck appeared in the spotlight beam on the passenger side of the van. Dorsey shot the deer in the head, then he and Shaun bailed out to retrieve it. The deer had fallen near the road, but on the opposite side of a woven-wire fence. I drove up the road, turned around, and came back to find that the men weren't ready to load the deer. Dorsey was lying along the fence out of breath, barely able to get up. He said he was worn out from trying to lift the large deer over the fence. Since this left Shaun trying unsuccessfully to pull the buck over the fence by himself, I jumped out to help. The deer was so large it took the two of us several minutes to get it over the fence and loaded into the van. All this time, Dorsey made no move to help; he just sat there, panting and watching.

We took the two bucks to Dorsey's house, gutted them, and then loaded them back into the van for safekeeping overnight; it was cold enough at night by then that we knew the meat wouldn't spoil. The next day we drove to the hunting and fishing store and bragged to the owners that we had killed a couple of nice bucks the night before and had the deer in the van. As was their usual mode of operation, the store owners handed us deer check forms and we filled them out ourselves. But we intentionally did not place the permanent, metal tags on the deer, as required by law.

Next, we took the two carcasses to a commercial meat processor who accepted deer. This particular processor, whom I'll call Jerry Ensell, knew the poachers and would accept their deer for processing whether or not they had the proper metal check tags attached. All of the suspects involved in this investigation—the store owners, the poachers, the meat processors, and others—knew one another and were buddies, and they all knew about the poaching that was occurring.

———

Throughout the deer-hunting season, we continued to shoot deer illegally with Dorsey and to take the carcasses to Ensell for processing. Shaun and I also continued to hang out at the hunting and fishing store, illegally tagging deer for the poachers who brought them in. We did this so that we could more easily keep track of the various numbers on the deer check forms and tags. That way, when it came time to take down these bad guys, we would know who had done what, who to arrest, and what more was needed in the way of follow-up interviews or interrogations by uniformed officers.

Shaun or I sometimes would wear a body wire, secretly taping our conversations with the poachers. On one occasion, we caught Dorsey on tape saying that if he ever did get caught poaching or doing illegal drugs, he wasn't worried about what the local judge might do to him; he said he had some dirt on the judge, and could buy him off if necessary. When we took down the poachers in this case, we played that tape for the judge, and he saw red. As a result, he hammered Dorsey, finding him guilty of more than twenty-five violations of state wildlife law, and sentencing him to pay a total of $4,770 in fines, restitution, and court costs. Dorsey also spent sixty days in jail, lost his Ohio hunting privileges for life, and was placed on probation for five years. He was sentenced not only for the deer violations but also for cocaine possession and other charges. Fifteen other poachers were also arrested in the case.

During the takedown, uniformed officers seized many illegal deer held by Jerry Ensell, the meat processor, and served search warrants on the hunting and fishing store. The owners of the store were not only shocked to learn that Shaun and I were undercover officers, but very hurt emotionally, as well, because they had grown close to us. In just a few months, they had taken a liking to us, even going so far as to invite us to meals with their families.

How does something like that affect an undercover officer psychologically? Can the process of cultivating people's trust and then ultimately turning them in mess with your mind? If I let my guard down, it could and did affect me. There were many times that I lay in bed at night, especially the night before a takedown, thinking how I actually controlled people's future. I knew exactly what was going to happen to the suspects the next day, and they didn't. They expected the next day to be just another ordinary day, while I knew their entire life was about to change. Most not only were going to have to pay a hefty fine but also probably were going to jail, possibly for many years. While it was true that the bad guy brought the impending grief on himself, the undercover officer still controlled what was going to happen. I hesitate to call it a God-complex, but it's something similar to that.

Such power, especially over people you have worked hard to get to know well and to spend time with, can and does work on you psychologically. However, the longer I worked under cover, the less that kind of thing bothered me. I gradually hardened myself to it, trying to maintain a psychological wall between myself and the bad guys.

After the takedown of an investigation, an undercover officer seldom sees the poachers again, and for good reason. But in this particular case, I did pass two of the bad guys in the parking lot of a restaurant one day. They waved as they pulled out in their vehicle, and I waved back, not fully recognizing them until they had driven past. It was a strange feeling.

To sum up this undercover investigation, Shaun spent more than a year on it. For me, though, it had been a relatively short case, involving only a few months of my time. I had arrived in the fall, just as the deer-hunting seasons were getting under way. Before I showed up, the investigation had been stalled; Shaun simply lacked the experience to cultivate the necessary contacts. Within hours of my arrival, however, I was 'coon hunting with the bad guys, and things took off from there. I believe Shaun was grateful for my help and instruction. Today, he still works undercover for Ohio's Division of Wildlife as one its best and most seasoned officers.

# 5

# OPERATION RIVER SWEEP

During my time as an undercover wildlife law enforcement officer, I was constantly amazed at how a seemingly small investigation could mushroom into a much larger one, eventually identifying and targeting many poachers. This was especially true of this investigation, Operation River Sweep, which I worked with Shaun, whom I had aided on Operation Tag.

Initially, the project targeted two groups of poachers in southern Ohio. By the end, though, the picture had changed. On the one hand, unfortunately, one of our main targets escaped prosecution, but on the other, evidence collected along the way let us prosecute several more bad guys. Here's how it all went down.

The primary area in which this project took place was a stretch along the Ohio River in Ohio's Adams and Brown counties. At the beginning of the investigation, in the fall of 1998, my undercover partner and I were living in and working from a safe house in Hillsboro, Ohio, just north of the project area. We had been investigating another case that we called Operation Mud Cat, since it involved fishermen illegally selling sport-caught catfish to pay lakes.

While living in Hillsboro, we received intelligence from our supervisor, Kevin O'Dell, about two separate poaching rings operating just to the south of us. One of the groups was headed by a poacher living in Peebles in Adams County, while the other was headed by a poacher living in Aberdeen in Brown County. The two poachers lived only about thirty miles apart, but apparently did not know one another.

The first suspect, the one from Peebles, was so extreme in his poaching that eventually we began referring to him as "the Hunter from Hell" (THFH), and the more Shaun and I got to know and interact with him, the more we despised him. But our main target in this investigation was the second suspect, the one living in Aberdeen. This poacher, named Louis Bramel Jr. (a.k.a. Junior Bramel), lived just a half-hour drive southwest of Peebles, along with two of his hunting buddies. The trio had been a thorn in the collective sides of local wildlife officers for many years.

From intelligence gathered about the poaching rings in Peebles and Aberdeen, and from complaints received from the public, we knew these poachers were illegally killing many big deer—especially large-antlered bucks—shining and shooting them mainly at night and bragging about their crimes to the locals. Initially, Shaun had been directed to investigate THFH and I had been assigned Junior Bramel and his two buddies, but because the poachers lived so close together, Shaun and I decided to work the two cases together.

Shaun tried several times to make contact with THFH, but for various reasons, he couldn't get it done. Eventually, he asked me to go along with him one day to try and break the ice. We drove by the suspect's house and noticed a souped-up Chevy muscle car sitting in the driveway. Shaun knew something about fast cars—in fact, they were his hobby—so I suggested we stop at the house, knock on the door, and see if THFH would answer. If he did, we'd begin talking with him about cars. I told Shaun to pretend he was interested in buying the Chevy. I also told him that I'd begin the conversation, but that since he knew more about muscle cars than I, he should eventually take over. He agreed, and we went for it.

Pulling into the suspect's driveway, we knocked on the door of the house, and a woman answered—THFH's wife. I told her we were in the area scouting for places to hunt, had seen the car sitting in the driveway, and wanted to know if it was for sale. Shaun then took over, saying he was looking to rebuild a car and might be interested in buying the Chevy. The woman told us that her husband wasn't home but that she expected him back shortly. We were welcome to come inside and wait for him, she added. Since she was very friendly, we took her up on her offer, talking with her for several minutes before THFH returned home. When he did, Shaun and I introduced ourselves, and we all went outside to look at the car.

Shaun talked a good while with THFH about cars but gradually steered the conversation toward hunting and fishing. THFH lit up when Shaun mentioned hunting, telling us about all the various species of game he hunted and the trophy animals he'd killed. We already knew much of what he was telling us from the intelligence given us on the case, but it was good to have it confirmed by THFH himself. Eventually, he said just what we wanted to hear: he invited us to go hunting with him sometime. We exchanged phone numbers and left, feeling good about our initial contact in the case. And no, Shaun didn't buy the car.

———

Soon after, I left for Aberdeen to begin my half of the investigation, traveling alone since Shaun's appearance made it unlikely that he would fit in well in that area of the state. I began scouting for a house to rent, staying in a local motel for a few days as I did so. During that time, O'Dell called late one night and asked me what I was doing. I told him I was in a motel room, watching TV, and trying to get the investigation under way. He shocked me by saying that the license plate number on my vehicle had just been run by local law enforcement officers. He knew this because of a safeguard called a "trap." If a uniformed law enforcement officer stops a vehicle and runs a license registration check, the license check goes through the national Law Enforcement Automated Data System (LEADS). If the vehicle is an undercover vehicle, the supervisor of the undercover officer assigned to the vehicle is automatically notified. This policy is added protection for the undercover officer, and in this case, it told us that someone was watching me.

I asked O'Dell when exactly the plate had been run and he told me. I told him that I had driven through a trailer court about 9:00 P.M. that night, looking for a place to rent. The trailer court was owned by Junior Bramel (the poacher I was targeting in this half of the investigation) and his family. The fact that my license plate had been run shortly after I'd cruised the trailer court indicated that Bramel might have connections with local law enforcement in the small town of Aberdeen. I still don't know why my license plate was run or by whom, but the fact that it was checked that early in the investigation was a concern. Who was watching me, and why? That incident would continue to play on my mind throughout the coming weeks and months.

A few days later, I drove back to the trailer court and stopped at the office, inquiring about a trailer to rent. Junior Bramel's mother managed the trailer court, so I spoke with her. She said she had an open trailer or two, and I asked the monthly rental price. When she told me, I said I was interested. She then asked me what I was doing in the area.

I told her I was from West Virginia but had been living recently in Hillsboro, Ohio. Since Shaun and I actually had been living in Hillsboro, I offered to give her the name and contact information of my previous landlord in that area as a reference if she needed it. I also told her my cover story, explaining that I was on disability after being injured in a coal-mining accident, that my girlfriend had recently left me, and that I was looking to make a fresh start in life. I added that I wanted to live closer to the Ohio River than Hillsboro, since I liked to catch big catfish and wanted to start fishing more often.

As I was finishing my rehearsed speech, she asked me right up front, "You ain't no game warden, are ya?"

Her comment caught me off guard, but I tried not to look too surprised. "Do I look like a game warden?" I asked.

"No, you don't," she said, "but I had to ask. We hate them damn game wardens around here."

She and her family no doubt did hate wildlife officers. After all, her son, Junior, had been caught poaching several times. Unfortunately, instead of slowing him down, these arrests had just made him smarter and harder to catch. Figuring I had better play up my good ol' boy role at this point, I agreed with her. "Yeah, I hate them damn game wardens, too," I said.

She ranted on about game wardens for several more minutes, saying they were all sneaky SOBs and telling me that she asked anyone who inquired about renting a trailer whether or not he or she was a game warden.

"You can't be too careful, ya know," she said. "They've tried to catch my son for years, so any stranger coming in here, I ask them who they are. . . ."

That comment seemed to support the possibility that either she or Junior had been the person who ran my license plate number, but if so, I had no idea how they'd done it. Vehicle registration information is supposedly available only to law enforcement personnel.

She eventually ran out of degrading comments about game wardens and took me to see one of the rental trailers. It was no showplace, but I told her it would do and paid a deposit. The trailer now became my safe house, from which I would conduct this undercover investigation. Junior Bramel and his wife lived in a house immediately beside the trailer court office, so close that I could see his house from my trailer. This meant my safe house was closer to the bad guys than I usually preferred for an undercover residence, but there was little else in the area to rent, so I took a chance on living in the trailer court. You might say I would soon be living right in the middle of the den of thieves.

I moved some furniture into the trailer a few days later and was sitting on the couch one night, watching TV, when a large cockroach crawled up onto the couch next to me. I had seen a few roaches in the trailer since moving in, but this one was way too friendly. I was eating a box of KFC fried chicken and the roach had probably smelled the food and come to investigate. I smashed the roach, finished my meal, then put the remainder of the chicken into the refrigerator and went to bed.

When I opened the refrigerator the next morning, I was disgusted to see several cockroaches climbing around in what remained of my box of chicken. I took the box out of the fridge and threw it in the trash, then stopped by the trailer court office later that morning and told the landlady, Junior's mother, about the roaches. "My trailer needs fumigating," I said sternly.

She reluctantly agreed, as she knew it would cost her money for an exterminator. I told her I was going to be away for the weekend and that she could have the job done then. The trailer was so infested with cockroaches that when I returned from my weekend away I counted sixty-four dead roaches of various sizes lying on the kitchen counter. I didn't even bother counting the number of dead roaches throughout the rest of the trailer, but the total was no doubt in the hundreds.

An even worse cockroach infestation occurred at a trailer across the street from mine. I came home one day to see two sheriff's cruisers sitting in front of this particular trailer, and neighbors from the trailer court standing around talking to the officers. Once the officers left, I went over and asked one of my neighbors what was going on. They answered with one word: roaches. It seems the trailer in question was so infested with cockroaches that the bugs were crawling all over the two young children who lived there, and the kids' parents had done nothing about it, even after several warnings from the local social services agency. The situation was so out of hand that the neighbors finally notified Children's Services. That child welfare agency stepped in, rescued the kids, and had the parents arrested.

Since no one was in the trailer, I walked over and peeked through one of the windows. I couldn't believe what I saw. There were so many roaches in that trailer that they were literally crawling up the windows and walls. I could see a mattress on the floor where the kids had slept, and the blanket on the mattress looked like it was moving there were so many roaches on it. The inside of that trailer was disgusting, and I felt sorry for those two little kids. But I tell this story to illustrate the kind of environment my neighbors and I were living in. If there had been hundreds of cockroaches in my trailer, there probably were thousands in the trailer across the street.

———

I had been living in my trailer for several weeks but still hadn't met Junior Bramel. The investigation seemed to be going nowhere. Shaun came to the trailer that weekend to visit, and I told him we needed to do something to get things moving.

So he and I took a drive into town. As we drove by a local restaurant, we spotted a pickup truck in the parking lot with a dog box in the back, a wooden crate used to transport 'coon hunting dogs. I told Shaun to pull into the lot, and I got out.

"Where're you going?" Shaun asked.

"Just stay put," I said. "I'll be back in a few minutes."

There were about a dozen people in the restaurant when I walked in, and I said in a loud voice, "Who owns that truck in the parking lot with the dog box?"

A thin guy sitting in the back of the restaurant spoke up and said he owned it.

I walked over. The man was sitting with a woman and two kids. I shook the man's hand and said, "Let me introduce myself. My name's Bill Stone, I just moved to the area, I like to 'coon hunt, but I don't have no one to 'coon hunt with. I seen your truck out in the parking lot, and I'd like to know if you'd like to go 'coon huntin' sometime."

Amazingly, the man said, without hesitation, "Well, I'm going huntin' tonight, and you're welcome to come along if you like." I asked him where he lived and what time I should be there, and he told me. I shook his hand again and walked back outside. When I told Shaun what had just happened, he shook his head in disbelief.

"You're amazing," he said. "I can't believe you arranged a hunt with a total stranger in less than ten minutes."

"Well, sometimes you just gotta be bold," I said.

That night, Shaun and I went 'coon hunting for the first time with Leonard W. McGowan and his father, Leonard R. McGowan, two poachers who would become secondary players in this undercover investigation. It was the younger Leonard who, unwittingly, would eventually lead me to Junior Bramel. While hunting with Leonard and his father, I learned that the younger Leonard not only knew Junior Bramel but had gone to school with him. Leonard had even lived in Bramel's trailer court for a time, the same place I was now living. Leonard and Bramel still saw each other occasionally and were close enough that Junior Bramel would lend Leonard money when he needed it.

That very first night Shaun and I went 'coon hunting with Leonard and his father, they carried a rifle into the woods. This was against the law because 'coon hunting season was months away. It was only spring, and 'coon season would not open until November. Leonard and his dad shot several raccoons that night after the dogs' barking signaled that they were treed. I was an experienced 'coon hunter and owned dogs of my own, and Leonard could see I knew what I was doing in the woods. That impressed him, which no doubt increased my standing in his eyes.

Soon I was 'coon hunting with Leonard and his father nearly every night, as the pair regularly shot 'coons out of season. The animals' pelts were worthless at that time of year, but the father-son team shot them anyway, to train their dogs—in 'coon hunting parlance it's called "putting fur in their mouth." They would shoot the 'coons out of the trees and the waiting dogs would tear them to pieces, a technique used to more quickly teach young 'coon hounds their life's work by getting them to recognize and find 'coons and only 'coons. The poachers were training the dogs to trail and tree raccoons alone, and not other animals, known as "trash" to 'coon hunters. In fact, though, Leonard didn't stick exclusively to raccoons on these night excursions. When he could spot wild turkeys roosting in trees, he would occasionally shoot them.

As our hunts continued, Leonard told me that Junior Bramel was starting to ask about me—who I was, where I was from, that kind of thing. Since Leonard had hunted with me many times by then, he vouched for me to Junior, saying that I was "cool" and could be trusted.

Eventually, Leonard and his father got so trusting of me that they allowed me to videotape our illegal 'coon hunts, videotapes that I knew would end up as evidence in a court of law. I'd get behind one of them with the camera as he shot a raccoon, the camera lens looking over his shoulder down the gun barrel as he made the shot. The tapes would show the gun muzzle and the raccoon in the tree and then follow the animal's descent when the gun was fired. After a night afield, we'd go back to Leonard's house, drink a few beers, and watch a replay of our hunt on his TV/VCR.

I videotaped our illegal hunts for weeks. I even encouraged the poachers to videotape me, which in turn, made them less wary when I videotaped them. In videotaping suspects, sometimes it's easier to do it overtly than covertly, especially once you've earned their trust. With Leonard, his father, and their friends, it was easy to do it openly. Eventually, they even started encouraging me to bring my video camera on hunts, as they enjoyed seeing themselves and their dogs on tape.

———

Several weeks later, when I stopped at the trailer park office to pay my monthly rent, I asked if Junior was around. I still hadn't met him and was getting antsy to do so. His mother said no, Junior wasn't home, but she added that he and some other guys played cards two nights a week—on Wednesdays and Saturdays—and suggested that I might find him at the card game. I asked her where they played, and she told me. I told her I didn't want to just show up without knowing anyone, so she said she'd tell Junior I was interested in playing cards and would ask him to come by and pick me up. That was just what I wanted to hear.

Sure enough, later that evening Junior Bramel stopped by my trailer. By that time I had filled the place with large, mounted deer heads, turkey tails, and big fish mounts, anything to make it look like I was a serious outdoorsman and possibly a poacher. Junior came in and immediately began looking over the mounted animals. I noticed that he paid particular attention to the large deer heads and their antlers. We talked some, and finally he asked me if I wanted to go play cards with him and some of his buddies. I said yes, of course. After months of trying, I had finally made contact with the number one target of this investigation, Junior Bramel.

When I arrived at the poker game, Bramel introduced me to half a dozen guys, some of them accompanied by their wives. I sat down and started playing cards with the group, and as the evening wore on these people began quizzing me about where I was from and what I did for a living, the normal questions you'd ask someone when first getting to know them. For me, though, the knowledge that I was in a room full of bad guys made the experience a real adrenaline rush, and not in a good way. I'd tried to prepare myself for it mentally as Bramel and I were driving to the poker game, but I was on edge as I sat at the poker table, surrounded by poachers. I could only hope that my stress didn't show and that if it did, they wouldn't suspect the real reason for my nervousness.

At this point in the investigation, I had no idea who I was getting myself involved with, other than Bramel. I didn't know, that first night, if these guys would cut my throat or accept me into their group. All I knew for sure was that I had to remain cool and play the part of a potential poacher. I had my cover story down pat, but I had to remind myself to concentrate on what I was saying when answering a question. I couldn't afford to contradict myself. At the same time, I had to try to play a decent game of poker. I didn't want to win too many hands and take their money, but I also didn't want to look completely inept at the game. My goal that first night with the group was simply to survive and be invited back.

During that first poker night, I finally met the two men our intelligence said were Junior Bramel's poaching buddies. But as the investigation went on, the only times I got to see Bramel and the other two guys were at the biweekly card games on Wednesday and Saturday nights; they didn't invite me to anything more than their poker games. I was getting frustrated, but I just had to bide my time and wait them out. In the meantime, I was continuing to 'coon hunt regularly with Leonard, his father, and a friend of theirs named Shay Wheatherspoon. We were constantly making illegal kills during these spring night hunts, and the poachers weren't fussy about the condition of the animals we shot. I specifically remember them shooting some female raccoons carrying unborn young inside them. This disgusted me, but I couldn't show any outward concern or emotion about it.

Once Wheatherspoon began hunting with us, our hunting talk widened to include turkeys. This began with his boasting about having bagged a couple of mature turkey gobblers near his house. As he told it, he saw the big birds strutting in a field one day and shot them at long range with a rifle. His actions violated the law in two ways, first, because it was illegal to kill the turkeys with a rifle—in Ohio, hunters may shoot turkeys only with shotguns, bows, and crossbows—and second, because the birds were out of season.

Every time Wheatherspoon and I got together, he'd retell the story of shooting those two big gobblers. After hearing the tale a few times and expecting to hear it yet again, I wore a wire and secretly recorded his admission. I also asked to see the turkeys' beards so that I had some tangible evidence that he actually had killed the birds. Wheatherspoon obliged by showing me the two beards on camera.

———

It was late April by then, and Ohio's wild turkey hunting season was about to start. At the poker game one night, the conversation turned to turkey hunting and Bramel remarked that he liked to turkey hunt but preferred doing it before the legal hunting season opened. He said the woods got too crowded with other hunters once the season began. This was the opening I'd been waiting for, so I got bold and chimed in.

"Me too," I said. "I like to hunt turkeys. Count me in if ya ever wanna go sometime."

Bramel surprised me by saying the words I'd been waiting months to hear. "Well, how about going tomorrow morning?"

I hadn't planned on going *that* soon, but it was the break in the case I'd been waiting for, and I couldn't pass it up. I quickly agreed, offering to drive the next morning, and telling Bramel I'd pick him up at 5:00 A.M. sharp. I hate getting up early, so inwardly I groaned at the thought of the early-morning start time, but I knew I had to do it. After the late-night poker game, it would be a short night.

Early the next morning, Bramel and I drove to Leonard's father's farm to hunt. The old man controlled a lot of property, and the woods there were filled with wild turkeys. Bramel and I both carried shotguns that morning, even though it was well before the legal turkey-hunting season. I also brought my trusty video camera, the one I'd been using to videotape the 'coon hunts with Leonard, Leonard's father, and Shay Wheatherspoon, although I wasn't sure I'd use it on my very first hunt with Bramel, unless possibly we killed a bird. However, I also had a second, hidden video camera, the same one I'd used during Operation Redbud. If need be, I could activate that camera, concealed in my turkey-hunting vest, and get Bramel on tape without him knowing it.

We hunted for turkeys until about midmorning but without success. However, we did come across a commercial deer feeder hanging in the woods adjacent to the property where we had permission to hunt. Hunters fill these feeders with corn to attract deer and other wildlife. The feeders are activated by a timer, scattering corn kernels on the ground at intervals throughout the day and night. Near the feeder was a commercially made hunters' treestand, placed there for deer hunting. The treestand and feeder, both legal for deer hunting in Ohio, were on property owned by a professional baseball player for the Atlanta Braves. He had bought the property, I later learned, for him and his friends to hunt on. Bramel and I were on the property illegally, hunting without permission.

Frustrated by hearing no turkeys gobble that morning, Bramel said nonchalantly, "I'm gonna steal that deer feeder and treestand."

"You are?" I said, trying not to sound too surprised.

"Yeah," Bramel said. "And I want you to take your van and drive around to the bottom of the hill and wait for me along the highway. I'll meet you there."

As Bramel proceeded to unchain the treestand from the tree, I quietly touched the "on" button for the small videotape recorder hidden in my vest and began recording him. When he got the treestand detached from the tree, I turned the recorder off, went back to my vehicle, and drove to the bottom of the hill where Bramel had told me to meet him.

As I pulled up, I could see Bramel running toward me, carrying the treestand. We quickly loaded it into my van, and he then went back into the woods and brought out the deer feeder. Combined, the treestand and deer feeder were worth several hundred dollars. Pleased with himself, Bramel next suggested we drive to the local gas station to get a sandwich and something to drink. We did so, but while we were there in pulled someone I didn't want to see: Alan Wright, the local uniformed wildlife officer, whom I had met a couple of times. Accompanying Wright was a second, younger officer, whom I didn't recognize.

I had no place to hide or no means of walking away from the situation, so I just stood there as the two wildlife officers entered the gas station and began talking with Bramel. All I could hope was that Officer Wright wouldn't recognize me. I had changed my appearance considerably since we had last seen one another, and I was counting on that being enough to get me through this chance meeting unrecognized.

Surprisingly, Wright was so focused on his conversation with Bramel that he never even glanced at me, let alone recognized me. I wasn't concerned about the younger officer; I didn't know him, so I figured he didn't know me. The officers talked for several minutes with Junior Bramel, while I stood within three feet of Officer Wright. He never looked my way.

The encounter was ironic in the extreme. Not only had we been turkey hunting out of season that morning but also we had stolen two valuable items, the treestand and the deer feeder, which were still sitting in our vehicle, just outside the gas station. The two officers eventually bought soft drinks and left, and I breathed an inward sigh of relief as they walked out. As Bramel and I climbed back into my van and closed the doors, he said disgustedly, "That dumb ass. . . ."

I didn't know what to say, so I said nothing. Soon Bramel continued. "If that game warden had any idea what we were up to this morning he'd have busted our asses, wouldn't he?"

"Yeah, I'm sure he would have," I said, nodding.

Officer Wright's conversation with Bramel had been about turkey hunting. Basically, the officer had been fishing for information, just as wildlife officers normally do when talking with known or suspected poachers. But Bramel was more than a suspected poacher. Officer Wright knew for certain Bramel and his cronies poached wildlife regularly, and he was trying his best to catch them.

Even the encounter with the wildlife officers wasn't the end of that memorable expedition. As we were driving back to Bramel's house to unload the stolen deer feeder and treestand, the feeder's timer kicked on, causing the feeder to spray us and the entire inside of my van with shelled corn. It scared us when the feeder suddenly engaged, but in retrospect it was pretty funny. I believed it served us right for having stolen a legitimate hunter's expensive equipment.

As soon as I got away from Bramel that day, I called O'Dell to inform him of what had just happened. I thought my supervisor should know that I'd been involved in a theft. I also asked him what he wanted me to do about the stolen items, if anything. He ran the situation up the chain of command, and the answer came back down for me to play the incident to the hilt, to remain undercover and continue my investigation. That made me feel better. I didn't want to make that kind of decision on my own and be called on the carpet for it later.

Bramel was not a big-time turkey hunter, meaning he didn't hunt the birds often. Nevertheless, our few preseason hunts together yielded enough evidence to charge him with hunting without a license, hunting prior to season, and stealing private property—solid but fairly minor charges.

———

Bramel had told me he was more interested in poaching deer in the fall than turkeys in the spring. Consequently, my real task that spring was to lay the groundwork with Bramel, building a rapport with him that I hoped would pay off big come autumn. In the meantime, Leonard, Leonard's father, and Shay Wheatherspoon had become my serious 'coon-hunting buddies. We were hunting hard, four or five nights a week, and all of it out of season.

An interesting side note here is that we would shoot our 'coons using CB caps, a light-powered .22 caliber ammunition. The poachers chose them because the light rounds make less noise than a regular .22 long-rifle cartridge; the guys reasoned they'd be less likely to get caught if a game warden couldn't hear them shooting. But often with the lighter loads they had to shoot a raccoon several times before it would be injured enough to fall out of the tree to the dogs waiting below.

After watching this for months, I finally said disgustedly, "If we're going to do this, we're going to do it right, with .22 high-powered, hollow-point ammunition. If any game warden hears us shoot, we'll be long gone before he can get here. If we keep trying to shoot these 'coons with CB caps, it's going to get us caught because we have to shoot so many shells." The poachers eventually agreed with my reasoning, and thereafter started using .22 long-rifle, hollow-point ammunition for our hunting. If nothing else, it was more humane for the raccoons.

I started bringing one of my own young 'coon hounds along with me on our hunts. I didn't want to bring a mature dog, because I wanted a dog that would not tree a 'coon on its own. That way, during the court trial I knew would follow this investigation, the judge or jury couldn't say I owned the dog that was doing all the treeing, leading these poor poachers astray. So I always brought along a dog that I knew couldn't tree a 'coon on its own. I'd even purposely say on the videotapes of our hunts how my dog wasn't treeing 'coons and the other guys' dogs were. I'd also ask any new guys hunting with us on a particular night to introduce themselves on camera. I'd ask them who they were, where they were

Operation Clanbake was the first long-term undercover operation I or the Ohio Department of Natural Resources, Division of Wildlife, was ever involved in. Initially, poachers were suspected of illegally killing white-tailed deer and walleyes, but the investigation eventually expanded to include other species of wildlife, such as waterfowl and wild turkeys. (ODNR, Division of Wildlife)

During Operation Clanbake, Doug Andrews (right) was a member of the Toledo poaching ring known as The Clan. Here he's pictured eating with Officer Don Carter and me (R. T. Stewart) at our "safe house" trailer in southeast Ohio. Our faces were blacked out when this photo first ran in *Wild Ohio* magazine to protect our identity for future undercover cases. (ODNR, Division of Wildlife)

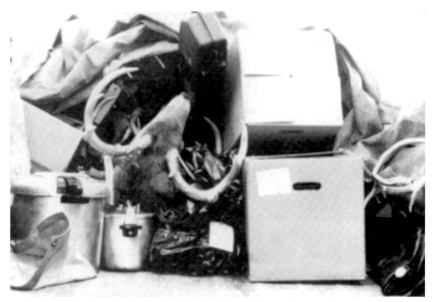

When search warrants were served at multiple locations during the takedown of Operation Clanbake, huge amounts of evidence were gathered, including firearms, whole deer carcasses, canned venison, mounted deer heads, mounted waterfowl, and even vehicles. (ODNR, Division of Wildlife)

Ron Kendrick was one of the ring leaders of The Clan during Operation Clanbake. He was charged with 10 wildlife law violations in Ohio's Ross County and 42 wildlife law violations in Gallia County. (ODNR, Division of Wildlife)

Operation Redbud lasted about a year and half and was the second undercover investigation of my career. It involved the poaching of some 100 wild turkeys and 60 white-tailed deer, as well as some birds of prey, in southeast Ohio. Pictured is Division of Wildlife Officer Mike Reed with just some of the evidence collected during the serving of search warrants. (ODNR, Division of Wildlife)

This "safe house" during Operation Redbud was in somewhat better repair than the house trailer we worked from in Operation Clanbake, but not much. An ideal safe house is located close to where poachers live but not too close; you don't want them dropping by unexpectedly. Pictured is Officer Don Carter in a contemplative moment during the investigation. (Author's collection)

During Operation Redbud, Officer Don Carter (left) and I spent an afternoon hunting mourning doves. Due to medical issues, Redbud was Carter's last undercover investigation. He retired from the Division of Wildlife soon after the end of this case. (Author's collection)

Would you believe this man was an undercover wildlife officer? Yep, that was me during Operation Redbud. I changed my appearance many times during my 18-year career undercover to better fit in with the ring of poachers I was trying to infiltrate. (Author's collection)

At the end of Operation Ego, this was the evidence seized at Mike Barker's residence near Charleston, West Virginia: nearly 70 deer heads as well as some full-body deer mounts, all with extremely large antlers. (ODNR, Division of Wildlife)

News media coverage—newspaper, radio, and TV—following a successful undercover wildlife investigation was always very positive and extensive. At times, reporters even accompanied our uniformed officers during the takedown of a case. Pictured are newspaper clippings from around Ohio describing the details of Operation Clanbake. (ODNR, Division of Wildlife)

Operation River Sweep, mainly involving the poaching of white-tailed deer, was a multi-year undercover investigation along the Ohio River in the southwest portion of the Buckeye State. It culminated with some 20 suspects being arrested and 180 charges filed. (ODNR, Division of Wildlife)

Occasionally, an undercover officer may have to kill wildlife illegally—or make it seem like he did—to maintain his cover with poachers. I would sometimes obtain dead animals from Division of Wildlife uniformed officers that I would then present to the poachers as having been taken illegally. Here, I'm holding a wild turkey. (Author's collection)

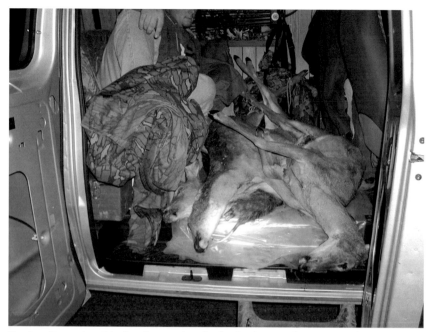

During Operation Stir-fry, this is what the back of my undercover van looked like the night we delivered the illegal white-tailed deer, shot in West Virginia, to the house full of Asian suspects in Cleveland, Ohio. (Author's collection)

This photo was snapped during the long-anticipated waterfowl hunt on Lake Erie with members of the DMC Club during Operation Take 'Em. Notice the late-model duck hunting boats, powerful outboard motors, and other equipment. These poachers had money and weren't afraid to spend it. (Author's collection)

The evidence seized in Operation Take 'Em amounted to tens of thousands of dollars in boats, shotguns, decoys, and other waterfowl hunting equipment. All of it was ordered by the court to be forfeited to the State of Ohio, Division of Wildlife. (ODNR, Division of Wildlife)

During Operation Take 'Em, I equipped my waterfowl hunting boat with cooking facilities, telling the poachers they could shoot the ducks and geese while I cooked breakfast. Not surprisingly, they thought that was a pretty good idea and took me up on the offer, no questions asked. (Author's collection)

from, and the names of their dogs. I was always trying to think ahead, trying to think what might look convincing on the videotape when it was eventually played before a jury as evidence.

Leonard had a wife and children, and he invited me to his house on many occasions for meals with his family. We became good friends, or so they thought—so good, in fact, that Leonard started dropping by my trailer any time of the day or night. This meant I couldn't get away and go to my real home for a break as often as I would have liked during this investigation because Leonard thought the trailer *was* my real home. That's not an ideal situation in undercover work, but I was stuck with the arrangement for the time being and had to make the best of it.

Leonard often had problems paying his bills, especially the high heating bills of the winter season, so occasionally he would ask me if I'd loan him money. His wife worked but he didn't, so often they would come up short on cash near the end of the month. He called me his "buddy Bill," and one day he called and said, "Bill, I need to borrow some money to pay my gas bill. My wife gets paid Friday, and if you lend me the money we'll repay you then." I always gave him the money, two or three hundred dollars per month, fully expecting to get stiffed for it at some point. In fact, I never did. Every Friday, without fail, Leonard would faithfully pay me back. O'Dell and I joked that the Division of Wildlife was paying a known poacher's heating bill.

A few times, O'Dell telephoned me while Leonard was at the trailer and I was in the bathroom or for some other reason couldn't get to the phone. Since this was before the widespread use of cell phones, Leonard could hear the message being left on the answering machine of my land line. To ensure that such messages wouldn't blow my cover, O'Dell began leaving messages for me in code. He'd say something like, "Hey, I'll give you five hundred dollars for that 'coon dog of yours we talked about, but not a penny more. If you're interested in selling, call me back." Translated, that meant my supervisor was putting another five hundred dollars into my checking account for this undercover investigation. Such coded messages left the bad guys none the wiser. It was a good thing we set up this system, because as time went on, both Leonard and Bramel began to spend quite a bit of time at my trailer, usually to get away from their wives.

———

By the fall of 1999, I had been investigating the Aberdeen poachers for about a year and Shaun had been gathering evidence on the Hunter from Hell and his cronies in Peebles for about the same amount of time. At this point, though, evidence of yet another group of poachers broadened and complicated our cases, eventually prompting us to combine all three investigations into a single case that ultimately became known as Operation River Sweep. The new evidence concerned illegal activity in Meigs County, which lay along the Ohio River a little more than one hundred miles east of our current areas of operation. Shaun was given a tip about waterfowl poaching by a group unconnected to the two poaching rings we had already identified. Surprisingly, it involved the local county prosecutor, a state highway patrolman, and other high-profile members of the community.

The intelligence given Shaun stated that this third group of poachers was regularly over-bagging on ducks and geese, as well as baiting—illegally using grain such as corn to attract waterfowl for hunting purposes—and other hunting violations. I couldn't help Shaun on the case because Meigs County is my home ground and we couldn't take the chance that one of the locals might recognize me. Regardless, we decided to work all three sets of poachers at once—THFH, Junior Bramel and his buddies, and now the waterfowlers in Meigs County—and call the broader investigation Operation River Sweep, since all the areas involved lay along the Ohio River.

In the meantime, back in Aberdeen, I continued my efforts to collect information and evidence. I was still playing poker with Bramel's group almost every Wednesday and Saturday night. I was also expanding my contacts, getting to know other people in town and consolidating my place in the trailer court. I got a nice boost around that time when I received my replacement undercover vehicle, a shiny new four-wheel-drive Ford cargo van, silver in color. I had already told the bad guys that I'd bought a new van and was awaiting its delivery, but they had no idea it would come equipped with state-of-the-art undercover surveillance equipment. A hidden tape recorder and video camera were built into the van and could be secretly controlled by me from the driver's seat.

When the van arrived, all the bad guys loved it. It was clear from the gleam in their eyes that they were just imagining the poaching we could do from such a vehicle. As a private joke, they nicknamed the van "Treestand." If someone said, "Let's go get in the treestand for a while," everyone knew that that really meant, "Let's go drive the roads in the new van and shoot some deer."

———

Two of Junior Bramel's closest poaching buddies, whom I'll call Steve Bray and Joe Riley, worked at the YMCA in Maysville, Kentucky, just across the Ohio River from Aberdeen, Ohio. Hoping they might talk more about their poaching than Bramel had to date about his, I decided to join that particular YMCA. My cover story for joining was that my doctor had recommended I swim regularly, since swimming would benefit the back muscles affected by my disability injury. Not long after I joined, though, an incident occurred that not only could have blown my cover but might have cost me my life.

At one of our biweekly poker games, Junior Bramel began talking with Bray and Riley—the two poachers who worked at the YMCA—about a bald eagle that had been shot and killed recently along the Ohio River. At the time, bald eagles were listed as a federally endangered species, although their growing numbers have since caused their removal from the endangered list. The incident was the talk of poachers, hunters, birder watchers, and wildlife enthusiasts up and down the Ohio River, especially since the U. S. Fish and Wildlife Service had failed to find the illegal shooter.

Anyway, as we were playing poker that night, Bramel and his two buddies hinted that they knew who had shot the eagle. Something—call it a sixth sense if you will—told me to stay silent, act uninterested, and keep playing cards. I did just that, letting the comment pass, and the conversation eventually turned to another subject.

I later found out, from Riley, that the poachers had been testing me that night. Even though I had lived in the community for a full year, regularly interacting with their group, they still had doubts, suspecting that I might be a game warden or other law enforcement officer. They had deliberately set me up by mentioning the eagle shooting, waiting to see if I'd bite. However, I'd kept playing cards and showed no interest in the eagle information, and this was very fortunate, since asking anything about the bird or showing even the least bit of interest could have jeopardized my safety and the entire year-long undercover investigation.

I've thought about that incident many times, wondering why the group was still suspicious of me after all the months I'd spent with them. Possibly it was because I had shown up out of the blue and they knew very little, if anything, about me. And while I seemed to fit right in with them and their poaching crowd, they may have thought I was too good to be true. As it turned out, their initial instincts were right. But they wouldn't find that out for several more months.

I believe most poachers know that undercover wildlife officers exist. But most, if not all, of the poachers I encountered during my undercover career believed they were too smart to get caught. They were sure they could spot a wildlife officer a mile away, that no undercover officer could infiltrate *their* poaching ring. Most poachers are suspicious by nature. Their involvement in illegal activities makes them very careful not to reveal too much about themselves too soon, especially around new people. It may have been just this natural caution that prompted these poachers to test me with the eagle story, but, whatever their motives, thankfully, I passed their secret test.

————

It came time for Shaun and me to visit THFH again, so we made the thirty-mile drive back up the road to Peebles. It was early fall by then, and we were starting to see bucks with their antlers rubbed clean of summer velvet. In other words, it was time for deer poachers to start getting serious about their illegal nighttime activities. When we got to THFH's house, he told us he'd already shot a few bucks that fall. That's what we wanted to hear, as we knew he'd be anxious to shoot more. When THFH saw my new van, he instantly fell in love with it. He knew all three of us could easily fit inside and still have plenty of room for illegal deer.

THFH wasn't someone I liked spending time with. In addition to poaching, he was into using illegal drugs, and he was always looking for ways to boost his income. One way he'd make extra money was by collecting old tires from people who wanted them disposed of, which he would then illegally dump in woods or along creek beds. He also didn't provide very well for his wife and child. THFH was just an all around bad actor, and as I said earlier, Shaun and I grew to despise him. Nevertheless, we needed to get close to him if we were to get the evidence we needed, so we were friendly and tried to act respectful of his skill as a hunter. We also were nice to his family. Since, as I've noted, he didn't treat them too well, we'd bring them treats when we visited his home. Every time we visited we'd take candy for the child and wine coolers for his wife, as we knew she liked them. As a result, the entire family looked forward to seeing us.

Later in the day on this particular visit, THFH decided that the three of us should sight in his new poaching rifle, a scoped .22 caliber magnum. He said we all needed to learn to shoot the same gun so we would need to take only a single rifle with us when we went poaching together. Shaun and I didn't want to shoot any deer ourselves if we could help it, but we did so occasionally to maintain our cover.

THFH started banging away with his rifle at a paper target about fifty yards away and, after several shots and sight adjustments, had the gun sighted-in perfectly. Since Shaun and I didn't want to shoot deer if we didn't have to, we wanted to figure a way of convincing THFH that his gun did not shoot the same for us as it did for him. I shoot left-handed, so when THFH handed me the rifle and told me to shoot at the bull's-eye on the target, I intentionally aimed at the lower right-hand corner of the paper and pulled the trigger. That's exactly where the bullet hit.

"I can't shoot this gun," I said, shaking my head. "It won't shoot for me like it does for you. I'm left-handed. . . ."

In reality, whether a person is right- or left-handed doesn't affect accuracy in shooting, but my excuse seemed to work, and I shot a second time just to convince THFH that my left-handedness ruined my aim. Once again, I took careful aim at the lower right corner of the target, pulled the trigger, and saw a neat, round bullet hole appear beside the first.

THFH grabbed the gun away from me, saying, "Gimme that . . . you can't shoot no deer like that!" This was just what I wanted to hear. He had fallen for my little ruse, never suspecting he'd been duped. For some reason, he never even offered Shaun a chance to fire his new gun.

After dark that night, the three of us piled into my new van and went poaching, driving the back roads looking for deer. We shot several, one a real nice buck, and THFH said he knew someone who would mount the deer's head without asking any questions as to whether or not it was legal. The next day, we drove the deer carcass to Harry Hackenberg, a shady taxidermist, who lived in the town of Peebles. Hackenberg took the deer, but seemed suspicious of us, asking THFH who Shaun and I were. THFH vouched for us, saying we were friends of his who drove him around while he did his "hunting."

A few days later, Shaun and I returned to Hackenberg, this time without THFH, bringing him a second buck that we claimed to have shot but that actually had been supplied to us by one of our uniformed wildlife officers. I had telephoned Hackenberg ahead, saying I had killed a buck, didn't have a tag for it, but wanted him to mount it. What Hackenberg didn't know was that I was recording our telephone conversation. He agreed to my request, telling me to bring him the deer as soon as possible—an agreement we got on tape. We had equally good luck when we actually brought him the deer, since I was able to secretly videotape the entire transaction. Hackenberg claimed to be a legitimate taxidermist, but he wasn't. He simply took people's money and never produced the finished mount.

Another night when the three of us—THFH, Shaun, and I—went poaching, I drove while THFH sat in the front passenger seat and Shaun in the back seat. We saw several deer standing in a field on the left-hand side of the road, so I drove past the deer, turned around, and came back. This positioned the van so that the deer were on its passenger side, allowing THFH to shoot from the front passenger window. Shaun turned the spotlight on the deer, they froze, and THFH started shooting.

The first deer dropped, and Shaun immediately shone the spotlight on a second deer. THFH aimed and squeezed the trigger a second time, dropping the second deer, and the rest ran. We prepared to retrieve the two animals we'd shot, but just as we opened the doors to the van, a shot rang out from near the spot where the two deer had fallen. Someone was shooting at us!

Apparently, there was a house in the woods beyond where the deer had stood—a house we hadn't seen—and whoever lived there was not happy about what we were doing. I couldn't tell whether the individual was shooting directly at us or not. Possibly, he was just shooting up in the air to scare us off, but we weren't staying around to find out.

We jumped back in the van, slammed the doors shut, and took off down the road. But in making our escape, we had to pass the driveway to the house. As we did, a second shot rang out, and there was no question this time as to whether or not the guy was shooting at us. The boom of the gun was much louder this time around. Whether the guy was using a rifle or shotgun, I didn't know and didn't care. All I knew was that the gun's report was *loud,* and we needed to get out of there, quick!

I tromped the gas pedal, driving as fast as I could, and we sped down the road. As I drove, I hunched down behind the steering wheel, trying to make myself as small a target as possible should the guy shoot again. Shaun flattened himself on the floor in front of the back seat, THFH was hugging the floor mat in front of the front seat, and it dawned on me that I was the only one of the three of us with my head still sticking up. By the way, all of this action was recorded by my new van's hidden videotaping equipment, so Shaun and I were able to review the incident later that night. We got a good chuckle out of watching it, but when it was all happening it was no laughing matter.

After we got away, THFH started acting tough, saying things like, "Let's go back there! I'll kill that SOB . . . No one's gonna shoot at me and get away with it!"

But there was no way I was going back to that house or anywhere near it. Not only did we not go back and retrieve the two deer we'd shot that night, we always avoided that particular road on later poaching trips.

———

The next day, I returned to my ongoing investigation in Aberdeen. Things had gotten a little too exciting for me the night before with THFH and Shaun, and I needed a break. I didn't like getting shot at, and I decided that a few nights of 'coon hunting was what I needed to relax. I might even take a swim or two at the YMCA.

A few days later, however, before I could make it to the Y, O'Dell called.

"Were you out hunting with anyone last night?" he asked.

"Yeah," I said. Why?"

"Were you out with Junior?"

"No. I was out 'coon hunting with Leonard and Shay. Why? What's going on?"

O'Dell then told me that the local wildlife officer, Alan Wright, had observed Bramel and two other guys spotlighting deer, and he had driven after them. In the car chase that followed, Wright had nearly caught them, but by the time the officer got Bramel to stop, his two companions had bailed out of the car, taking the gun and spotlight with them. This left Wright with no evidence on which to arrest Bramel. O'Dell feared that one of the guys who fled might have been me. When he learned it wasn't, he said, "Keep your ears open . . . See if you can find out who was with Junior last night."

A few days later, I finally made it to the YMCA, where I followed my usual swim with a soak in the hot tub. I was glad to see that no one was in the large hot tub; I would have it to myself. I had only been soaking in the luxuriously warm water for a few minutes, though, when about a dozen large women—and I do mean large—walked up to the hot tub dressed in swimsuits and asked me if I was about ready to get out.

"Nope. I just got in," I said. "But you can get in, too, if you like," I said, grinning. "There's plenty of room." I was hoping they wouldn't take me up on my offer.

One of them said, "You've got more nerve than the last guy we found in here. We were able to run him off."

"Well, I've never been known to be too intelligent," I said. "But I'm staying in here 'til I'm good and cooked. Suit yourself . . ."

As I said, the hot tub was large, so all dozen of the women proceeded to get in with me, raising the water level so much it nearly spilled over onto the floor. The situation was turning out to be pretty comical, especially after they sat down and we started teasing each other, One said something like, "You're embarrassed to get out, aren't you?"

"Yeah, you're right," I answered. "With twelve lovely young ladies like you in here with me, I'm so excited right now that I'd embarrass myself if I stood up."

They got a kick out of that comment, but eventually, I got out and began toweling off in the locker room. That's when Riley, one of Bramel's poaching buddies who worked at the YMCA, walked in. Without any prompting from me, he came over and started telling me about the car chase he and Bramel had gotten into a few nights earlier with the local wildlife officer, Alan Wright.

"Really?" I said. "Tell me about it."

Riley then told me the entire story—who was involved and how and when it all happened.

"You're kidding," I said, coaxing him on.

"Nope," he responded. "I'm not . . . When the game warden tried to stop us, Junior dropped me and Steve off with the gun and spotlight, and we ran into the woods and got away. I didn't make it home 'til the next morning."

That night, I called O'Dell and told him I knew who was with Bramel the night Officer Wright chased him. He asked me if I had recorded what Riley told me, and I had to tell him no, that all I had been wearing at the time was a towel. He said, "Well, you need to figure out a way to get the guy's confession on tape." I had no idea how I was going to do that, but I told him I'd give it some thought and come up with something.

The next day, I looked at a county map and located where the shining and shooting of the deer had taken place, as well as the car chase. I then explored the area in my van, driving along the same route and along other roads in the area. I wanted to familiarize myself with the location, and as I did a plan started coming together in my mind.

I knew that Riley liked to drink beer, so I told him I'd drop by sometime, pick him up, and we'd drive around and drink some beers together. He said that sounded like fun, so a few days later I gave him a call. Riley said he was available, so I drove over to his house and picked him up. My plan was to take him on an apparently random drive, but end up on the road where the car chase had occurred. I was hoping he would recognize the area and repeat the story, which I could then get on videotape in the van.

Sure enough, as we drove the back roads and drank a few beers, a light seemed to come on in Riley's head as we neared the area of the car chase. "Hey," he said, right on cue, "this is the road where Junior and us shot that deer and then the game warden chased us!" Riley then proceeded to rehash the entire story, only this time with my van's videotape recorder running. The recorder had an on/off button located on the left side of the steering column, and I slipped it on without the poacher ever suspecting a thing.

Riley couldn't have recalled more detail about the incident if I had been interrogating him. He went on and on about how the three of them had outsmarted the game warden and about how proud they were of themselves. I called O'Dell the next day and told him about my ploy, telling him I had taped enough evidence to arrest Bramel, Bray, and Riley for the spotlighting and the subsequent car chase. O'Dell was pleased, and he told me to continue the investigation, hunting with the bad guys whenever possible and collecting more evidence.

————

Following the car chase, Bramel got word via the grapevine that he now topped the Division of Wildlife's most-wanted list for that area of Ohio. As a result, he decided to lay low and refrain from poaching for a while. That slowed the investigation considerably, so in late winter the decision was made to end all three of the undercover investigations making up Operation River Sweep, taking down all of the poachers at once. After all, other undercover cases were being planned elsewhere in the state, so we decided to make what arrests we could from these investigations and move on to greener pastures.

As we were winding things down, however, I decided to add one more bad guy to those we hoped to arrest. I heard of a guy in the area, whom I'll call Ed Cox, who was butchering illegal deer, so I decided to take him an alleged illegal deer to see if he'd accept it. When I did, I ended up going to the wrong house by mistake. The man answering the door, whom I'll call Lou Viers, said, "I'm not the guy you're looking for, but I cut up deer, too."

"Well, this deer ain't exactly legal . . . ," I said.

"I don't care," Viers said. "I'll cut it for ya."

"Have you ever butchered deer before?" I asked.

"Oh, yeah," Viers replied. "I do it all the time."

So I gave him the deer I was supposed to give to Ed Cox and then called O'Dell to request a second deer. I took that deer to Cox, and he too agreed to do the work with no questions asked. Now I had evidence on two fly-by-night butchers. Moreover, they led us to still more bad guys, since we were able to identify the customers of both Viers and Cox from their records, seized when uniformed officers served search warrants at the takedown of the case.

Another interesting twist in this case is that when I went back to Viers to pick up the meat from the deer, he told me he also did taxidermy work. That was good to know, I told him. If I killed anything worth mounting, I'd bring it to him. A few days later, I showed up with an illegal hen turkey, one that had been evidence in a previous case and was sitting in a Division of Wildlife evidence freezer. Since we were getting close to the end of this investigation, I wanted that turkey in Viers's freezer when we made the arrests and served the search warrants.

———

Once we started winding down all three branches of Operation River Sweep, we notified wildlife officer Alan Wright that Shaun and I had been working under-cover in his area for nearly a year and a half. We also played him the videotape I had made of Joe Riley telling me about the car chase incident. Wright was not only amazed to see it but also very pleased, because he knew that Junior Bramel, a poacher he had been chasing for years, would soon be going to jail.

Unfortunately, the takedown in Shaun's waterfowl case in Meigs County had to be put on hold. The main target of the investigation died unexpectedly, before the search warrant could be served on his residence, and our supervisors made the decision to end that case at a later time, after the guy's funeral. They reasoned that arresting the other Meigs County poachers for wildlife law violations while they were mourning their friend's death would give the Division of Wildlife a black eye.

When the younger Leonard McGowan was arrested in the takedown of Operation River Sweep, and he and his wife learned my true identity, they both broke down and cried. They had grown so close to me that the discovery that I was an undercover wildlife officer was a great shock. In fact, they could hardly believe it. They just couldn't understand how their "buddy Bill" really could be the person the arresting officers said he was. Also arrested were Leonard's father, Shay Wheatherspoon, Steve Bray, Joe Riley, and, of course, our primary target, Junior Bramel. All told, twenty suspects were arrested, 180 charges were filed, and five search warrants were served.

When Junior Bramel was arrested, his mother threw a fit. She told the ar-resting officers that she should have gone with her first instincts about me. "I knew he was a game warden from that very first day he came to rent a trailer," she said. "I should have listened to what my conscience was telling me. . . ."

When the search warrant on Junior Bramel's residence was served, it became evident that his crimes were not limited to poaching. Officers discovered an indoor marijuana growing facility in the basement of his house. The one time I had been in Bramel's basement during the undercover investigation, his mother had quickly hustled me out, closing the door to its back room. Obviously, there was something in there she didn't want me to see, but I had no idea what it was until the search warrant was served.

Everyone arrested in the various cases was convicted. Unfortunately, THFH evaded arrest and prosecution by going to Florida just a week before the takedown. He didn't leave from fear of wildlife officers; instead he fled the state because he thought the law was looking at him for illegally dumping all those used tires. In any event, he just got lucky. And we couldn't extradite him back to Ohio because none of the wildlife violations we had him on were felonies, only misdemeanors. We thought we might be able to grab him later, when we got word he was scheduled to return to Ohio to attend a friend's wedding, but he never showed.

The original targets of Operation River Sweep were two poachers who killed large-antlered deer, but the investigation ended up nabbing many more poachers, most of whom dabbled in a bit of everything. The sweep had been a success, but the numbers of those arrested and the range of their violations pointed to a discouraging fact about that region. It seemed that in that particular part of southern Ohio, poaching was regarded as an acceptable, almost routine, way of life for many people. Just about everyone I contacted in this investigation was violating wildlife laws in one way or another. Their philosophy seemed to be, "Do what you want, and if the game warden catches you, well, sorry about your luck." They saw wild animals as theirs for the taking and didn't think it mattered how, when, or where they did their hunting. When it came to wildlife, the local culture seemed to assume that anything goes. Hopefully, this investigation began changing that thinking.

# 6

# OPERATION CORNERSTONE

The tiny town of Conneaut, in Ashtabula County, Ohio, lies in the extreme northeast corner of the Buckeye State, bordering Pennsylvania and Lake Erie. Despite its size, Conneaut is an international deep-water port for freighters on the Great Lakes, as well as a popular sport-fishing destination. This investigation, which was conducted in and around Conneaut, was titled Operation Cornerstone for its location, since Ashtabula County is known as the Cornerstone of Ohio.

The fish most sought after by sport anglers in the area is the yellow perch, a small species highly prized for its excellent, mild taste. The selling of perch, or any other sport-caught fish for that matter, is illegal in Ohio. Only licensed commercial fishermen are permitted to sell their catch. Yet because of its popularity, the yellow perch is a favorite with poachers, and intelligence coming into the Division of Wildlife indicated that local anglers were poaching yellow perch by the tens of thousands to sell illegally. In the fall of 2000, therefore, I was assigned to investigate the matter and do something about the situation if the reports turned out to be true.

The three main targets of the investigation were reported to be selling sport-caught yellow perch from Conneaut's Lakeshore Marina and the local Moose Lodge, which stood directly across the road from the marina, very near the public boat-launch ramp. I was living in Steubenville, Ohio, at the time, along the Ohio River, working several undercover projects simultaneously. To begin this case, I met with the Division of Wildlife law enforcement investigator working the Conneaut area, and he filled me in on the intelligence he and other officers had gathered so far, information about the suspected poachers that had been piling up for several years. Area wildlife officers had previously arrested several suspects on misdemeanor charges, but the officers knew many of the bad guys were still selling fish illegally, a felony. The money was too good for the poachers not to take a chance, and they considered getting caught just a cost of doing business.

One of the reports stated that Lakeshore Marina was skimming yellow perch from sport anglers who had their catch cleaned there. This means that when a sport angler dropped off his fish to be cleaned—the legal limit was 30 yellow perch per angler per day—the facility would clean the perch but keep a few fish fillets for themselves. Thus if a charter boat containing six sport anglers (known as a six-pack charter) brought in a limit catch of 180 perch to be cleaned, the fishermen were unlikely to bother counting the number of fillets they received in return. Since Lakeshore filleted thousands of perch each day, they could make quite a bit of extra money on the side by pocketing a few perch from each group of anglers. At the height of the summer fishing season, anywhere from four to eight people worked at the facility, cleaning fish and skimming perch. At that time, yellow perch sold for about eight dollars per pound on the black market, about half the price they sold for in fish, seafood, and grocery stores.

Since I am a southern Ohio boy, I had no experience fishing on Lake Erie. I had plenty of experience fishing for catfish on the Ohio River, but I was completely ignorant about the perch and walleye fishing that went on at Lake Erie. This investigation was, therefore, going to be a big learning experience for me, but I planned to use my ignorance to my advantage to gain an in with the poachers. I planned to tell our suspects that I was new to the area, had little knowledge of Lake Erie, and wanted to learn more about the lake and how to fish for perch. I didn't know how else to approach the case, and I thought that playing up my inexperience just might work.

My first visit to the area was on a weekend in early spring. I wanted to somehow gain entrance to the local Moose Lodge, but knew I needed a membership to do so: the lodge didn't accept just anyone walking in off the street. The fraternal club known as the Loyal Order of Moose has chapters and lodges across the United States. As with most private social clubs, its lodges allow in only members or friends of members. Moreover, Conneaut's lodge required potential members to go through a background check and then be voted in by its existing members. As an undercover officer, I needed to avoid that process. Somehow, I had to come up with a way to get around the usual requirements.

As luck would have it, one day not long after beginning this operation, I was in Weirton, West Virginia, just across the Ohio River from where I was living in Steubenville, when I drove by a Moose Lodge there. A sign out front read,

"Taking Applications for New Members," so I pulled in and asked about joining. The guy behind the bar said simply, "Give me twenty-five dollars and sign here." This lodge required no background check, no vote by the lodge members, no nothing. The club obviously needed bodies, and if a person had twenty-five dollars, he was accepted as a new Moose Lodge member. No questions asked. Congratulations.

This worked into my cover story perfectly, as I was planning to tell the suspects in Conneaut that I was from West Virginia to explain my southern Ohio accent. The Moose Lodge in West Virginia issued me a temporary membership card, and I used it a few times to socialize at that lodge, drinking a few beers and chatting with my fellow members. I did this to build my cover, just in case the Conneaut Moose Lodge ever happened to call Weirton and ask about me. Now the West Virginia lodge would have to vouch for me, saying that they knew me and that I was a member in good standing.

———

Back in Conneaut, I picked up a local newspaper and saw that a guy had some used fishing reels for sale. I was looking for Penn 320 reels for catfishing, so I gave him a call. During our phone conversation, he told me that while he was a construction contractor during the week, he guided smallmouth bass fishermen on Lake Erie out of Conneaut on the weekends.

My undercover partner at the time was Jim Baker, and the two of us dropped by to see the fishing guide that evening and ended up talking with him for several hours. I purchased a fishing reel from him and got his business card. Now that we had made a contact and knew a local angler's name, our next stop was going to be Lakeshore Marina, the suspected den of our thieves. Our plan was to take the bass guide's business card with us, show it to the people at Lakeshore, and ask if the man was a reputable fishing guide or not. In fact, we didn't care whether the guide knew the difference between a bass and a bluegill; we just needed an excuse to make our first visit to Lakeshore.

During that initial visit to the marina, I led the people there, including the owner, whom I'll call Bruce Jones, to believe that my partner and I were in the area scouting for places to fish for bass during the coming summer. I also told them I enjoyed wheeling and dealing in fishing tackle and was looking for any used Penn 320 reels they might hear of. I spun them a cover story I'd used successfully in past undercover investigations: that I'd been injured working in the West Virginia coal mines and now lived on disability payment checks. This gave me the time to fish and hang out at the lake all summer. That cover story would open a lot of doors for me during this investigation.

Jim and I next made the rounds of yard sales in the area, trying to meet the locals and learn some names, just as I'd done during the preliminary stages of previous undercover investigations. This early in the case, we were trying to learn the area and identify and sort out all the players. I had photos of some of the suspects from intelligence reports, but for others all we had were names.

A few weeks later, I received my permanent membership card for the Moose Lodge in Weirton, West Virginia, and used it to make my first visit to Conneaut's Moose Lodge. Walking in with Jim Baker in tow, I showed my card to the guy behind the bar, who examined it and announced to the dozen or so people in the club, "Gentlemen, we have with us today Bill Stone, a fellow Moose member visiting from West Virginia, and his guest!" All the bar patrons applauded. So much for trying to make a low-key entrance and maintain a low profile.

The protocol was that since we were visitors, the first round of drinks was bought for us by the Moose Lodge, after which we took our turn. My undercover partner wasn't allowed to buy drinks because he wasn't a Moose member, but both of us got right down to business, working the crowd and trying to get to know people. Jimmy Baker had an advantage, though; he was a Cleveland Indians baseball fan. This was a great bond; Cleveland is just sixty miles west of Conneaut along the lake shore, and it seemed everyone in the Moose Lodge was an Indians fan.

Baker and I ended up talking to people at opposite ends of the bar, and every time he needed another bottle of beer he'd holler at me across the room, "Hey, Bill, buy us another round!" I made a joke about it, saying loudly for all in the bar to hear, "For someone who's not allowed to buy any alcohol, you're sure free with *my* money." Everyone laughed at that and seemed to enjoy hearing Baker and me go back and forth at one another. So every time someone in the bar needed another drink that night, they'd holler to Baker, "Hey, buy us another round, will ya . . . ?" And Baker, of course, would then holler to me. I probably ended up spending at least one hundred dollars that evening buying everyone drinks. But this ultimately worked to our advantage, because it was the start of me becoming known to the guys in the club as the "money man." They believed I had money to spend, although in reality the money I was spending so freely came from the Division of Wildlife.

As Baker continued talking with several members about batting averages and ERAs, I sat on a bar stool, watching TV and socializing with whoever happened to sit down beside me. After a while I said to the guy seated to my right, kind of offhandedly, "Ya know, I've come up here to the lake from West Virginia a few times and tried to catch some yellow perch, but I just haven't had any luck. And I'm tired of it. I can't seem to catch 'em and I don't know how to catch 'em. If I had my druthers, I'd just sit on this barstool, drink beer, watch TV, and let someone else catch 'em, then I'd buy the fish from him . . ."

My bar buddy, whom I'll call Charlie Haller, surprised me by saying immediately, "Well, hell, I'll sell you some fish."

"Do you have yellow perch?" I asked.

"Yeah. . . ."

"How much you want for them?" I asked.

"I'll sell you perch for eight dollars a pound. And I'll even go get 'em right now, if you want."

"Sure," I told him, "go get 'em. I'll be sitting right here on this barstool until you get back. And when you come back, park beside the silver van in the parking lot . . . that's my vehicle."

"Okay," Haller said, and left the bar.

I got Baker off to the side, informed him of what was happening, and told him to stay in the bar when Haller returned. We didn't know if Haller would eventually become a major player in this investigation or not, but either way we didn't want to spook him by showing too much interest. I did not recognize his name from any of the intelligence reports we'd received, but at this early stage in the investigation we didn't know where he would lead us, so I didn't want to take any unnecessary chances.

About an hour later, Haller returned to the Moose Lodge, walked up to the bar, and tapped me on the shoulder. We went outside, where he had parked his vehicle beside my van, just as I'd instructed him. Opening the double doors on the passenger side of my van, I got out a set of weighing scales I'd purchased just for this investigation. I hung the scales in the open doorway, directly in front of the hidden video camera I had mounted in the van, and then turned on the camera without him seeing me do it.

Haller removed a cooler from his vehicle filled with packages of frozen yellow perch fillets, and I started weighing the packages, one at a time. The weight of each package was marked on it, but I told him I wanted to make sure of the weights. He seemed a little suspicious of the scales, so I tried to put him at ease by explaining that I always weighed the fish the first time I did business with someone.

"It's nothing personal," I said. "I just want to make sure I'm getting my money's worth."

And when I paid him, instead of just handing him the money, I counted out the bills for the camera to record, "Twenty, forty, sixty. . . ." I bought eighty dollars' worth of yellow perch fillets that very first night at the Conneaut Moose Lodge. And before we were through with the transaction in the parking lot, I also made sure to ask him, on camera, where he got the fish.

"I caught 'em myself . . . from the lake," Haller admitted proudly.

After making the buy, we went back into the bar and he told me he had buddies who also had perch they would probably sell me. "That's just what I'm lookin' for," I said. "Spread the word, will ya? I'm tired of driving all the way up here from West Virginia, spending a lot of time and money and not catching anything. If I can buy fish, that's just what I want."

When Baker and I finally left the Moose Lodge late that night, we were feeling pretty good, not only because of the amount of alcohol we'd consumed, but also because we had successfully made some first contacts and our first buy of fish. As we left, we copied down license plate numbers of the vehicles sitting in the parking lot, just in case any of the targets we were looking for owned any of the vehicles.

The next day, I ran Haller's name through the Division of Wildlife's records of previous arrests, but he came back clean. So as far as we knew, he was not going to be one of the major players in Operation Cornerstone. As I said earlier, all of the people we initially targeted had records of previous arrests for violating Ohio's wildlife laws on sport fishing. Ironically, when we finally wound up this case after a year and a half, Haller avoided arrest and prosecution because the statute of limitations on him had expired.

———

During the first phases of this investigation, Officer Baker and I visited the Conneaut area mainly on weekends, staying in a cheap motel. We usually arrived on a Thursday night and stayed through Sunday. But even a cheap motel can eventually become costly if you stay too often, so we began looking around the area for a house or cabin to rent. We eventually found a small cabin near the lakeshore. It was rough, but the owner rented it to us for the entire summer at a rate lower than it would have cost us for weekends alone. We soon moved in, bringing with us a small boat for fishing in Conneaut Harbor. We wanted the locals to think we were just your average summer fishermen.

In the evenings, Baker and I would occasionally build a campfire behind the cabin and sit around the fire, talking and drinking a few beers. The man who owned the cabin lived only a couple doors away, and often he and his girlfriend would come over and join us. During one of those first few visits, I told the couple about buying some perch from one of the locals at the Moose Lodge, adding that we were interested in buying more. I repeated the story I had told Charlie Haller, about not having the fishing knowledge or skill to catch perch myself. The couple listened quietly to my story, and then the woman remarked, "If you're interested, my dad sells fish to people."

"He does?" I said, trying not to sound too anxious.

"Yeah. He's got a fish-cleaning shed out behind his house, and he sells perch to people all the time. As a matter of fact, he's stopping by our place later tonight. If you're serious about buying some fish, I'll tell him to come over and see you."

"We'll be here," I said, popping open a can of beer and handing it to her. "Send him on over."

Sure enough, about an hour later, an older gentleman showed up and the woman introduced him to us as her dad, whom I'll call Joe Gordon. After we had chatted for a few minutes, Gordon said, "My daughter tells me you're lookin' to buy some fish . . . that right?"

I told him yes, yellow perch, and he said, "Well, I go fishin' every morning, and sometimes in the evening, too. How many pounds you want? As much as you need, I can get it for you."

I dickered with Gordon a little on price, finally settling on eight dollars per pound, the same price I had paid the guy from the Moose Lodge. Then he said, "I can have some fish for you tomorrow, if you want them that soon. Just stop by my house about noon." He gave me the address, and the next day Baker and I got there about midday, just as Gordon had instructed.

Joe Gordon had a small building behind his house where he cleaned fish, complete with a homemade scaler. The scaler was a metal drum hooked up to a small, electric motor. He'd put about a dozen perch inside the drum at a time, and when the motor was plugged in it rotated the drum by way of an attached belt. The tumbling of the perch inside the drum knocked the scales off the fish before they were filleted. It was an impressive setup, and by the looks of the place we guessed this guy had been cleaning perch this way for many years. We bought about a hundred dollars' worth of fish from him that first day.

One of Gordon's fishing buddies, who had been helping him clean the fish as we watched, told us he worked in Pennsylvania growing mushrooms and that he could get us all the mushrooms we wanted to buy. He said he stole the mushrooms from his employer. I told him we were interested. I also told Gordon that we'd be back the next weekend, and that I'd give him a call to see if he had more fish by then.

"You just call during the week and put in your order," he said. "I'll have your fish ready when you get here."

Gordon was not one of our main targets, but at least we had broken the ice in this case and bought illegal fish from two of the locals. We hoped they might eventually lead us to our targets. We later learned that Gordon was poaching so many yellow perch he was regularly supplying an area restaurant with fish. Our intelligence suggested that Lakeshore Marina was also supplying local restaurants with perch. It turned out this was a very common practice. During the eventual takedown of this case, we examined the records of all the suspected restaurants in Conneaut and although Lake Erie perch dinners were a major feature on all their menus, not one restaurant had purchased any perch from licensed commercial fishermen for the previous eight years! Hmmmm. . . .

––––––

As soon as we began making connections in this investigation, though, a problem arose: we were soon buying so many fish we were running out of money. The Division of Wildlife would give us only three or four hundred dollars at a time for "buy" money, and I could easily use that up buying fish in the first day or two of a long weekend at the cabin. Eventually, I began using some of my own money to supplement our allowance from the Division, figuring I'd recoup it somehow, later in the investigation. When my boss found out what I was doing, he wasn't too happy about it, but I knew I had to buy the perch when they were available.

My previous supervisor, Kevin O'Dell, would not have cared that I was spending my own money to buy fish, but since he had recently been promoted to assistant wildlife law enforcement supervisor, he was out of the loop on decisions concerning undercover officers. My new boss, whom I'll call Donald Kramer, went strictly by the book, something that is not always convenient in undercover work. I understood that he was new to the job and learning to supervise undercover officers, but Kramer had never been one himself so he couldn't fully understand our needs in the field. I really think Kramer was afraid that if an undercover officer under his command got into trouble, it would reflect poorly upon him and jeopardize his chances for advancement within the Division of Wildlife. It often seemed to us that he gave greater priority to not screwing up—and preventing his undercover officers from screwing up—than to doing what it took to catch the bad guys. This was frustrating when we were working hard, isolated from our colleagues and families. Thankfully, Kramer didn't remain supervisor of the Covert Investigations Unit for long; within a year or two he had been promoted out of our hair. In the meantime, however, he put a crimp in our style, blocking the actions that would have allowed us to wring all the bad guys out of this investigation that we possibly could.

———

As the investigation progressed, Officer Baker and I continued dropping by Lakeshore Marina and the Moose Lodge, showing our faces and getting to know the locals. We were trying hard to make contact with the three suspects originally identified as the main targets of Operation Cornerstone. One of these was the marina's owner, Bruce Jones. The second was Jones's good friend, Raoul Erdman, known as Corky, and the third was Walter Kaczoroski, known as Wally. All three of the men owned large charter-fishing boats that they docked at Lakeshore, boats worth tens of thousands of dollars.

Baker and I also regularly made the rounds of the local bars, restaurants, and even a local strip club a time or two, because some of our targets reportedly hung out at these places. We went to the strip joint, Cherries, only in the line of duty, of course. The women working the club occasionally would ask me what I did for a living. I always told them I was a go-getter.

"What's a go-getter?" they'd ask.

"Well," I'd say, "I take my wife to work in the morning, come in here to drink beer and look at you in the afternoon, then when my wife gets off work, I go get 'er." When they asked Baker what he did for a living, he'd always point to me and say, "I work with him."

One evening at the Conneaut Moose Lodge, a guy came in and sat down beside me at the bar. I didn't know his name, but I remembered seeing him earlier that day at Lakeshore. I noticed he was deeply suntanned, like many of the fishermen in the area, so I offered to buy him a beer. We talked some, and he eventually introduced himself as Jason Heinbaugh and told me that he was the first mate on Corky's charter boat. He also said he helped clean fish at Lakeshore and told me he made extra money selling perch on the side.

I then told him the same thing I had told everyone else in the club who would listen—that I wanted to buy as many yellow perch as possible. I told him that I knew how to catch catfish—even showing him a few photos of large cats I'd pulled from the Ohio River—but complained that I didn't know anything about perch fishing. Finally, he made me the offer I was waiting for. "Well, if you want to buy perch, I'm just your man."

I asked him how much he could get for me, and he said, "As much as you want." "Are you serious?" I asked. He nodded, but demanded $8.50 per pound.

I hesitated, just to add a little suspense, and then responded, "Well, Jason, I'm a businessman myself, just like you, just trying to make a buck. And I have buddies in West Virginia who want to buy fish from me, but I need to make at least a dollar per pound profit to make it worth my while. Can we deal?"

He said he understood, and immediately dropped his price to $7 per pound. "That way, we'll both make a little money," he said. "How's that?" And he stuck out his hand for a shake.

"It works for me," I said, and shook his hand on the deal.

I had dickered with Jason on the price so as not to seem too anxious to make a buy. You never want to appear too anxious when making your first buy from poachers, as that can make them suspicious. I also let him know I'd already bought fish from Gordon two or three times, and Jason said he knew Gordon. This bolstered my credibility with Jason, helping to put this poacher at ease.

I asked Jason if he could sell me any perch right then, and he said he could but that he'd have to go home and get it. I told him I'd wait at the bar until he got back. About half an hour later the phone rang, and the bartender asked if there was a Bill Stone in the bar. I raised my hand and took the receiver, all the time wondering who knew to look for me at Conneaut's Moose Lodge. The caller was Jason.

"Hey, Bill," he said. "I don't have as much fish in my freezer as I thought, but I've got a fishing buddy here in town who has some perch he'll sell ya. You interested in buy from him?"

"Sure," I said. "If the price is the same. Seven dollars a pound?"

Jason said yes, the price would be the same, and I told him to bring me as much fish as he and his buddy, whom I'll call Eric Staley, had. He offered to bring Eric with him to the bar, which was great because I needed to make a visual identification of the guy. Things were now starting to roll in this investigation, and our fishing "net" was growing ever larger.

Money was the enticement for these poachers, rather than the ego that drove many of the deer poachers in my previous undercover cases. These fishermen had easy access to the lake's fish, and if they could trade yellow perch for quick cash, they were all for it. They were looking for buyers, and I was filling that niche. They didn't limit themselves to individual buyers, either. Baker and I soon learned that some of the poachers in the area had contracts with Conneaut restaurants to supply them with fish. If you weren't part of the inner circle of poachers, though, you weren't invited to sell to the restaurants, the source of the big money for the poachers. Many of the small-time poachers in the area had extra fish they wanted to sell but few buyers. That's what made them so willing to take a chance and sell to relative strangers like me and my undercover partner.

Jason and Eric eventually returned to the Moose Lodge that night, and I went out to the parking lot to make the buy. Just as I had when making my first buy in Conneaut from Charlie Haller, I opened the side doors of my van and hung the weighing scales in the door opening. When I did this, though, the two poachers began looking at me suspiciously.

"Look," I said. "I buy ginseng and a little marijuana from guys sometimes, too, and I just want to make sure that if a guy tells me a package weighs a certain amount, it really does. I'm weighing these packages of perch to make sure the weights match what's marked on them. If they do match, I'll never use these scales again. If we're going to do business, we need to be able to trust each other. Okay?"

They seemed to agree with my logic and reluctantly nodded. I began weighing the packages of perch in front of the hidden video camera in my van. The weights were close enough to accurate that I took out my money. And, just as I'd done before, I counted out the bills for the camera to record, "Twenty, forty, sixty . . ." I now had Jason and Eric hooked, and in the weeks and months to come they became regular suppliers as well as eventual big-time players in this investigation.

Remember the guy who offered to sell me the stolen mushrooms? As the investigation proceeded, we discovered that he was a part-time cook in the kitchen at the Moose Lodge. And as I became more acquainted with him throughout the summer, he invited me to help him cook at the lodge on weekends. He told me he'd been a cook in the Navy, so knew his way around a commercial kitchen. Seizing the opportunity, I said, "Ya know, I've always wanted to learn to cook. Would you teach me . . . ?"

"Hell, yes," he said. "The next time you're at the lodge, you come back to the kitchen, and I'll show you a thing or two about cooking."

I took him up on his offer, not only because it was an opportunity to get deeper into the Moose Lodge and closer to the poachers who came and went there, but I really did like to cook and wanted to learn more about it. And here was a chance to learn from a guy who knew what he was doing. He just didn't know what I was really up to.

———

About that time I started wearing my white cowboy hat, my trademark. I had soon learned that to get deeper into this group of poachers I had to convince them I had money. So as I started cooking more and more often at the Moose Lodge, I made sure that I showed up looking sharp. These were not the low-life poachers I'd had to deal with during most of my undercover career; many of these guys were professional businessmen in the community. I had to make them believe that I had money, too—money to spend on buying perch.

Many of the poachers lived in homes worth hundreds of thousands of dollars and owned late-model, state-of-the-art fiberglass fishing boats. So I had to clean up my good ol' boy act in order to fit in. I cut my hair, trimmed my mustache, and always made sure I had on clean, pressed clothes when I went to the Moose Lodge to cook and hang out.

I even went so far as to contact the U.S. Fish and Wildlife Service (USFWS), asking to borrow several outfits of expensive western clothing that the federal agency made available to its own undercover officers. Since many of the bad guys at the Moose Lodge wore expensive cowboy boots, I had the USFWS send me boots made from the skins of endangered species. Some even came complete with jackets trimmed in leather to match the boots. The agency also sent fancy, expensive hat bands for my cowboy hat, made from various snakeskins.

All of this clothing was high-dollar, and the poachers knew it. They would comment about my clothes from time to time, especially my boots. One pair of boots was made from the skin of sea turtles, which was hard to obtain. I even had a leather coat trimmed with caiman skin on the collar. In addition, I sometimes wore a vest made of snakeskin. It was the kind of wardrobe only a man with money could afford. The ironic part of this charade was that we were conducting this operation on a shoestring budget, yet I was always dressed to kill.

———

By mid-summer, the poachers had fallen so completely for my act that it got to be humorous. When they spotted my van in town for the weekend, they acted like kids running toward an ice cream truck. Poachers would literally line up, waiting to sell me their fish. I could easily have spent a thousand dollars every weekend buying illegal yellow perch—and sometimes I did. My buys were limited only by the money I had available.

Much of the illegal fishing in this case took place in the mornings. These poachers often began fishing at dawn so they could catch their fish and get off the lake before it got too hot. By noon, most of the fish caught that day had already been cleaned and placed in freezers. Knowing that, I'd show up about noon or even later to make my buys. That schedule worked well for me: I could sleep late and still obtain the evidence we needed against the bad guys.

A few weeks later, I called Jason, told him I was coming up to the lake for the weekend, and asked him if he had any fish for me. He said he did, and asked how much I wanted, offering to provide me as much as one hundred pounds of perch fillets per week, if I wanted to buy that much.

"A hundred pounds per week?" I asked.

"Yeah, I can do that," Jason replied, and bragged that he and his fishing buddy Eric regularly caught double or even triple their daily limits of yellow perch. And if the fishing was really good, he said, they would make two fishing trips per day, one in the morning and another in the late afternoon. I told him I was interested in his offer to supply one hundred pounds of perch per week but needed to wait until after the Fourth of July holiday. I told him I had some other things I needed to attend to and couldn't make such a big buy until then.

In fact, I was stalling for time enough to get more money from my supervisor, Donald Kramer. There wasn't enough money in the investigation's bank account to buy one hundred pounds of perch weekly at seven dollars per pound. Plus, I didn't want to sound too anxious to make such a big buy.

I finally made contact with one of the three original targets of the investigation one morning at Lakeshore Marina. I had gone there looking for Jason, and when I couldn't find him, I asked the guys if anyone had seen him. They hadn't but suggested that he might be with Corky (Raoul Erdman), who was one of our prime suspects. They recommended that I call Corky, and when I told them I didn't have his phone number, they dialed the number and handed me the receiver.

Corky answered, and I launched into my story. "Hi, I'm Bill," I told him. "I'm looking for Jason. Is he with you? He was supposed to sell me some fish."

"How much do you want?" Corky asked. "I'll sell you some. . . ."

That was just what I wanted to hear. "I need about twenty pounds," I told him. "Can you do that?"

"Yeah," he said. "I've got twenty pounds. Come on over to my house, and I'll fix you up." He told me to ask the guys at the marina how to get to his place, and they gave me directions.

I drove to Corky's house, knocked on the door, and he invited me in. He then took me to his freezer, dug out several bags of yellow perch, and handed them to me. I asked him when he'd caught the fish and he said, "Oh, sometime this summer, maybe a month or so ago. I forget exactly when." I asked him if he'd caught them himself, and he said he had, with the help of a few friends he had invited along on his boat that day. I carried the perch out to my van, but before paying Corky, hung the weighing scales and weighed the packages, just as I had done when dealing for the first time with the other poachers.

And, just as the other poachers had, Corky questioned me using the scales. I gave him the same line I'd used with the others, saying that if he and I were going to do business, we needed to be able to trust one another. Knowing that I'd try and lure Corky outside to make the buy and give him his money, I'd already turned on the videotaping equipment in my van when I'd pulled into his driveway. As a result, all I had to do was open the side doors to my van, hang the scales, and begin weighing the packages of fish to get Corky on camera. I counted the money out to him, just as I always did, and when we were done he said, "Whenever you need more, just let me know."

"I'm sure I'll be back in touch," I said, grinning, shook his hand, and left.

Corky was willing to deal with me because Jason, who was first mate on his charter boat, had vouched for me. Jason had told Corky that I'd already bought fish from him and could be trusted. Jason had also told Corky that I had money to spend and would likely buy as much fish as I could get. Corky even commented that he had heard I had a contract with Jason to buy one hundred pounds of perch fillets per week. I told him I did, although Jason hadn't sold me that many fish at one time as of yet. Corky asked me why I was buying so much fish, and I explained that I was supplying people back in West Virginia, making money on the transactions. Corky seemed to accept that explanation, and as far as I could tell he now trusted me.

The third main target in the investigation, after Jones and Corky, was Walter Kaczoroski—a real catbird, in my opinion. Wally was divorced, and he liked to drink and chase women. Ironically, given his lifestyle, he lived with his mother. Like Corky, Wally was a good friend of Jason's, so he too offered to sell me fish, and I started buying from him. By this time, I was buying fish from so many people I was completely out of money by the end of most weekends.

———

The Fourth of July came, and I made it a point to be at the cabin that weekend, knowing that most of the poachers would be around for the holiday. I had been invited to Jason's house for a cookout, and when I got there he and Eric, his fishing buddy, were sitting at a table on the backyard patio. About half a dozen other guests had already arrived. I walked in to the party wearing my cowboy hat, and sat down across the table from Jason and Eric.

We hadn't been talking long when Jason said, "Bill, we've got something to tell you."

"Okay," I said. "Shoot."

Eric started, "Bill, I want you to know that I worked for the U.S. Coast Guard, and. . . ."

All I heard were the words Coast Guard, and I went ballistic, not giving him a chance to finish. "You're telling me you work for the Coast Guard? Are you telling me that after I've already bought illegal fish from you guys that you two are cops? Did you guys set me up? Are you wearing a body wire?"

"Hell, no, we're not cops," Eric stammered. "We didn't set you up!"

"Well, I know I ain't no cop," I said angrily. "And I ain't wearin' no wire. And we're going to prove that to each other right now, gentlemen. Strip off your shirt and pants!"

They looked incredulous, but when they saw me stand up, peel off my shirt, unbuckle my belt and drop my pants, they did the same. Within seconds, all three of us were standing with our shirts off and our pants down around our knees, stripped down to our underwear. People at the cookout couldn't believe what they were seeing; most likely they thought all three of us had suddenly gone insane.

Once we each saw there were no body wires present, we pulled our clothes back on and sat down. Eric finally said sheepishly, "You didn't give me a chance to finish, Bill. . . . What I was trying to tell you was that I was recently fired from the Coast Guard for failing a drug test. I just wanted you to know that in case it made any difference to you about buying fish from us. Is our deal still on? One hundred pounds per week?"

By that point I had calmed down, so I said, "Yeah, It's still on." Then I smiled apologetically and added, "Hey, you guys put me on alert, man. . . . After buying all those fish from you and Jason already, the first thing I thought when you said 'Coast Guard' was that I was getting busted."

The party eventually resumed as everyone relaxed, but what that little impromptu strip-tease had done was remove any suspicion Jason and Eric may have had that I was a cop and couldn't be trusted. What they didn't realize, however, was that in fact I was wearing a wire. I had hidden a small body wire in the crown of my cowboy hat, and it had recorded our entire conversation.

When I returned to the lake the next weekend, Jason and Eric had the hundred pounds of perch ready and waiting for me, just as they'd promised. The downside was that at seven dollars per pound, the buy cost me seven hundred dollars, money the investigation's budget could barely afford.

———

As the summer wore on, my partner and I returned to the rental cabin most every weekend, spending time with the poachers either at the Moose Lodge, Lakeshore Marina, or the local strip joint. We kept telling the bad guys we had girlfriends, and they kept encouraging us to bring them with us to the lake some weekend. Baker and I got to talking about that and figured we needed to show up with at least one woman to maintain our cover story, so we called Kramer, our supervisor, for advice.

I asked Kramer if the Division of Wildlife had uniformed female wildlife officers that might be able to join us undercover for a weekend or two, and he gave us some names. I knew the few female officers mentioned and didn't think any of them were suitable, so I asked Kramer if we could use our wives instead. His answer was a resounding no; that was definitely not an option. Finally, I said, half jokingly, "Well, we've been hanging out at a strip joint in the area. How about if we hire two of those women to be our girlfriends for a weekend?"

Kramer floored me by saying, without hesitation, "If you do, just make sure you get a receipt."

In the end we dropped that idea, since Baker thought his wife would probably kill him if she ever found out. This left us back at our original idea of bringing in one of the Division's female officers. We selected an officer I'll call Sheila, and she agreed. She became my "girlfriend" for a few weekends that summer, playing her role well. Sheila's presence helped confirm our stories in the eyes of the poachers, and soon we added to the rapport we were building with them in yet another way: Baker began playing golf with them. Some of the poachers enjoyed golf, and since Baker did too, he'd play a round or two with them occasionally.

As the investigation lagged on, Baker and I tried to spell one another. Sometimes he would go to the cabin alone for the weekend, and sometimes I would. By switching off, we hoped to give each other occasional breaks from the work while maintaining our momentum and continuing to infiltrate deeper and deeper into this group of fish poachers.

Summer eventually gave way to fall's cooler weather while I continued buying perch from Jason. Then one day he told me he couldn't continue supplying me with my standard weekly order of one hundred pounds of fish because the fall weather was hindering his fishing trips. He said the more frequent winds and storms of autumn meant he couldn't get out on the lake as often, and the fishing was less predictable. But he added that he had quite a few buddies scattered through the town of Conneaut who had fish in their freezers and were willing to sell to me. Would I want fish from them? I told him yes, and promised to get back to him when I was ready to buy.

Excited about the prospect of making a huge buy from many different people, I called Kramer, my supervisor, and told him that if he could get me five thousand dollars to make a gigantic buy, we could take down all the remaining poachers in Conneaut and wrap up the case. To my great surprise and disappointment, he refused to authorize that amount, saying that five thousand dollars was just too much money. To add to my disappointment, my personal life was starting to fall apart about that time. In fact, it was my personal problems that caused us to wind up this investigation much earlier than it should have been.

————

In September 2001, on Labor Day weekend to be exact, I was home with my wife for a few days when she informed me that she was leaving me. She told me it was because of my job as an undercover officer; I had been gone too much over the years. She said that my use of our personal money to make buys of the illegal Lake Erie yellow perch had been the last straw. We had been married twenty-two years at that point and had raised two children together, a son and daughter. I was devastated.

My wife had asked me several times over the years to quit undercover work and go back into uniform. She believed that a return to somewhat regular hours would allow me more time at home and be better for our marriage. I kept telling her I would do as she asked, but I never did. I liked undercover work too much, and I believed my skills were better suited to undercover investigation than to work as a uniformed officer. When my wife announced that she was leaving, though, I decided the job wasn't worth sacrificing my marriage.

I contacted my friend and former supervisor, Kevin O'Dell, and told him I needed out, that my wife was leaving me and I wanted to try to salvage my marriage. He couldn't believe what I was telling him, but I finally convinced him I was serious.

"Well, it will take a little while to get you back in uniform, R.T.," Kevin said, "but it can be done. Officer Baker will just have to take over Operation Cornerstone and finish it out." I told him that I understood that the transfer would take time, but I also made it clear to Kevin that I needed to make the switch as soon as possible.

I went back to the cabin once or twice in September to pursue the investigation, but with everything on my mind concerning my wife and our marriage, I just wasn't myself. On top of those worries, my father had just been diagnosed with cancer. Then came the attacks of 9/11—the destruction of the World Trade Center and damaging of the Pentagon by terrorists. And finally, to top it all off, I arrived at the cabin one weekend to discover that someone had broken in and stolen all of my fishing tackle. Everything combined to make it a very black time in my life.

Over the next several months, the Division of Wildlife began making arrangements for me to return to uniform. Yes, I had requested the change, but the thought of going back into uniform and working as a regular wildlife officer assigned to a specific county was killing me. By that time in my career I had been undercover for about a dozen years, and I just couldn't wrap my mind around doing anything other than undercover work. I loved it. It was who I was. Looking back on it now, I believe my entire personal identity was wrapped up in the job.

I knew that uniformed wildlife officers were needed and performed a valuable service in the protection of natural resources, but I just couldn't see myself doing that job again. I don't know how to describe my feelings except to say that I felt as if going back into uniform would take away my manhood. I had proven to myself and others that I could do the job of an undercover officer and do it well. Hell, I'd been doing it successfully for more than a decade. I felt that undercover wildlife law enforcement work was a perfect fit for me and my talents, and I didn't want to take a step back.

I was literally losing sleep worrying about my marriage, my dad, my job, my country, and anything else I could think of to worry about. Things were not good. My wife and I had a long talk about the situation, and she told me that even a transfer back into uniform might not save our marriage. I remember her saying specifically, "I can't promise I'll stay with you, R.T., even if you do give up undercover work."

Given her warning, I eventually made up my mind that there was no use in me giving up the profession I loved when doing so couldn't guarantee my wife would stay with me. I chose to continue working as an undercover officer and see what happened with my marriage. In any event, my wife left me on October 1, 2001, and by December 12 we were officially divorced. Ironically, Kevin O'Dell went through a divorce at about the same time.

———

Getting back to the case, I had two thousand dollars of the five thousand I needed to make the major perch buy. But Kramer, my supervisor, told me that I had to spend the two thousand before he could get me more. "That's just the way the system works now," he explained. So that weekend, I spent the entire two thousand dollars I had buying perch. By Sunday afternoon I had bought so many perch fillets that I couldn't fit them all in my van—hundreds of pounds of fish.

Word spread throughout Conneaut that I was buying perch like they were going out of style, and people came out of the woodwork to sell them to me. Soon, though, I was out of money. If I'd had just a few thousand dollars more, I could have bought fish from nearly all the remaining poachers in town, but my lack of funds forced me to stop. That's how frustrating undercover work can be. Not only do you have to put up with the bad guys, but at times you also have to battle your own supervisors and administration to get what you need to do your job.

In this case, because I couldn't get the additional money I needed to make the big buy I'd hoped for, I was unable to identify any more poachers in addition to those we'd already identified and gathered evidence on. As a result, Operation Cornerstone began to wind down.

Over the time I had invested in this case, amounting to more than a year, I had built up such credibility with the poachers that one of the three top targets in the investigation, Walter Kaczoroski, invited me to his house several times to eat steak suppers with him and his mother. When I mentioned Wally's invitations to some of the other poachers, they remarked that I must be special for some reason, because Wally didn't invite anyone to his house. He obviously liked me, and he even invited me to go to Florida with him for the winter. He told me he always took a lot of perch with him when he went—to sell, of course.

Wally also told me that he worked for a commercial fish processor while in Florida and made extra money skimming fish, just as he skimmed yellow perch from the sport anglers who had their catches cleaned and filleted at Lakeshore. I saw Wally's invitation as an opportunity to broaden the investigation out of state, so I asked my supervisor for permission to leave Ohio. It did not surprise me when he said no. Whereas O'Dell would have gladly let me go, Kramer instead chose to turn over the evidence we'd collected on Wally to the Florida Fish and Wildlife Conservation Commission, letting them pursue that part of the investigation from their end.

Baker and I visited Conneaut intermittently over the winter, occasionally showing up at our old haunts to maintain our contacts with the poachers. However, little fishing went on during the winter, so there weren't many fish to buy, and our money supply had likewise dwindled.

———

Operation Cornerstone officially ended in late May 2002, just as the yellow perch fishing was beginning to pick up again for the summer. We had plenty of evidence against two of the three original targets, but had failed to draw in the third target, the marina owner, Bruce Jones. I had asked to buy fish from him several times, but he was always very evasive and never sold me any. He was likewise very careful not to predispose himself during any of our conversations. I was sure he was poaching but believed that he sold all his fish to local restaurants, so that he didn't need to sell to individuals like me. Jones was so cautious that I doubted we would be able to indict him even if we spent more time on this project. As a result, the Division of Wildlife decided to go with what we had, taking down the poachers we had been able to gather evidence against and ending the operation.

One reason we decided to end the project when we did was from concern that pursuing it for another year might look bad to the courts and the general public when the case finally went to trial. Since tens of thousands of yellow perch were being poached annually, a longer investigation might prompt people to ask why we hadn't taken steps to stop the slaughter sooner. We also felt that allowing the poachers to keep operating through another season would be unfair to the legal sport anglers fishing in the area; after all, the poachers were literally robbing the law-abiding fishermen of yellow perch. Finally, we wanted to protect the perch population itself from overexploitation. The mission of Ohio's Division of Wildlife is to protect and conserve the state's fish, game, and other wildlife populations. To quote from the agency's Mission Statement itself, "We are dedicated to conserving and improving the fish and wildlife resources and their habitats, and promoting their use and appreciation by the people so that these resources continue to enhance the quality of life for all Ohioans."

In short, a protracted investigation might have given the Division of Wildlife a black eye. Nevertheless, I was disappointed that the case was ending without netting all the poachers. I believed I had bought out everyone else's fish and had worked my way down to the last few big poachers. Now I was going to have to let them go.

The takedown was carried out on Fourth of July weekend in 2002. Because of the tens of thousands of illegal perch caught and sold during this case, the restitution payments imposed on the poachers were much larger than the fines. But the real significance of this case was the nature of the charges.

Eight poachers were arrested and indicted, and every one of them was found guilty. These convictions were especially significant because they marked the first time anyone in Ohio had ever been arrested and convicted for the commercialization of wildlife under a felony statute. Before Operation Cornerstone, all wildlife law violations, whether they involved illegal commercialization or not, were considered misdemeanors under Ohio law. The classification of their crimes as felonies was a big surprise to some of the poachers. Several of them had been arrested for wildlife law violations before and only had to pay small fines—fines they'd shrugged off as the price of doing business. None of them had ever been sent to jail. What they didn't know was that Ohio wildlife laws had changed and that illegal commercialization of wildlife was now classified as a fifth-degree felony. So when Corky was arrested, for example, he told the arresting wildlife officers, "Just give me my ticket. I'll pay it."

He was shocked to hear the officers say, "No, Corky, this time you're coming with us." They handcuffed Corky and the other poachers and took them all to jail. There they were ordered to put on orange inmate jump suits and then were taken to the county courthouse to appear before a judge.

The judge didn't seize their expensive fishing boats as evidence. The Division of Wildlife had specifically asked the court to refrain from seizing the boats, because the agency didn't want the responsibility of storing them for the months leading up to and during the trial. The judge did make it clear to the poachers, though, that if any piece of equipment or fishing tackle was removed from their boats without his permission before the trial commenced, they would forfeit all the equipment and tackle, and their boats, to Ohio's Division of Wildlife. The poachers were badly scared when they learned they were being arrested for felonies, but they were doubly afraid of losing their boats, equipment, and fishing tackle, so they abided by the judge's orders.

I am quite proud of my involvement in two cases that marked a more serious view of the illegal commercialization of wildlife in Ohio. My first-ever undercover case, Operation Clanbake, marked the first time illegal commercialization of wildlife was proven in an Ohio court. Following that milestone, it had taken years to strengthen the laws so that poachers selling the proceeds of their crimes were now charged with felonies rather than misdemeanors. Now, as a result of Operation Cornerstone, there were felony convictions on the books for the illegal commercialization of wildlife. I had been heavily involved in both undercover investigations—conducted a decade apart—and I believed we were finally making significant progress in the war against wildlife poachers in the Buckeye State.

# OPERATION STIR-FRY

In the fall of 2001, during Operation Cornerstone—the undercover investigation described in chapter 6, concerning the poaching and illegal sale of sport-caught yellow perch from Lake Erie—I received a telephone call from West Virginia's Department of Natural Resources. The caller was Captain Wadsmen of that department's Division of Wildlife, an officer I had worked with during Operation Redbud and a few other undercover projects.

"Hey, R.T.," Wadsmen began, "I've got something here you might be interested in. We just took into custody a couple of individuals with seven dead, illegal deer in the back of their pickup truck. And one of the guys told us he and his buddies were on their way to Cleveland, Ohio, to sell the deer to an Asian buyer. Are you interested in taking their place? One of the poachers said he'd cooperate and go along with you."

Maybe I should have thought twice before answering, but I didn't. "I'm on my way," I said. "I'll be there in about an hour."

The cooperative poacher, whom I'll call Don Cobb, had agreed to go along with me on the delivery of the deer to Cleveland in exchange for leniency on the charges facing him. Nevertheless, I was apprehensive. The situation was potentially very dangerous. I didn't know anything about Cobb or where exactly he would be taking me. I had used witting informants—informants who knew my identity—before in undercover cases, but this was the first time I had ever begun an undercover investigation in exactly this way.

I called my former supervisor, Kevin O'Dell, explained the situation, and told him I needed someone to go with me to meet the Cleveland connection in this poaching case. "I'm available," he said, and told me where to pick him up on my way. I was glad Kevin was coming along, as I trusted him completely in such situations.

When I arrived at the Parkersburg office of West Virginia's Department of Natural Resources, I asked Captain Wadsmen if he had already tuned up Don Cobb. "Tuning up" means explaining to a suspect what is expected of him. In this case, Wadsmen described to Cobb all the charges he would face in the state of West Virginia, unless he cooperated fully with West Virginia's and Ohio's wildlife officers, including me. After thinking it over, Cobb chose to cooperate.

Captain Wadsmen told me that this particular group of poachers claimed to have been selling illegal game to their contact in Cleveland for several years. He also said that while he didn't think Cobb would rat on me once we got to Cleveland, there were no guarantees. Since I had never before put myself in such a situation, I decided I needed to make my own judgment about the informant. I told the captain I wanted to talk to Cobb. Alone.

I walked into the interrogation room where the poacher was sitting and introduced myself. Don Cobb was a young man in his early twenties, tall and stocky, a typical West Virginia farm boy. He didn't look violent, but my instincts told me not to turn my back on him. He looked plenty strong.

"Are you willing to help us?" I asked.

"Yeah," he said, without looking up.

"Can I trust you?"

"Yeah."

I had no idea what cameras or tape recorders may have been recording us as we talked, so I ended the brief conversation and took Cobb outside. Once I had him beside my van, where I knew no one else could hear or see us, I told him I wanted to frisk him, just to make sure he did not have a weapon. He allowed me to do that, and I gave him a thorough pat-down. The last thing I wanted to deal with during a long drive to Cleveland in the middle of the night was a bad guy in my van pulling a gun, knife, or other weapon.

After searching him, I spun Cobb around to face me and pointed my finger at his face. "I have no idea where you're taking me tonight," I said, "but I've already talked to my partner, and if you get us into trouble, even a little bit of trouble, you're the first one going down. Do you understand me ?" He nodded. I didn't explicitly say that Kevin or I would shoot him, but he knew what I meant, especially when I opened my jacket just enough to let him see I was armed with a handgun. I wanted this guy to know we were serious, to believe we would shoot him if things went bad. But I didn't want to say that inside the office where my words might be recorded. Outside, where there were no cameras, I could tell him whatever I wanted.

During the drive from West Virginia to Cambridge, Ohio, to pick up Kevin O'Dell, the informant never said a word. When Kevin got into the van, he immediately pointed to Cobb and asked me, "Did you tune him up?"

"Yep. . . ."

He then turned to Cobb and asked, "Do you understand what this officer has told you?"

"Yes, sir."

"Do you understand what we're getting into? That this could be a very serious, dangerous situation?"

"Yes, sir."

"Good, then let's go."

That's all Cobb said, and away we went, headed north. As we drove, I was preparing myself for whatever might happen, and I could feel my adrenaline begin to build as we neared Cleveland.

I had received the initial call from Captain Wadsmen about 7:00 P.M. I had then driven first from southern Ohio to West Virginia to pick up the informant and the seven dead deer, then back to southern Ohio to pick up Kevin, and finally to Cleveland. When we arrived at our destination, it was well past midnight—about 2:00 or 3:00 A.M., as I recall.

I followed Cobb's driving directions to a house in the city. Despite the early hour, all of the lights in the house were on, although the windows had been covered with plastic so no one could see in. All my senses were screaming at me to be on high alert, and I was as tense as a cat as we walked onto the front porch. An Asian met us at the front door, motioning for the three of us to come inside. The man looked to be in his mid-thirties and was slight in stature, maybe five and a half feet tall at the most. Another half a dozen Asians were inside the house, talking to one another, but since none of them were speaking English, I had no idea what they were saying. I couldn't tell if they were talking about us or if they even cared that we were there.

Eventually, one of the Asians asked Cobb, in English, who Kevin and I were. That's when Cobb finally broke his stoic silence, saying we were his hunting partners. He also told the Asians that they would not be dealing with him anymore after tonight—that Kevin and I were taking his place. I was pleased with how Cobb was handling himself so far, but I was not even close to letting down my guard. Cobb then asked the Asians where they wanted us to put the deer we had brought, and they led us to a garage connected to the house.

When the garage door opened, I couldn't believe my eyes. Several species of wildlife lay dead on the floor. In addition to many deer carcasses, there were also raccoons and even possums. I noticed that though the deer had been field dressed—their intestines removed—they retained their other organs, such as heart and lungs. I backed my van up to the garage, and we unloaded the seven dead West Virginia deer. I then asked the Asians if they were going to eat the deer we had brought, and they shook their heads no.

"We no eat, we no eat," they said. "Others eat. . . ."

What they meant, we learned later, was that they were selling the deer and other animal carcasses to a Chinese restaurant in Cleveland. The restaurant used the meat in sweet-and-sour "pork" recipes, as well as in other dishes.

Many of the wild-animal carcasses in the garage looked as if they'd been lying there quite a while. So long, in fact, that their eyeballs had sunk into the skulls. I didn't know how anyone could eat that meat. It made me gag just to think about it.

We went back inside the house, where the other Asians were sitting around drinking, although what they were drinking I didn't know. The oldest woman in the room seemed to be in charge, so I asked her if they were drinking coffee. She said yes, and I told her that I'd like to have a cup, if she didn't mind. I then remembered what I had just seen in the garage, and asked her what kind of coffee it was. "Folgers," she said, which made me feel somewhat better; at least I recognized that brand and knew that it was unlikely to give me food poisoning, as long as she used a clean cup.

We stayed for about half an hour, drinking coffee and socializing a bit with the group, trying to get to know the various players. They finally paid us for our seven deer—about fifty dollars per animal—and told us they wanted to buy more wildlife, especially a bear if we could get one. They also made a request. If we did manage to get a bear, they asked us not to gut the animal; they wanted it whole. They told us they used everything in the animals they bought: intestines, heart, lungs, everything. They were particularly interested in a bear's gallbladder, believing the bile to be a powerful aphrodisiac.

We exchanged phone numbers with the group, and left shortly thereafter, none too soon to my way of thinking. That first meeting with the Asians had been successful but very stressful, too. I was glad to get out of there.

———

We continued selling wildlife to this group of Asian buyers on and off throughout the winter. When spring came, they asked us to bring them snapping turtles as well. So my undercover partner and I started setting baited turtle lines in lakes and ponds and catching turtles to sell. When we made our deliveries, the Asians always directed us to carry the live snapping turtles down to the basement of their house. They would eventually kill and clean the turtles in the basement, but in the meantime the live turtles just walked around on the cement floor. With a basement full of large live turtles in a confined space, you can imagine the smell.

It was also interesting to note that once the summer growing season began, the Asians planted literally every square inch of their property with something edible: vegetables as well as herbs. You name it, and they probably had it growing there. The property looked as if it had been plucked from a Chinese village and set down in the middle of Cleveland, Ohio.

Within about six months we knew that this investigation—dubbed Operation Stir-fry for its obvious Asian restaurant connections—wasn't going to get much larger than it already was, so we decided to take it down. After all our efforts, though, we wanted to bring the case before a court that would treat wildlife law violations seriously—more seriously than a Cleveland court probably would. Large, municipal courts that deal daily with all kinds of serious crime rarely give wildlife cases the attention they deserve. Knowing this, we wanted to somehow lure the bad guys out of the city to a more rural county and make the arrest there.

To accomplish this, we offered to sell our Asian buyers the black bear they wanted, along with some ginseng. Since Jim Baker, my undercover partner at the time, was the Division of Wildlife's ginseng expert, he had access to several pounds of the dried root that we could use as bait to tempt the Asians. We talked them into meeting us in Cambridge, Ohio, about one hundred miles south of Cleveland. We chose that area because Cambridge is located in Guernsey County, whose courts took a dim view of wildlife law violations.

To obtain a black bear carcass, I called wildlife officers I knew in Pennsylvania and West Virginia. Since Ohio has only a small population of black bears, they are classed as an endangered species within the Buckeye State and there is no open hunting season for them. In these two neighboring states, however, black bear hunting is allowed, and I reasoned there would likely be a black bear in a freezer somewhere we could use. I was right. We received two black bear carcasses within a few days, one from each state.

Baker and I drove to the Asian buyer's house in Cleveland one final time to set up the bear and ginseng buy in Cambridge. We brought more snapping turtles with us and informed the Asians we were getting them a bear. But we also told them we wouldn't bring the bear to them. If they wanted it, they would have to come to us. They wanted the bear so badly they agreed without hesitation, no questions asked.

Since my partner was still relatively new to undercover work at the time, he had already made a few mistakes, and during that last visit to the Asians before the takedown, he made another, which luckily turned out to be humorous rather than dangerous. As we were talking with the Asians at their house, Baker suddenly had to use the bathroom. He excused himself, leaving me alone with the bad guys. I spent the time telling them exactly when and where they could pick up the bear and ginseng from us. Baker came back a few minutes later, and we left. Getting into my van, he confessed, "Man, I screwed up. . . ."

"Again?" I asked, hoping it wasn't anything serious.

"Yeah," he said. "I got a sudden case of diarrhea and forgot to turn off the tape recorder in my pocket before I went into the bathroom. I got all the noises on tape."

I had to laugh. Then, pointing toward the hidden videotape camera in the van, I told him, "And I just got your confession on videotape!" Baker lived in fear that I would someday play that videotape at his retirement party, but when the time finally came, I was merciful. It was just fun holding the threat of it over his head for years.

———

We planned to implement the takedown of Operation Stir-fry in the parking lot of a Ruby Tuesday restaurant in Cambridge. We placed two officers in an unmarked vehicle parked across the street, where they could videotape the transaction. In addition, several uniformed officers stood by out of sight, awaiting our call to emerge and make the arrests after the illegal transaction was completed.

The Asians were supposed to meet us at 1:00 P.M. on a weekday afternoon, but the scheduled time came and went and no one showed. I wasn't too concerned, having learned from my years of undercover work that bad guys are seldom on time. We waited another hour, and finally I got a cell-phone call from one of the officers waiting across the street.

"We've got a problem," the officer told me.

"Relax," I said, "They'll be here. . . ."

"No, I'm not talking about the bad guys," he said.

"What is it, then?" I asked.

"The boss has got to go pick up his kids at three o'clock from school. Says he's got to leave if this thing doesn't happen soon."

"What!" I said.

The officer was referring to Donald Kramer, my new supervisor, who was waiting with him in his vehicle. Kramer had recently taken over the Covert Investigations Unit from Kevin O'Dell, and this was his first time in the field on an actual takedown in an undercover investigation. I couldn't believe what I was hearing. After I had worked six months on this case, the takedown might be jeopardized because my boss had to leave early to pick up his kids? It was unbelievable—and very frustrating.

"You tell him he needs to get on the phone and make other arrangements, because we're not leaving!" I said. "The bad guys will be here eventually. Just sit tight."

I was disgusted, to say the least, especially in light of how accommodating my previous boss had been. Under O'Dell, for instance, we always had a debriefing session after the takedown of a case that usually lasted long into the night. After the work was done, we'd drink some beers, talk over the case, unwind, and celebrate yet another successful project. Now my new supervisor wasn't even prepared to stay a few extra minutes after the planned time to see the takedown through, let alone most of the night. I was frustrated that Kramer wanted to leave early and frustrated with the Asians for not showing up on time. In the meantime, all we could do was continue to wait.

The bad guys finally arrived about two hours later. I should say "bad guy" in the singular, because only one showed up, the man who had been the main buyer at the house in Cleveland. I had the bear carcass inside my van, lying near the doors on the passenger side. That way, when the doors were opened, I could videotape the transaction.

The Asian pulled his truck into the restaurant parking lot, parking beside my van. As he did so, I turned on the hidden video camera, then opened the doors of my van on the passenger side. We also had set up a body wire communication system so that the officers videotaping the transaction across the street could hear the conversation.

I sold the guy the black bear right there, in the restaurant's parking lot during the middle of the afternoon. Even though we were in a public space in broad daylight, only the Asian and I could see the bear. No one coming and going nearby could see it, because it was still in my van. The black bear carcass was frozen whole. As the buyer had requested, it had not been field dressed. He looked the carcass over carefully, and I assured him the bear was in good condition. Then he said, "Big bear . . . good bear."

Taking money from his pocket, he paid me the price we had agreed upon, several hundred dollars. Once I had the cash, I decided to have a little fun with the guy while Baker was selling him the promised ginseng.

"I know exactly what you're going to do with that bear's gallbladder and this ginseng," I joked. "You're going to use it to make love to some woman, aren't you?" The man grinned.

I then asked him, "Does that stuff really work? Does it really make you stiff for hours?" He nodded and kept grinning. Baker knew I was putting the guy on and rolled his eyes at me when he knew the Asian wasn't looking.

After a few minutes, the Asian paid Baker for the ginseng and we transferred the bear into his vehicle. Baker and I then closed and locked my van and walked into the restaurant to get something to eat and watch the takedown. Just as the Asian was pulling out of the parking lot to head back to Cleveland, he was swarmed by uniformed wildlife officers, their vehicles blocking him in with lights flashing and sirens blaring.

Jumping out of his vehicle, the Asian pointed toward my van and told the uniformed officers, "They have bear! They have bear!"

"No," our officers said. "You have the bear now. Open your vehicle . . ."

The officers then spread-eagled the guy over the hood of his truck, frisked and handcuffed him, and hauled him off to jail. While all of this was going on, Baker and I were sipping beer and watching the show in the parking lot from our seats at a window table in Ruby Tuesday.

Within minutes, people started running into the restaurant, telling anyone who would listen what was going on outside. Baker and I played up the situation for all it was worth. "Really?" we said, looking surprised. "Some guy got arrested for having a bear in his truck?"

"Yeah," they said. "A live black bear! And some game wardens caught him!"

The Chinese restaurant in Cleveland that had been serving illegal game was never cited for any wildlife law violations. We couldn't prove the meat was being used by the restaurant, since this operation took place before DNA testing was in widespread use for wildlife crimes. The single guy we arrested in Cambridge was the main buyer from the house in Cleveland. We decided to let it go at that and not arrest any of the other Asians living in the home.

Despite our success in Operation Stir-fry, the case ended on a sour note for me, with a parting shot by my supervisor. In the future, Kramer told me, if I wanted to work with the West Virginia Department of Natural Resources on an undercover case, I would have to get his approval first. In the past, if wild-life officers from West Virginia called me requesting my help, I'd just go. My previous supervisor had been fine with that arrangement. Once Kramer took over, though, I had to clear all of my out-of-state forays with him beforehand, which took time. The unwieldy new system worked poorly, and the relationship I had developed over the years with Captain Wadsmen and his undercover unit slowly deteriorated. This was very disappointing to me. I had been on the job as an undercover officer about ten years by then, had proven myself in the field time and again, and had made useful contacts with undercover officers in other states. Yet none of that seemed to matter to my new supervisor. Despite such frustrations to come, I was happy that day. This particular cooperative venture had ended in success. Through Operation Stir-fry, we cut at least one connec-tion between poachers and Asian buyers.

# 8

# OPERATION CAMP KILL

Sometimes you work hard, but in the end have little or nothing to show for it. Such was the result in Operation Camp Kill, which took place near Cambridge, Ohio, beginning in 2002. The Division of Wildlife took on this case in response to many complaints from the public over the poaching of deer and some wild turkeys.

The main target of the investigation was a group of poachers operating from Camp Kill, a very plush hunting camp. The camp was so nice, in fact, that no one was allowed inside the house wearing boots. It had spotless wall-to-wall carpeting, so once inside the door, you were expected to take your hunting boots off to help keep the place clean. Obviously, this camp was very different from most of those I'd worked before.

My fellow undercover officer, Jimmy Baker, initially worked the case alone, although it overlapped with Operation Cornerstone, an investigation we'd undertaken together, as partners. Baker had been working the Camp Kill case for about a month without success. Our intelligence told us that most of the poachers he was trying to contact were from northeast Ohio, with a few additional guys coming from other parts of the state.

Donald Kramer, my supervisor, phoned me at the safe house I was occupying, near Steubenville, Ohio, and asked me to collaborate with Baker for a while, to see if together we could make contact with the bad guys. I suggested to Baker that we bring along one of my 'coon-hunting dogs and go knock on the door of Camp Kill. "We'll see who answers and pretend we're just two 'coon hunters looking for a place to hunt," I said. So we drove to the camp one evening, and, sure enough, the suspects' vehicles were sitting in the driveway. As planned, we drove up, got out, and rapped on the door.

A man opened the door, and we introduced ourselves. Then, explaining that we had come into the area hoping to go 'coon hunting, I asked him if he cared if we did some hunting in the woods behind his house. The man, whom I'll call Rick Beeler, said he didn't mind. "Help yourselves," he added. We talked to Beeler a few minutes longer, and he asked where we were from. I told him that I was originally from West Virginia, near where the Hatfields and McCoys had held their long-standing feud along the Tug River. I made that story up just to keep the conversation going, but it worked. It seemed Beeler was related to one of the two feuding clans. "That so?" I asked. "Which one?"

"The Hatfields," Beeler answered.

"Well, we got problems then," I said, "because I'm related to the McCoys." I was just joking with him, and he took it all good-naturedly. We later learned that he was the number one target of the investigation.

Before we headed into the woods, Beeler told us to stop back at the house when we finished hunting that night. We set off behind the bad guys' camp with my dog, 'coon hunting for a few hours. Once we were out of earshot, Baker commented that he was surprised I had made contact with the group as easily and quickly as I did. "Just knocking on their door and introducing ourselves sure beats trying to make contact at a sporting goods store or some other way," he added.

As Beeler had requested, we stopped back at the house after we quit hunting. Four or five other guys were in the house that night, in addition to Beeler, but he didn't introduce us to them. Nevertheless, Baker and I chatted for a few minutes with the group. I told them where I lived, in a general way, and remarked that Baker and I were thinking about coming back to hunt in their area during deer season. I said we were thinking about staying in a small campground nearby. The bad guys surprised us by saying we could park our camper on their property instead. They even offered to let us plug into one of their electric outlets at no charge.

"No, we wouldn't do that," I responded, "but we appreciate your offer." I was concerned about getting too close to this group of poachers too fast. My experience had taught me that it was better to keep poachers at arm's length until I had a clear idea of who all the players were and how they operated. Also, I didn't want to seem too anxious. When we eventually left that night, Baker and I believed we had made a good first contact.

———

When the the season for hunting deer by gun opened in late November, Baker and I returned to go deer hunting in the area. We stayed in a small camper with a pop-up top that we trailered to the public campground near Camp Kill. The weather was cold, snowy, and just plain nasty. We didn't have any heat in the trailer—in fact, our drinking water froze—so Baker went to town and bought a small ceramic heater that he slept with at night to keep warm. Meanwhile, I was still freezing every night. I knew we had to make a change. The next morning, I finally said, "Bake, we got to do something."

"Like what?" he asked.

"We need to somehow get some heat in here."

We went deer hunting that morning, and about noon we stopped by the poachers' cabin. As we talked, I told them how cold we had been the previous night, and they repeated their earlier offer for us to pull our trailer to their camp, park it just off the driveway, and run an extension cord to the electric outlet in their cabin.

"Hell, better yet, why don't you just come on inside and stay here with us?" they offered. "We got extra beds that aren't being used. . . ."

Despite our discomfort, I hesitated. I told them I wasn't too sure about that, and asked if my hunting buddy and I could think about their offer. Again, I didn't want to jump too quickly or seem too eager. I was afraid that once they stopped to think about the situation they might become suspicious. If possible, I wanted them to beg us to come stay with them.

We hunted with the group two or three days that deer season. They killed several deer, but we were never actually with them when they did, so we didn't know if they shot the deer legally or illegally. The deer were all legally tagged, but, from some of the stories these guys were telling, we weren't too sure if they had been legally killed; one person in the party may have shot and killed a deer while someone else tagged it. We had no proof of such actions, but the hunters' talk made us strongly suspect that some illegal activity was going on. At this point in the investigation, though, we weren't trying to collect evidence. We were simply trying to infiltrate the group of poachers. Only after we had accomplished that task could we start building solid cases against these men and collecting the evidence needed to back them up.

About a month later, during the muzzle-loader deer-hunting season, we returned to hunt again with the men at Camp Kill. Again, they invited us to stay with them in their cabin, but I remained evasive, yet polite. I told them my hunting partner and I were going to take a drive to look for deer, and that we'd discuss their offer then and let them know our decision. They were okay with that, so Baker and I left.

As Baker and I drove around and discussed the situation, I asked him what he wanted to do, and he said he wanted to take the suspects up on their offer. I still wasn't sure. I explained that the poachers might say and do some unexpected things and that he would have to be prepared for whatever they asked. "It won't be like spending just an hour or two with them," I warned him. "If we move in, it'll be twenty-four/seven contact, and that can be dangerous."

Baker assured me he could handle it, so I eventually relented.

"So you want to stay in the lions' den, do you?" I asked him.

"The Lion's Den?" he asked, "The adult book store in town?" Baker wasn't much of a Bible scholar. I told him I meant we would be living in the lion's den, as Daniel had done in the Old Testament. Baker looked embarrassed when I explained my meaning, and by the way, his comical comment about the "Lion's Den" followed Baker throughout his undercover career. Not that I ever mentioned it to him again, of course.

About dark, Baker and I returned to Camp Kill and had a few drinks with the guys. Then they asked us what we had decided. When we told them we wanted to stay with them, they said we were more than welcome, and told us to bring in our gear and stash it upstairs. When we did, we found that the second floor of the house was a large, open room with a dozen beds. Like the ground floor, it was clean and comfortable, with wall-to-wall carpeting and mounted deer heads hanging on the walls.

During the evening, I was talking with two or three of the suspects when Baker informed me he was going upstairs with the small group he had been talking to. I asked him what they were going to do, and he said he thought they were going to smoke some dope—that is, marijuana. I immediately began to worry about how Baker might handle the situation, but I had warned him things would be different once we were living on the inside. Baker and the group of guys went upstairs, and for about forty-five minutes I could hear them talking and laughing.

When they came back down, I asked Baker how he was doing, and I could see his eyes were about to bulge out of his head. He realized he shouldn't have gone up there. The men he had been with had clearly offered him some dope, a situation he didn't know how to handle. Obviously, I couldn't ask him any details about what had happened while we were in the suspects' house, but later he told me they did smoke marijuana. I didn't know if Baker had ever smoked marijuana before or not, but I soon noticed him starting to eat up every snack he could find in the house, the "munchies" being a side effect of marijuana use.

When it came time for all of us to go to bed that night, I was the one sleeping closest to the stairs, with Baker sleeping in the bed beside mine. When we got up the next morning and were getting ready to go deer hunting, I asked Baker how he'd slept.

"Man, I didn't sleep a wink," he said. "I was just too nervous and wired. My adrenaline was really going. I was afraid someone might shoot me or cut my throat. I never slept at all. . . ." He then asked me how I had slept.

"I slept good," I said.

"How can you do that in a situation like this?" he asked.

"Well, I knew you probably wouldn't be able to sleep, so I figured I was safe. You didn't know it, but you had me covered, partner. I slept just fine." Baker knew he'd been had, but he was learning the hard way about undercover work and that living with bad guys is not easy.

For the rest of that week, we hunted with the group of poachers, killing a few deer. We also watched them shoot a couple of deer illegally from the road. We were starting to build evidence on a few individuals, mostly regarding small offenses, but at least it was a start. The group told us they had killed quite a few deer during the rut in early November; hearing that, we figured that this investigation was going to run at least another year.

Before long, we were meeting more players and had gathered evidence for fifteen to twenty charges on three or four members of the group. The poachers came to Camp Kill only occasionally; it wasn't like they were there constantly. We eventually discovered that one of the group was a taxidermist, living in Marietta, Ohio. The unfortunate part of that discovery was that Baker had arrested the guy previously, and there was a chance that if the taxidermist came to the cabin, he might recognize Baker.

———

Winter ended, and the next spring, as wild turkey–hunting season approached, we contacted the group again to see if they would be hunting. We went over to the cabin and hung out with them for a couple days prior to the opening of the season, but they were leery about inviting us to hunt turkeys with them as they were hunting woods they didn't have permission to be in. Rather than beg to join them, we acted as if we had our own places to hunt and didn't need to go with them. We even killed a couple of birds and showed them off to the poachers at Camp Kill. In fact, we had killed the birds legally and tagged them properly, but we took the tags off before bringing them to the poachers' camp to make them believe the birds had been poached. As a result, our suspects invited us back inside Camp Kill, and we accepted, hunting with them from the cabin for a few days.

The next morning, we set off with one of the poachers to hunt wild turkeys, but though we heard some birds gobble at first light, our own calls didn't produce a single bird. Then, just about noon—legal quitting time for turkey hunting in Ohio—we were standing in a field near some large, round hay bales when we saw a hen turkey come out of the woods and start walking toward us. All three of us quickly sat down against the hay bales and pulled on our camouflage face masks. I started calling, and the hen eventually came so close she literally walked over Baker's outstretched legs without knowing he was sitting there. I thought the poacher with us would shoot her, but he didn't. To my surprise and disappointment, he let her walk off. After the hen left, we all three stood up. Baker was very excited about the hen coming so close that she had actually stepped on him.

"Man," he blurted out, "that hen was so fired up I couldn't tell whether it was her calling or R.T.!"

Inadvertently, Baker had used my own initials rather than my cover name of Bill. I was shocked and alarmed, but I thought fast for a way to cover his blunder.

"R.T.?" I asked. "You mean 'real turkey'?"

Baker laughed nervously and said, "Yeah, that's what I meant, real turkey." He knew he'd screwed up bad and that I was about ready to kill him. The poacher didn't seem to suspect anything, but you never know what or how much a person notices in a situation like that.

Two days later we were back at the poachers' cabin, enjoying a turkey dinner and fish fry, complete with wild morel mushrooms and various other tasty side dishes, when another screwup occurred. During the meal, I was eating outside at a picnic table with six of the poachers, and Baker was inside the cabin with two or three more. As I was eating, a beeping sound started emanating from under my shirt. It was the tape recorder that I had hidden there, taped to my chest to record the suspects' conversations. Until that moment, I didn't know that when the recorder's batteries got low, it started beeping.

I had no idea what to do when I heard the beeping, so I did nothing. I just kept eating, my head down, my mind racing. I didn't acknowledge the beeping sound in any way. It was a tense moment. My feet were screaming at me to run, but my mind was telling me to stay put. The hidden recorder beeped only about six times, but it seemed like six thousand times to me. All the guys at the table were staring at me, but I just kept eating as if nothing unusual was happening. When the beeping finally stopped, I got up and walked to the grill, supposedly to get another piece of meat. In reality, I was putting some space between me and the bad guys so that if things went bad, I could get out of there as quickly as possible. Baker would be on his own.

This incident occurred just two days after Baker had accidentally called me R.T. in front of one of the poachers. Taken together, the two slipups could very well be raising suspicion among the poachers. When Baker came out of the house a few minutes later, he noticed I had a strange look on my face. "What's wrong?" he asked.

"Are you done eating?" I asked in turn. When he said no, I overruled him. "Yeah, you are," I said. "We need to get out of here. . . ." So we left shortly thereafter, and I explained what had happened with the hidden recorder.

We immediately drove to town, searching for any electronic device that might make a beeping sound similar to that made by my tape recorder. We planned to buy whatever we found, return to Camp Kill, and show it to the poachers to explain the sound they had heard. None of the gadgets we looked at made a similar noise, but luckily, one of our fellow undercover officers had a pager that beeped similarly, though more loudly, than my recorder. We took the pager and went back to the poachers' cabin the next night, having arranged for the officer who owned the device to call his pager number at a certain time so it would beep. The plan worked perfectly. Baker and I were sitting on the back porch of the cabin drinking beer with the bad guys when the pager went off, beeping loudly.

I reached into my pocket, pulled the pager out, turned it off, and put it back in my pocket. I wanted the bad guys to see the pager and see me turn it off, but I intentionally didn't make a big deal about it. It's not like I pulled it out, waved it around, and commented on it. I just took the pager out of my pocket, turned it off, and put it back into my pocket, and no one ever commented about it or the sound. Baker and I hoped the demonstration had covered one of our blunders, but there was no way of knowing for sure. From then on, I never wore a body wire to the camp, just in case someone was suspicious enough to search me.

It had been more than a week since Baker had accidentally called me by my real initials in front of the poacher, and I hadn't yet said anything to him about it. Eventually, though, I knew I had to address his blunder, so one day, as we were driving together, I opened by saying, "By the way, Bake, we need to have a little talk."

He knew what was coming, and said, "This has been killing me, R.T., and I've been waiting to talk to you about it for the past week. I want you to know I've lost sleep over the incident. I'm surprised you haven't said anything about it until now." Baker told me he had even gone so far as to mention the incident to a fellow undercover officer, commenting that I hadn't yet said anything. The other officer, knowing me, replied to Baker with just two words: "He will."

"Bake, you're a good man," I told my partner. "But you need to realize that when your adrenaline gets going, you have to keep your thoughts and wits about you. Because if you screw up one more time, you're working undercover on your own. I'm not putting myself in jeopardy needlessly because of your screwups. So don't let it happen again."

"Man, I feel a lot better now," Baker said in response. "This thing has bothered me since the day I did it. I promise you, R.T., it won't happen again."

———

As Operation Camp Kill progressed, we discovered that our suspects weren't killing as much wildlife illegally as we had originally thought they might be. We also discovered, though, that they were dishonest in other ways, breaking a range of laws concerning things other than wildlife. They were getting more and more involved with illegal drugs, both using and selling. And we also suspected them of stealing ATVs, yard tractors, and any other light vehicles they could get their hands on. One of our suspects was a long-haul truck driver, and frequently at the cabin we overheard him talking about taking stolen equipment to other states to sell.

Eventually, I got to meet the taxidermist from Marietta, whom I'll call Ray Cullen. Cullen was disgusting and scary at the same time. I can honestly say I've never met a more racially prejudiced individual in all my life. His attitude toward African Americans was unbelievable, as the following incident demonstrates.

Some of the Camp Kill poachers, including Cullen, wanted to make a trip to Cape Hatteras, North Carolina, to go fishing for tuna—or, as Cullen called it, "sitting in the fighting chair," referring to being strapped into a chair on the back deck of a charter boat and fighting a tuna. He asked if I wanted to go along on the trip, and I said yes. I asked him when the group was going, and he said, "Tomorrow." I couldn't believe they wanted to go that soon, but I was willing. "Okay," I said. "Let's go!" I should have called my supervisor for permission to leave the state while on duty, but I didn't. But I had done similar things before and gotten away with them, so I didn't think too much about the decision at the time.

I asked Cullen how to find his house in Marietta, and he told me to drive down a certain street until I came to the "marble orchard," then turn left.

"Marble orchard?" I asked. "What's a marble orchard?"

"A cemetery," Cullen told me. That was the way this guy talked, in strange references. I showed up at his house to stay the night, as we were planning to leave for North Carolina early the following morning. I already knew he was racially prejudiced, but I had no idea just how deeply until that night, when, to pass the time, he showed me a videotape he had made. The video showed Cullen and a couple of his buddies, supposedly from Florida, hurting a black man they had tied to a tree. During the portion of the tape I saw, the black man was begging for his life. I didn't see him killed or dead, but Cullen claimed that he and his friends had killed the man near the end of the tape. "Don't tell anyone you seen this," he warned.

At this point, I was starting to seriously question what I had gotten myself into. I felt I had no choice but to continue my charade with Cullen, but I made up my mind never to turn my back on him. And I notified my supervisor about the contents of the tape as soon as I could.

The next morning, we drove to Cape Hatteras and got a motel room, anticipating the next day's fishing trip. The following morning, I got up early and took two Dramamine tablets to prevent seasickness. I'm susceptible to motion sickness and knew there was a chance I might get queasy while on the ocean, so I wanted to take preventive measures. The only problem was that Dramamine tablets make me sleepy. Very sleepy. . . .

Unfortunately, our plans fell through. That particular day was so windy that the charter captain with whom we had booked canceled our fishing trip, and the poachers, instead of staying another day, hoping for the weather to improve, all wanted to drive back to Ohio. I had driven the group to North Carolina in my undercover van, and now the Dramamine had kicked in big time. I could hardly keep my eyes open, but I didn't want to let anyone else drive my van for fear they would notice the buttons on the steering column that controlled the hidden video-tape equipment. In addition, my vehicle was owned not by me but by the state of Ohio, and only state employees are permitted to drive state vehicles. If anything bad happened, I didn't think the state would make an exception for poachers.

We piled into the van and took off for Ohio, and somehow I made it all the way to West Virginia without falling asleep at the wheel. Eventually, just after dark, we stopped for gas, and I got out and started pumping the gas while the other guys went into the station's little convenience store. Within just a minute or two, however, they all came running out the door, yelling "Drive! Get in the truck and drive!" I had no idea what was happening, but I jammed the gas cap back on and we jumped in the van and took off. It was then I realized that the poachers had just robbed the store! They began talking over their exploit excitedly and showing me their haul. I couldn't believe what I was hearing. They had stolen knives, fishing reels, and other outdoor equipment, and to top it all off, I hadn't even paid for the gas I had been pumping when they poured out of the store. It had all happened so fast! I figured the store probably had security cameras that caught the robbery and my van on tape, but there was no way of knowing for sure. Thinking quickly, I turned on the hidden videotape recorder in my van, hoping the tape would show that I'd had no prior knowledge of the robbery and had played no part in it.

There was one unexpected side effect: the robbery completely counteracted the Dramamine. I was now wide awake, and when I finally got back home, I was a nervous wreck. I figured that I had really screwed up this time and that I might be in serious jeopardy of losing my job. After dropping off the poachers at their homes, I immediately called my supervisor, who went off the deep end. He not only yelled at me for going out of state without his permission, but he couldn't believe that I had also been involved a robbery—at least to the extent of driving the getaway vehicle. He told me to document everything I could concerning the robbery and my involvement in it and then wait for the phone call to come from West Virginia law enforcement. Surprisingly, it never did. To this day, nothing has ever resulted from that robbery.

————

The year rolled on, fall arrived, and eventually it was time again for the opening of the deer–gun hunting season. As a result, Baker and I once again found ourselves at Camp Kill, ready to go hunting with the bad guys. On the very first day of the season, however, Rick Beeler, our primary target, had a hemorrhoid attack, bleeding so severely that we had to take him to the local hospital. He remained there the entire week, which put a damper on the group of poachers at Camp Kill. As a result, no one hunted much, legally or illegally. In addition, there was conflict in the group, probably having to do with the illegal drugs some of them were using, selling, or both.

Because of these developments, Baker and I decided to leave and come back a month later, during the season for hunting deer with muzzle-loaders, as we had the year before. When we returned this time, though, the cabin wasn't anything like it had been just one month earlier. Even from the outside, it looked neglected and messy, with junk lying around where none had ever been before. It obviously wasn't being kept up. When we knocked on the door, a woman answered. I told her who we were and asked to speak to one of our former hunting buddies, but she said the particular poacher we asked for wasn't there, adding that he was on the road, driving an eighteen-wheeler cross-country. From the open door I could see the interior of the cabin, and it looked like a disaster area. It wasn't anything like the tidy, well-kept hunting lodge it had been only weeks earlier.

I asked the woman if anyone from the group was hunting, and she said, "No, no one's huntin' and no one's planning to . . . far as I know." I asked her what had happened to the group, and she didn't give any details, just said they'd had a falling out. When I did finally make contact with Beeler, the poacher who had been in the hospital, I got the impression that he was using illegal drugs heavily, and that he and his girlfriend—the woman who had answered the door—were now living in the cabin full-time. The appearance of the house suggested that both of them were abusing drugs and didn't care much about taking care of the place or themselves.

Baker and I returned to Camp Kill two or three more times over the following months, but we never found anyone hunting. As a result, this undercover investigation just kind of petered out. Although we had some evidence of a few wildlife law violations, we didn't have enough to make much of an impact, so we didn't pursue charges against anyone in the group. As for the evidence we had gathered on other illegal activity, evidence pertaining to illegal drugs and possible stolen property, we turned it over to local law enforcement authorities. All told, Baker and I had about a year and a half invested in working this case, and in the end, we had nothing to show for it.

We never officially closed the investigation; we thought that if the Camp Kill group ever got back together again we'd have an automatic "in" with them. But to my knowledge that never happened. I believe illegal drug use took down this poaching ring before we could. Either way, the good news was that this particular group of poachers was no longer killing wildlife illegally. This eventually led to the decision not to devote any more time or effort to this operation, and we pulled out.

Something else that played into our decision to abandon the case was the fact that we had recently taken down Operation Cornerstone, and the Camp Kill poachers had said that they knew some of the fishermen targeted in Operation Cornerstone. A connection between the two groups of poachers might put us in jeopardy, so we decided to cut our losses at Camp Kill. All in all, this was a disappointing case; Baker and I had invested a lot of time and effort with little or nothing to ultimately show for it. But that's the bald truth about undercover work. Sometimes things work out, and sometimes they don't.

# OPERATION TAKE 'EM

The final major investigation of my eighteen-year career as an undercover officer in wildlife law enforcement concerned the illegal hunting of waterfowl in the tristate area of Ohio, Indiana, and Kentucky. The investigation got its name from the phrase waterfowl hunters use in the blind, when ducks or geese are decoying and the birds are finally within shooting range—"Take 'em!"

The investigation began on July 7, 2004. I remember the specific date because just a few days earlier, on the Fourth of July weekend, I had moved into a safe house in Ross, Ohio, with Shaun, my undercover partner. Our safe house was small, but it was a much better dwelling than we were used to, as it actually had air conditioning and heat.

The complaint that originally spurred this investigation concerned deer poaching rather than waterfowl poaching. Our intelligence indicated that a ring of deer poachers was operating out of a bar named the Farm, located near Oxford in southwestern Ohio. This bar was actually a fairly nice place—not your typical poachers' bar. It did have mounted deer heads on the walls, and even a large moose head, but all the mounts were well-done and recent. Out back, the bar had an outdoor pavilion and stage, with a large sign over the stage that read Hillbilly Fest, referring to an annual country music festival held at the bar in midsummer.

In an attempt to make my first contact with the poaching ring, I spent quite a bit of time at the bar, just as I had when beginning other undercover operations. After several months had gone by without the targeted poachers showing up, though, I started casting a wider net. I frequented other bars in the area and visited sporting goods stores, but still I couldn't find the poachers, let alone meet them. In the end, I never did—at least, not in time to gather evidence on them. I'll explain later. . . .

Eventually I learned why I had failed to connect with this specific group of poachers. It turned out that the local uniformed wildlife officers had already identified the group and had recently arrested several of its members. The remaining poachers that we had targeted were therefore lying low. Not only were they not doing anything illegal, they weren't even venturing to the bars I was frequenting.        In defense of the uniformed officers, they did not know I was in the area attempting to begin an undercover investigation. They were just doing their job, and doing it extremely well. Nevertheless, their actions hindered my efforts to get this particular undercover operation started.

My new supervisor, Will Thompson, and I had considered telling the uniformed officers that I was in the area but thought better of it. I was working several undercover cases simultaneously out of the same safe house, and we were concerned that if we told the uniformed officers of my presence, someone might inadvertently blow my cover. Since the resulting fallout would affect several cases, not just this one, we decided to say nothing and give the investigation more time to develop.

The owner of the Farm bar was Chris Hill, an avid deer bow hunter and fisherman. One night when I was at his bar, Chris was in the kitchen, cooking venison steaks. He came out and asked me if I wanted to try one, and of course, I took him up on his offer.

As I sat at the bar and ate my steak—which was very good by the way—Hill started talking about hunting and how he processed the many deer he shot. I told him I had a meat grinder, a meat saw, and other deer-processing equipment that I used to butcher my deer. I then added that I had just moved into a rental house and didn't have room to store the equipment. "Would you like to borrow it for a while?" I asked him.

He immediately took the bait, saying something like, "Yeah! That's great. We're partners, man . . . you're my buddy now!"

In fact, I had brought the deer-processing equipment along with me on this investigation for just such an opportunity. So the next day, I took all of the equipment over to his garage and left it there. Hill even gave me a key to the garage. This happened in October, during the early part of the deer bow-hunting season. I had already been working on this investigation for more than three months.

I was back at the bar a few days later when Hill came through the front door and asked, "Who owns the large silver van in the parking lot?" I said I did, and he asked, "Is it four-wheel-drive?"

"Yes, it is," I answered. "You wanna take a look at it?" Hill agreed at once.

When I opened up the van and he saw I had 'coon dog boxes inside, plus all of my fishing tackle and other outdoor equipment, he fell in love with it. Hill was already pleased with me for loaning him my meat-processing gear; now his interest in my van made him very friendly toward me. I was making progress.

———

The season for hunting deer with guns opened near the end of November, and I needed at least one large, antlered buck to show off to the guys hanging out at the bar. I contacted my supervisor at the Division of Wildlife with my request, and he in turn contacted our uniformed officers in the area. My plan was to display the buck to the guys at the bar, claiming I had killed it illegally by shooting it at night. I thought that might loosen a few tongues and encourage them to tell me some of their own poaching stories.

Tom Burroughs, a local wildlife officer I knew and trusted, got an antlered buck for me. When I told him where I was living he said the name of the street rang a bell with him. Apparently, he and his fellow officers were keeping an eye on a poacher now living on the same street, just cattycorner to Shaun and me, in fact. The poacher, Shawn Harris, had recently been arrested by the state of Indiana for spotlighting deer, and the wildlife officers of both states had him under surveillance.

As it turned out, I had noticed Harris already because he wore a lot of camouflage. He also had an English setter that occasionally ran loose in the neighborhood; it had nosed around in our yard from time to time. I told the local wildlife officer that I would try and meet Harris, and as it turned out, Harris became an unexpected and valuable asset in Operation Take 'Em.

I finally met Harris one day later that fall, while I was unloading equipment from my van after hunting waterfowl. Dressed in camouflage as usual, he was standing outside his house, looking my way, so I decided this was as good a time as any. I walked across the street, introduced myself, and started talking to him about duck hunting.

Harris jumped right into the conversation, telling me that he enjoyed waterfowl hunting and that he did some taxidermy work to earn extra money. He then remarked that he also loved catfishing. Since catching big catfish is one of my passions, this immediately gave us a common interest, and I invited him over to my house for a beer. That initial meeting went so well that throughout the remainder of the fall and winter we visited back and forth quite a bit, getting to know one another.

During one of our visits, Harris mentioned that he had recently bought a used boat, which he planned to fix up and use for catfishing on the Ohio River. Since by that time, I was hoping to be invited to go fishing with him from time to time, I offered to help Harris rebuild his boat. Doing so was enlightened self-interest, since I wanted the boat to be as safe as possible. The Ohio River is a large, powerful body of water with a strong current and is not to be taken lightly. Harris took me up on my offer, and we worked on the boat off and on throughout the winter, constructing a new floor and making other improvements. As a result, Harris began feeling more comfortable around me, and he started introducing me to several of his hunting and fishing buddies—buddies whom I suspected were poachers like him.

———

Over this period I was still hanging around the Farm bar, mainly on weekends, attempting to make contact with the main target of this investigation, but I still was having no luck. I couldn't seem to even locate the guy, let alone make contact with him. In fact, I couldn't find anyone who knew him. Intelligence received through my supervisor said that he and his fellow poachers were still lying low. I had been spinning my wheels on this operation for about six months, and we were about ready to shut down, pull out, and begin a new case in another area of the state when something happened that changed our minds.

My supervisor, Thompson, called one day and told me that the Division of Wildlife had recently received intelligence about another man living in the area who was supposedly a big-time waterfowl poacher. If I happened to come across this guy, Thompson told me, I should take him on as our new main target and begin working him (try to get close to him).

The Division of Wildlife became aware of this new poacher because of a chance encounter. Wildlife officer Ryan Kennedy had stopped at a gas station when he saw a vehicle pulling a large, duck-hunting boat and trailer sitting at the gas pumps. Although Kennedy did not work undercover, he happened to be in plain clothes that day. He began talking with the hunters and learned they were on their way home from a duck-hunting trip to Lake Erie. Soon they were bragging about their kills to Kennedy, showing him all the ducks they had shot— well over their legal limit—as well as photos of previous trips. The photos likewise showed kills that were well over the legal limit for waterfowl. The officer hid his identity from the poachers, and after they left the gas station, he called wildlife officers in the southern part of the state to tell them of the situation. These local officers were able to find the poachers before they got home and arrested them, including their apparent leader, Myron Hamilton. They were charged and convicted, but unfortunately, their punishment was only a small fine.

Hamilton's name surfaced again a few weeks later, when he attended a fundraising banquet for Ducks Unlimited, a national waterfowl conservation group. For some reason, Hamilton bragged about his poaching to several people at the banquet, saying that he would kill as many ducks as he wanted whenever he hunted, since even if he was caught it would cost him only a small fine. Needless to say, that did not sit well with members of the organization, and they reported him, noting to the Division of Wildlife that the license plate on Hamilton's hunting vehicle was "Duck Mag," which stood for Duck Magnet. Now Hamilton was our new primary target, although at this point, a year into the operation, I still had met neither the main target of the original deer-hunting investigation, nor Myron Hamilton, the duck poacher.

———

I continued to hang out with Shawn Harris, the poacher who was practically my neighbor, going catfishing with him on the Ohio River, throughout the following summer and into the fall. He and I became good buddies, or so he thought, doing practically everything together. We fished mainly at night, usually near Tanner's Creek in Indiana. Our favorite fishing spot was near the Argosy Casino, a large riverboat that had been converted into a floating gambling palace.

One night, Harris confided to me that after dark he and some of his buddies would break the locks off of people's boats docked in the area and steal whatever they could find: including fishing tackle, electronic sonar/GPS units, and life jackets. Harris and his friends stole other things as well. During daylight hours, they would drive the roads near their homes and look for goose decoys in people's yards, decoys the home owners had placed there as lawn decorations. Harris and his buddies would then return after dark and steal the decoys, which they used to hunt waterfowl. I did not know the extent of these thefts until one day Harris showed me about six dozen decoys he had accumulated in his garage, most of them expensive goose decoys made by the Big Foot Company.

Harris told a humorous story about one of these nighttime forays. He and his friends had located six goose decoys sitting in front of a house. But when they returned that night to steal them, they found the property owner had wisely chained all six decoys to a tree. I would have liked to have seen the would-be thieves hit the end of that chain while running at full speed with a goose decoy under each arm.

One of the first hunting seasons to open each fall is the season for mourning doves, which are federal, migratory game birds. Harris and his buddies liked to hunt them, and I joined them a time or two. Harris was good at shooting the small, fast-flying birds. Although doves are not easy to hit, Harris overbagged (that is, shot more than the legal limit) nearly every time he went hunting. As a result, I was able to gather evidence for various charges against him concerning mourning doves.

The next game species to which this group of poachers turned their sights was deer. Soon they were spotlighting and shooting deer illegally at night. They began doing this so early in the fall that the bucks they were shining and shooting still had velvet covering their antlers. I didn't go with them on those hunts, saying I didn't want to get caught poaching. As it turned out, I didn't need to go with them to gather evidence of their crimes. The poachers bragged so much about the numbers of deer they were killing at night that I challenged them, demanding proof before I believed them. "Here," I said, "take my video camera. Show me what great hunters you are. . . ." Not surprisingly, they took me up on my offer, even saying on camera before they'd shoot a deer, "This one's for you, Bill!" using my alias name. They would then pull the trigger, and the camera would record the deer falling. It was pretty thoughtful of them to gather my evidence for me!

---

I had warned the poachers that if they weren't careful they'd likely get caught, and sure enough they did. But to my way of thinking that wasn't good, because it slowed down my investigation.

It was Harris's own bragging that got him and his ring busted; he, like most bad guys, couldn't seem to keep his mouth shut about his illegal activities. It happened this way. Harris went to a meeting of Delta Waterfowl—a waterfowl conservation group similar to Ducks Unlimited—and started boasting about how many mourning doves he had shot already that fall, obviously well over the limit. His listener called the local wildlife officer and reported Harris's claims. Unfortunately, this officer took it upon himself to begin his own mini-undercover investigation of Harris, without seeking approval from his superiors. This plan of action interfered with my investigation, but of course the officer hadn't intended that. He had no idea I was even in the area, let alone already gathering evidence on the same poacher. The officer telephoned Harris and arranged to meet him, on the pretense that he wanted some taxidermy work done. The two then arranged to go dove hunting together, and during the hunt, the officer observed several violations of wildlife law. At Harris's house, he also found evidence of the illegal deer hunting Harris had been doing with his friends. As a result, uniformed wildlife officers arrested Harris a few days later and served a search warrant on his house and surrounding property. This local investigation was dubbed Operation Velvet, as all the illegal bucks Harris and his buddies had killed were shot in late summer or early fall, when the antlers of the white-tailed bucks were still covered in velvet.

Just as the uniformed officer didn't know of my investigation, my supervisor and I didn't know of his. The one saving grace in all of it was that Tom Burroughs, the local wildlife officer who had told me that Harris was living on my street, called Thompson, my supervisor, to warn him about the impending arrest and search of Harris's home. Burroughs also arranged to be in on the arrest and search, since he was concerned that they might somehow lead to my safe house—which they ultimately did. Thompson advised me not to be home on the day scheduled for the arrest of Harris.

Not surprisingly, when Harris was arrested he ratted on me, telling the wildlife officers where I lived and testifying that I had been along on some of the illegal dove hunts. As a result, several wildlife officers came to my house and knocked on the door. But when no one answered, Burroughs told the other officers that he would handle the follow-up investigation, saying something like, "The charges against the guy living here are trivial. I'll come back and follow up with him later." Essentially, he kept the other officers away from me and my undercover residence. It was a tricky situation, but Burroughs handled it well, which I very much appreciated. The incident could have blown my cover.

Even though Burroughs preserved my cover, Operation Velvet was bad news for me. It made the front page of the local newspaper and was covered by area TV stations. Harris's arrest and the consequent publicity seriously messed up my own operation. Everything I'd been working on for more than a year kept getting sidetracked by our own officers. As a result, my undercover investigation would now have to be prolonged. The entire episode was frustrating for me.

Because of Operation Velvet, Thompson and I decided I should back off from Shawn Harris for a while. This was partly because Harris had ratted on me to the uniformed wildlife officers who had arrested him. Harris didn't know I knew that bit of information, but I realized now that I couldn't fully trust him—no honor among thieves, I guess. When Harris eventually came over to tell me that he had been cited by wildlife officers and that they were looking for me too, I played dumb.

As we talked, however, Harris told me something else that changed the situation yet again. He said he had been duck hunting on the Miami River recently, and gotten into an argument with another hunter about who had permission to hunt where. Once they settled their dispute, though, they had ended up hunting together for the rest of the day. Harris then told me the other hunter's name, and when he did I nearly fell off my chair: he had been hunting with Myron Hamilton, the same waterfowl poacher I had been told to watch for. As in other operations over my career, I just got lucky. It was amazing. I'd hung out with Harris for more than a year, building up great credibility with him, and now he had led me to Myron Hamilton without knowing it.

I coaxed more information about Hamilton from Harris and he filled me in. "Yeah, he's got a big duck-hunting boat, and he's got a license plate on his truck that says 'Duck Mag.' He's one hell of a serious duck hunter. . . ."

When Harris finally left my house that night, I called Thompson to tell him the good news. Needless to say he was very pleased.

"I know I told you to back off Harris for a while," he said, "but he's about to become your best buddy, again, R.T. Go get him. . . ."

After nearly two years, this investigation finally had a focus and a main target—Myron Hamilton—as well as an official investigation name: Operation Take 'Em.

———

A few days later, Harris told me he was going duck hunting that weekend and asked me if I wanted to go along. I told him sure and asked who all was going. He told me he was supposed to meet Hamilton and a few of Hamilton's buddies, which was just what I wanted to hear. He then asked me if I would drive my van and stop by and pick him up. Harris had already told Hamilton that I was a friend of his and that I would be coming along on the hunt. "I told him you were okay," said Harris, vouching for me. It was just the foot in the door I needed.

On the day of the hunt I picked up Shawn Harris well before daylight, and the two of us drove to Myron Hamilton's house. I didn't know what to expect, but when we arrived at the address, I was shocked. My best guess was that the house alone was probably worth nearly a million dollars. A gate at the end of the driveway had ornate, cement pedestals on each side, and the entire neigh-borhood reeked of money. I thought to myself as we drove up the driveway, "I may have to step up my game a bit to pull this one off."

As Harris and I approached the house, we saw Hamilton's truck sitting there, a large, late-model, twin-cab, four-wheel-drive diesel pickup, a vehicle worth at least fifty thousand dollars. Sitting nearby was a camouflaged duck-hunting boat, a twenty-foot Triton, no doubt worth tens of thousands of dollars.

We got out of my van and Harris introduced me to Hamilton. He was a good-sized man in his late thirties, fit and trim. My first instincts as a wildlife officer were always to quickly size up the people I met, both physically and mentally. Hamilton looked like he could handle himself in a fight. He also seemed to carry himself confidently.

I had trailered my fourteen-foot duck-hunting boat behind the van that morning, but now, looking at Hamilton's much larger, state-of-the-art craft, I felt like a rookie. Thinking on my feet, however, I quickly turned the situation to my advantage.

"Ya know, Myron," I said, "I just started duck hunting a few years ago and this boat is all I have for now. I'm getting more serious about waterfowl hunting, though, and looking to buy a bigger boat eventually."

I wanted Hamilton to think I was an inexperienced duck hunter eager for him to teach me more about the sport. I was playing to his ego, which is pretty large in most poachers. If a bad guy believes he is better than you, rather than competing with you, he is more likely to accept you and open up to you more quickly. It worked. He was flattered, especially since Hamilton was about ten to fifteen years younger than I. After we got to know one another, he started calling me "Dad."

The first time you hunt with a new group of poachers, you're always a little leery about how the day will go, so I was definitely on edge. Besides Harris, Hamilton, and me, a fourth guy went hunting with us that day, a friend of Ham-ilton's nicknamed Hippie. Hamilton's nickname was Sensei, a Japanese word for a teacher of martial arts.

We had a good hunt that first day. We killed a few ducks, but no one over-bagged; since there weren't many ducks flying, there was not much opportunity to do anything illegal. Hamilton had a lot of questions for me during the hunt, but I had anticipated that, and I returned the favor. Looking back on it now, I believe he was testing me, feeling me out. He was subtle about it, but I'd been through it so many times before, when first meeting other poachers on other undercover investigations, that I was actually comfortable with the exchange. I was still on guard, however, taking great care about what I said and how I said it.

I eventually sensed that Hamilton had intimidated the other members of his small poaching group. He had a quick temper, which he used to keep the others cowed. I didn't put up with his intimidation, even that first day. I wasn't being cocky or putting him down, but I wanted him to know where I stood. I'd argue with him when others wouldn't. I'd tell him jokingly, "Just because you're bigger than me, Myron, that don't mean nothin'.' . . . And if there's ever a fight between us, one of us is going to get whipped, but the other one is going to know he was in a fight."

I never said who would win the fight, but I wanted him to know that if he ever chose to take me on physically he'd end up knowing he'd bitten off more than he could chew. The other guys in the group couldn't believe I talked to Hamilton the way I did, especially when I had just met him. Surprisingly, though, Hamilton seemed to like the way I treated him. I think he enjoyed the verbal sparring back and forth. He even commented on it. "You know," he said, grinning, "you and me, we're just like two big range bulls circling each other, about to battle for dominance." That comparison was fine with me. And his statement was more accurate than he knew.

Later I heard a rumor that may partly explain his dominance over the members of his group. Apparently, Hamilton had gotten into a fight as a juvenile in which he shot and killed a man. If his hunting buddies believed the tale, they may have assumed that since he had already killed someone, he might kill again, if provoked. I still didn't understand why everyone was so intimidated by Hamilton, but that may have been one reason.

———

About a week later, Harris and Hamilton showed up at my house unannounced. I didn't have time to even look around the place to make sure it was the way I wanted it before the two poachers were at the door. Since it was too late to worry about it, I opened the door and invited them in. We talked a while, and I showed Hamilton the mounted deer heads I had hanging on the walls. He then suggested we go to the local restaurant and get something to eat.

At the time, a new undercover wildlife officer—I'll call him Mike—was just starting to work with the Covert Investigations Unit and had been assigned to shadow me for a few days. I was supposed to talk with Mike, coach him a little, and fill him in on the basics of undercover work. Thompson had been adamant, however, when he told me, "Do *not* get Mike directly involved with any bad guys yet. He's not ready." Well, Mike hadn't been at the safe house for more than an hour when Harris and Hamilton came knocking at the front door.

"Oh, shit!" I said, peeking out the window at the two poachers standing on the front porch.

"What?" asked Mike, his eyes widening.

"Bad guys," I said. "Just keep your mouth shut, and don't say anything unless someone asks you a direct question . . . got that?" He nodded, but I could sense panic in him. This was definitely going to be his baptism by fire.

Mike ended up doing a great job. I introduced him to the poachers as a hunting buddy of mine. He kept his mouth shut as I had instructed him, not speaking unless spoken to and giving very short answers when he did talk.

During our meal at the restaurant, Hamilton surprised me by saying, "Bill, I'm having a birthday party for my wife tonight at our house, and I'd like you to stop by." I found the invitation rather awkward. I had only met Hamilton once before, the day we had duck hunted together, and now, even though there were three of us seated at the table with him, he was asking only me to his party.

"Would you like to come?" he asked, pressing me for an answer.

I was somewhat taken aback, but said, "Sure!" I was willing to do most anything to get closer to this poacher.

Hamilton then said, "I just ask one thing, Bill. Don't embarrass me . . . okay?"

"I'll tell you what," I said, a certain seriousness in my voice. "I won't intentionally do anything to embarrass you, your wife, or myself. I promise."

"Fair enough," he said. "The party's at 7:00. See you then."

I believe Hamilton invited me to the party without inviting Harris or Mike because he saw me as closer to him in age and maturity than the others. I also think he believed me to be his equal and didn't look at the others in quite the same way.

Once we had all finished eating, Hamilton and Harris left the restaurant, and Mike could finally breathe a sigh of relief. We returned to the safe house, where I showered, shaved, and put on my best clothes: clean shirt, tie, sports coat, and expensive snakeskin cowboy boots. As I was going out the door, I told Mike I would be stopping by the local florist on my way to the party.

"Why?" he asked, and I gave him a little undercover advice.

"If a suspect is married or has a serious girlfriend and you get his woman to like you, she doesn't resent her man spending time with you. But if she doesn't like you, it makes it tougher for him to get away as often as he'd like. Remember that." Mike said he would, and I headed out the door.

On my way to the florist, I telephoned Hamilton, told him I was bringing a present for his wife and asked him her favorite color. "Now, remember what I told you," he said. "Don't embarrass me. . . . Don't be bringing any underpanties as a gag gift or anything like that to the party."

"Don't worry," I said. "Just tell me her favorite color." And he did.

I had the florist place a bouquet of flowers in a vase, and when I arrived at Hamilton's house I introduced myself to his wife and handed them to her. "Happy birthday," I said, as graciously as I knew how. The room was full of people, but I caught Hamilton's eye where he sat at a table across the room. When he saw that I had just given his wife a vase full of flowers in her favorite color, he gave me the thumbs-up sign. Obviously, he was impressed by my gentlemanly gesture, and she seemed to be, too.

I chatted with various people at the party that night, but I didn't drink any alcohol. I had stopped any serious drinking by that time in my life, opting instead for soft drinks when the beer, wine, or hard stuff were offered. I'd been having problems with high blood pressure, and my doctor had advised me to stay away from alcohol. Also, I was afraid to drive home under the influence, as there seemed to be cops around every street corner in that neighborhood. No need to take a chance with this investigation if I didn't have to.

Most of the men at the party, I learned, were avid waterfowl hunters, so it was easy to strike up a conversation with them. About halfway through the evening, some of us got into a Texas Hold 'Em poker game. The stakes were high by my standards—one hundred dollars just to sit in on the game—but I bit the bullet and paid my hundred bucks so as not to appear cheap. As I had expected, the entire evening was an upscale event.

When it was all over, I had kept my word to Hamilton by not embarrassing him, his wife, or myself. I also made sure to leave the party at an appropriate time, not too early and not too late. This wasn't my first rodeo, which is a good way to describe my behavior that night. And as I pulled my van out onto the street and headed home, I felt pleased about my first contact with Hamilton's hunting buddies and his wife.

————

Over time, I continued to cultivate Myron Hamilton, until he believed we were close friends. As a result, I told Thompson that the investigation was now going well and that we definitely should continue it. The group of poachers even invited me to go duck hunting with them to Lake Erie, telling me they had killed many ducks over the limit there the previous year, each receiving only a small one-hundred-dollar fine after being caught. I played dumb to that bit of information, but I knew quite well what this group of poachers had been up to and their reputation.

Hamilton also informed me that he was part of a small group of six or seven poachers that he called the DMC Club. I was never quite sure what DMC stood for, because I heard a couple of different names—Duck Member Club and Duck Murdering Club. To become a member of this exclusive club, you had to be asked to join. You also had to have intentionally violated a waterfowl hunting law, as witnessed by other members of the club. Each member had a hat printed with the letters DMC on the front and his individual nickname on the back.

When I wasn't hanging out with Hamilton or Harris, I was back at the Farm bar, still trying to make contact with the deer poacher supposedly operating from there. I was at the bar so much that I even started helping the owner, Chris Hill, tend bar and do a little of the cooking. Eventually, I discovered that the two groups of poachers—the ones at the Farm bar and the members of the DMC Club—knew each other. Members of the DMC Club had even met at the Farm bar a few times. Imagine that!

———

Early that next spring of 2005, Hamilton wanted to go to Illinois to hunt snow geese, and he asked me along on the trip. At that time, the state of Illinois had a special spring season for snow geese because the birds were getting so numerous they were damaging their northern nesting grounds in Canada. Since biologists recommended that the population be thinned, bag limits in the United States were raised and a spring hunting season was initiated.

I told Hamilton I'd like to go along on the hunt, but in fact I didn't want to go without another undercover officer being along. I just felt the trip would be safer that way. When you're by yourself on an undercover trip, it's more difficult to gather evidence and keep an eye on everyone. So I asked Shaun, my undercover partner, to go along. He was living in the same safe house as I and working on other undercover investigations. I had already introduced Shaun to the group of poachers several months earlier, so they knew him, liked him, and wouldn't have any problem with him going along.

Before leaving on the hunting trip, I called the undercover unit of Illinois's wildlife law enforcement division and told the officers there we were coming, letting them know where we would be while in their state. I also advised them that we would be hunting with a professional waterfowl guide the first day and then possibly hunting by ourselves the last two days of the trip. The Illinois officers told me they knew little about the hunting guide we had hired, but they thanked me for letting them know our group would be in their state. They also offered help if I needed it.

We killed a few snow geese on the first day of the hunt, but nothing to brag about. In the process, however, we met a couple of local hunters, to whom we offered twenty-five dollars each if they would show us around and introduce us to local landowners. We hoped to get permission to goose hunt on private property, learn the area, and eventually hunt by ourselves without a guide.

It was during this process of traveling around trying to meet landowners that we drove into a public park where no hunting was allowed and saw a small flock of snow geese sitting along the edge of a pond. The vehicle ahead of my van, containing members of the DMC Club, stopped, and the poachers bailed out, loaded their shotguns, and started shooting. Seeing what was happening, Shaun and I jumped out of our vehicle and started shooting at the geese, too. When our guns were empty, we all ran to the pond, gathered the dead geese, threw them in the back of our vehicles, and took off. When it was all over and we were out of there undetected, members of the DMC Club were impressed.

"Man, you guys are just like us," they said. "Great shooting!"

Poaching during broad daylight in a public park was not my idea of a smart move, and I was surprised we didn't get caught. But it had been a spur-of-the-moment thing, and I had taken the chance of participating because I was determined to get closer to the DMC Club. As it turned out, it was a good move. Shortly after that incident, members of the DMC Club presented Shaun and me with our own club hats. We were now official DMC Club members. The poachers actually had a small ceremony for us as they handed us our club caps and gave us our club nicknames.

I wasn't thrilled with my nickname. Unfortunately for me, the movie *Brokeback Mountain* had recently premiered, a story of two homosexual cowboys. Since I usually wore a cowboy hat and since my alias was Bill Stone, the DMC club members jokingly nicknamed me Brokeback Bill, printing BBB on the back of my hat, letters that also stood for the size of certain steel shotgun pellets used for waterfowl hunting. Everyone in the DMC club knew the double meaning, and all I could do was endure the joke.

A few days later, I proudly wore a new cowboy hat into the Farm bar. It was late on a Saturday night and the bar was packed. When Chris Hill, the bar's owner, saw me walk in wearing my hat, he picked up the microphone and said over the public address system for all to hear, "Ladies and gentlemen, may I have your attention, please. Brokeback Bill just walked through the door!"

Of course, I was embarrassed, and everyone in the bar had a good laugh at my expense. But I told myself that the ribbing was worth it: I was now in deep with the DMC Club, accepted as one of their own. "We'll see who eventually has the last laugh," I told Hill; he had no way of knowing what I meant. My DMC hat remained a source of laughs in the bar for months, but I continued to wear it to show allegiance to the club. And as a matter of fact, I still have it somewhere, hanging on a hook in my closet.

To grow closer yet to Myron Hamilton, I often asked his advice about buying a larger duck-hunting boat. I even let him read my fictitious disability insurance claim for worker's compensation, the official-looking papers having been drawn up by a lawyer friend of mine. I told him that when my settlement money finally came through, I was going to buy that bigger duck boat I'd been dreaming about. "As a matter of fact, Myron," I joked, "if the money's good enough, I might even buy you a new one, too. But don't hold your breath."

As a result of our many conversations, Hamilton actually began looking for a used boat for me to buy. In the back of my mind was the thought that if I was going to eventually hunt on Lake Erie with members of the DMC Club, I needed a boat seaworthy enough to handle the big water. So I had Thompson put out the word to area wildlife officers that I needed a relatively large, stable boat that could be converted for duck hunting. They eventually located a twenty-footer that had been used by one of the Division of Wildlife's fish-management crews as a work boat.

I towed the boat home and worked on it throughout the summer, making it into a superb duck-hunting boat. I built a wooden blind on it, painted it in camouflage colors, and even installed a small cook stove. The blind had three roomy, comfortable seats, complete with shotgun shell holders and other extras. Hamilton would stop by every once in a while to check on my progress, and he seemed impressed. He was convinced I now had a boat worthy of Lake Erie, and we looked forward to the various waterfowl hunting seasons opening that coming fall.

In the meantime, though, Chris Hill invited me to a Fourth of July party at his house. That party marked the second year of this undercover investigation. During a poker game that night, and for no apparent reason, the conversation turned to the subject of undercover officers. The group members were smoking marijuana as they played cards. I don't know if that had anything to do with it or not, but if you're doing something illegal your subconscious seems to keep reminding you of it.

"Bill would make a good undercover cop," remarked one of the players as he dealt the cards.

"Why do you say that?" I asked. I was trying to act nonchalant about the comment, but I could feel my blood pressure beginning to rise.

"Well, you just would," he said. "You have a certain knack of being able to talk to about anybody about anything."

I just kept playing cards and didn't respond to the guy. I don't know for sure, but looking back on it now I think the group may have been testing me that night. As far as I knew, they had no reason to suspect that I was an undercover wildlife officer. Perhaps the fact that I didn't smoke marijuana with them that night made them suspicious. Whatever prompted the poacher to make that comment about me, though, I knew the group well enough by then to believe that my best course was to say nothing; trying to defend myself by denying I was an undercover cop might backfire, deepening any suspicion in their minds.

Similar tests—the bad guys subtly questioning that you might be an undercover officer—seem to come up at least once during most undercover investigations. The suspects' involvement in illegal activities must be constantly on their minds, fostering distrust. Recent publicity about Operation Velvet, both on the TV news and in the local newspapers may have added to their tension, keeping the subject of undercover officers fresh in their thoughts.

When people ask me what I told poachers when they questioned me directly about being an undercover wildlife officer, I respond that there is no pat answer you can use to diffuse the situation. Each time a poacher asked me that question, I gave a different answer. Each time I had to think on my feet, quickly coming up with the answer I judged would be most plausible to the particular group of poachers I was infiltrating. An inexperienced officer may feel a bit of panic the first time he or she is asked such a direct question by a bad guy. I know I did. But before going out into the field, the officer should know enough about undercover work to expect such questions and to be prepared to give a believable answer.

———

Despite my invitation to Hill's party and the fact that I was still stopping in at the Farm bar now and then, the emphasis of my investigation had changed. One new element was my growing involvement with José Hernandez-Maldonado, nicknamed Ho. He owned a construction company. He also owned and operated a mechanical bull that he rented out to bars for people to ride. I had first met José at the birthday party for Hamilton's wife. At that event, José had on a big cowboy hat and a pair of expensive, exotic-leather cowboy boots, worth hundreds of dollars. He saw my fancy cowboy boots and we hit it off, sharing stories. Once I got to know José, he gave me occasional work transporting and operating his mechanical bull. Eventually I came to find out that most of José's buddies were cowboys. It was just coincidence, but I fit right in with that crowd. Many of the expensive western clothes I wore in this investigation were the ones I had used in Operation Cornerstone, the yellow perch poaching case on Lake Erie. If you recall, the clothing had been provided for me by the U.S. Fish and Wildlife Service. I even contacted them to get more clothes, especially expensive boots. Cowboy boots seemed to be what caught the eye of most poachers, and the more elaborate and expensive the boots, the better.

Besides owning a mechanical bull, José also owned a large fishing boat he kept docked at Lake Erie, and one day he invited me to go walleye fishing with him and some of his friends. Since everyone in this group had good jobs paying excellent wages, money was no object to them, and on their fishing trips everyone expected to pay his share of the expenses at the end of the day. They split evenly whatever the trip happened to cost in the way of gas, food, bait, and so on; you were expected to pay what you owed, no questions asked. For me, hanging out with these well-heeled poachers was very different from my usual operations; I was used to investigating relatively poor poachers and working on a shoestring budget to do it.

I'm glad no one took pictures of me that first day, because I was dressed like a "dude," at least in my own opinion. I had on a pair of khaki shorts—I'd hardly ever worn shorts in my life—and a pair of new deck shoes. I couldn't have felt more out of place, but I was trying to fit in, and that was what the others in this group wore to go fishing on the lake. On this first trip, we caught more than our daily allowable limit of walleyes, a result I later learned was standard procedure for Jose and his friends.

To fit in with Ho, I was playing the role of a high roller, and one evening at the Farm bar, that got me thinking of a popular country song, "Save a Horse, Ride a Cowboy," which had the lyrics, "Throwing down a hundred dollars and buying a round of Crown [whiskey] for the bar . . ." I told the barmaid, "You play that particular song for me on the juke box, and I'll buy a round of drinks for everyone in the bar." So the barmaid went over to the juke box, slipped in a quarter, and played the song.

What happened next I couldn't believe. The deer poacher I had been hunting for more than two years was at the bar that night, and he came up to me and introduced himself, thanking me for the free drink. "Well," I thought to myself, "at least I got to meet you, buddy. But, fortunately for you, I've shifted to bigger fish. . . ."

Although Thompson assigned Shaun to the Farm bar to work the deer poacher and his friends, he had redirected me to other targets. Moreover, even Shaun had little luck in his assignment. The poacher I had finally met after two years continued to go straight, or at least lie low, when it came to wildlife law violations. The contact never turned into anything.

———

Meanwhile, in addition to working José and his fishing crowd, I continued to cultivate Hamilton and the DMC Club. Hamilton and his poaching group began the hunting seasons that fall by hunting mourning doves, and I went along. One day when the doves weren't flying too well, the group started shooting anything that flew as target practice, mainly songbirds such as chimney swifts and swallows. In all, they probably killed a hundred or more nongame birds that day. The same evening, a flock of Canada geese landed in the field where we were, but far out of range. So the next day we went back to the same field to set up closer to where the geese had previously landed. As the poachers had hoped, the geese returned to the same spot, and we ended up shooting plenty that evening—well after legal shooting hours and using illegal lead shot.

Next that fall, we went waterfowl hunting with a professional guide. During the hunt, Hamilton introduced me to a separate group of hunters, a group that the DMC Club regarded as rival. The two groups would eat at the same local restaurant, each bragging to the other about how many ducks they'd killed illegally. This was a break for me, since it allowed me to bring more poachers into the investigation. I began hunting with the other group from time to time, as well as with members of the DMC Club. We had already discussed videotaping some of our hunts, and I said, "I got a video camera we can use. . . ." The poachers told me to bring it along the next time we hunted.

One day, not too long thereafter, we were hunting wood ducks along a creek, and I attached my video camera to a tripod, set it up behind the blind, and turned the camera on. The resulting tape shows all of us participating in an early-morning waterfowl hunt where we killed a few ducks and geese but nothing major. That evening, though, we scouted for places to goose hunt and got permission on a local farm, and when we hunted there the next morning, we killed more than twenty geese, well over our limit. We loaded the extra, illegal geese into my van, and I drove the dead birds back to our safe house, stashing them inside the garage. I then drove back to the hunting field, where we had left three dead geese in the field to account for the blood and feathers on the ground. I had no more than stepped out of my van when we were approached and checked by the local, uniformed wildlife officer.

I had no idea who he was, as he was a younger officer I had never met before. He checked us over thoroughly and found no violations. But had he arrived an hour earlier, we all would have been arrested. After the officer left, we shot another limit of geese and then headed for home. We decided not to take any more than the legal limit the second time, as we knew the wildlife officer was in the area and might still be watching.

The regular duck hunting season finally rolled around later that fall, but when I went out with my fellow DMC Club members, it was early enough in the season that the ducks just weren't migrating yet, and there wasn't much to shoot at. The poachers and I did manage to kill some birds by shooting before and after legal hunting hours, but we just weren't bagging the large numbers of waterfowl these guys were used to shooting, and they were getting frustrated. They were more than willing to violate the law, but ducks and geese just weren't around yet in any significant numbers.

Eventually, the DMC Club members let me in on a little secret. When the hunting got tough, as it was now, they had a special honey hole they hunted. It was a shallow rock quarry that had filled with water, and they baited it with corn to attract waterfowl. They then hunted over the corn, which was illegal since corn is very addictive to waterfowl. Hamilton was upset because some of the guys weren't paying him for their share of the corn, so I pulled out a twenty-dollar bill and handed it to him, saying, "Here, I'll give you some money for corn. If we're going to hunt the stone quarry, I'm in for my share."

During the court trial following this case, Hamilton's attorney tried to argue that because I had given Hamilton the twenty dollars, I was the one who had bought and placed the corn in the quarry—the old entrapment argument. Luckily, the videotape from the wood duck hunt showed Myron talking about already having illegally baited the area himself, so the lawyer's argument fell flat. We hunted two days later in the baited rock quarry, and Mike went along to videotape the hunt. Given the ducks' addiction to our corn, we easily killed more ducks than we were legally entitled to.

During the hunt, I inadvertently received some serious, permanent damage to my hearing. I shoot left-handed, so I positioned myself on the far right side of the hunting blind. That way, I could swing on a duck flying far to the right better than a right-hander. Some ducks decoyed into the quarry pond, landed on my side of the blind, and I stood up to shoot. However, the hunter to my left rose up at the same time, stuck the muzzle of his shotgun in front of my face, and pulled the trigger. The muzzle blast was so intense that both of my ears began ringing immediately. I dropped my gun and walked away. The blast had given me an instant headache, and the shot had been so close to my left ear that I thought my ear drum burst. Mike had recorded the incident on videotape, with the other hunter saying, "Man, I got ya didn't I? I'm sorry. I shot too close. . . ."

"Yeah, you got me all right," I said, my ears ringing severely.

My left ear hurt so bad that later that day I went to the hospital to have it checked out. My ear drum wasn't broken, but the concussion from the shot had caused severe hearing damage, hearing loss I still suffer with today. The other hunter never should have shot that far to his right, but things like that sometimes happen when hunting with guys you don't know, guys who may be a little too anxious to kill something. Avid poachers tend to be careless in that way.

We hunted at the baited quarry pond several more times that fall before the local ducks—those that were left—simply moved out, migrating farther south for the winter.

———

There were few ducks in southern Ohio at the time, so the DMC Club members decided that it was time to make the long-awaited Lake Erie hunting trip we'd all been talking about for the last year. About a dozen of us planned to go, leaving the Friday morning after Thanksgiving Day and taking three boats with us. Two of the poachers rode with me in my van; Hamilton brought three or four guys in his truck; and still more guys rode in a third vehicle that was also jammed with hunting equipment. We planned to take the large ferry boat across from the Catawba Peninsula to South Bass Island, where we would stay and hunt for several days.

While we were waiting in line to load our duck-hunting boats and trucks onto the ferry, a guy working the ferry boat saw our camouflaged clothing, boats, and other gear and walked over to ask the obvious question, "You guys duck hunters?"

"Yeah," we said, thinking him an idiot.

The guy then proceeded to tell us about a group of duck hunters who had been caught by game wardens the previous year after overbagging on South Bass Island. "Yeah, they had hundreds of ducks over the limit," he claimed. He was talking, of course, about Hamilton and the DMC Club, not knowing that they were standing right in front of him. The guy droned on and on, saying things like, "Yeah, them hunters was dumb asses from somewhere down in southern Ohio. . . ."

I kept egging the guy on, saying things like, "Really? How dumb were those hunters?"

Hamilton's face just kept getting more and more red with anger until finally he couldn't take it any longer. "If you're going to talk, buddy," he finally said, stalking forward and getting in the guy's face, "get your facts straight! I'm one of the hunters the game wardens caught, and you haven't told anything right about that story yet!"

Hamilton's size, combined with his angry demeanor, intimidated the ferry boat employee; his eyes opened wide and he backed away, apologizing. But no amount of apologies could change Hamilton's disposition. The incident had pissed him off big time. Eventually, we loaded our boats and tow vehicles onto the ferry and crossed to the island. As we rode the waves, I couldn't help chuckling to myself about the scene I had just witnessed.

Given their arrests by wildlife officers the previous year, Hamilton and his fellow the DMC Club members had a plan to cover their poaching this year. One member of the group traveled separately on the ferry boat, keeping his distance from our main group. He did not wear any camouflage clothing or have any hunting gear in his truck; he looked instead like a maintenance man going over to work on the island's many businesses or summer homes. I'll tell you more about him later, but keep that guy in mind.

Once we reached the island, we checked into the local motel and made our first duck hunt of the trip at dawn the next morning. We killed so many ducks that day I couldn't keep track of them all. With nearly a dozen guys shooting, it was impossible to watch everyone at once. I didn't know who shot what, but suffice to say we were all well over our daily limit. My excuse for not shooting more was that I had a cook stove in my boat and told the guys I'd cook them all breakfast if they shot my limit of ducks for me. They were more than happy to do so.

Back at the motel, a poker game was the evening's entertainment, but we didn't play for money. Instead, we played for steel shotgun shells, using the individual shells as you would poker chips. Steel or other nontoxic shot is required for waterfowl hunting, but it isn't cheap, generally costing double, or sometimes even triple, the price of standard lead shot. Moreover, every hunter in the poker game knew that if he bet all his shells and lost, he would have no way of hunting the next day, since there were no steel shot shells to be bought on the island.

Two of the guys did lose all their shells in the poker game that night, so the next day, they had to sit and watch the rest of us shoot. No one in the group of poachers offered to give them any shells. The guys got so desperate to hunt that they begged to buy back their shells, but no one would sell them any, not even a few.

Being a southern Ohio boy and not used to big water, I feared hunting on Lake Erie more than I did being with the bad guys. As one of the five Great Lakes, Lake Erie is serious big water. People drown there every year. And we were hunting just at the time of year when fall storms are most frequent and intense. The overall stress of the hunt, on top of the stress of working undercover, must have become too much for me, because the next morning when we got up someone looked at me and said, "What's wrong with your eye?"

"I don't know," I said, and walked over to look in the mirror. What I saw shocked me. Blood vessels had burst in my right eye, and the eyeball was extremely bloodshot. That told me my blood pressure must be up, likely sky high. My eye didn't hurt, but nevertheless I was concerned as to what it all might mean, although not concerned enough to refrain from going on the hunt.

That day we overbagged as usual. When we finally got ready to leave the island, we cut the breasts out of the illegal ducks, put them in plastic bags, and gave them to the guy who had come to the island in a separate pickup truck. He, in turn, then put the duck breasts on top of his truck's spare tire, which was located underneath the truck bed, completely out of sight. That way, when the rest of us left the island, we had only our legal limit of ducks in possession; the guy who had driven separately had all the illegal ducks.

He got on the same ferry as the rest of us, but you never would have known he was part of our group. He did not fit the typical profile of a waterfowl hunter, and we never spoke to him during the half-hour trip back to the mainland. He was simply a guy driving a pickup truck. It was a pretty smart way of averting suspicion, and it worked. As we came off the ferry, uniformed wildlife officers checked the rest of us but waved him on down the road.

On the drive back to southern Ohio, my van's engine began missing and running rough. We made it home, but I later came to find out that the number eight spark plug had blown, a common defect with that type of engine, and the engine had developed serious mechanical problems. By the time I made it home from the trip, I was stressed like never before. Not only had I spent the past several days living with the poachers round the clock, but now my undercover van was in need of major repairs. Needless to say, my blood pressure was way up—and the next day was the start of the gun deer-hunting season in Ohio, the biggest opening day of any hunting season of the year.

——————

My plan had been to quickly shift gears and hunt deer that next day with Chris Hill and some of the poachers from the Farm bar, and I still hoped to do that. That evening, I received a phone call from one of the local wildlife officers, saying that he had a large, freshly killed buck deer that I could use if I needed it. I picked up the deer carcass and took it to the Farm the same night, telling the guys at the bar that I had killed the deer illegally. The deer was so big that all the guys wanted their pictures taken with it. That was helpful to the investigation, because we needed photos of all of them anyway.

However, the next day—opening day—I got a second phone call from the wildlife officer who had given me the deer. In a panic, he told me that the guy from whom he had gotten the large deer had first shown it to a park ranger, who in turn had taken photos of the deer and posted them on the Internet. This particular deer had an unusual rack with drop tines, making it easily identifiable. This news added further to my stress, although as it turned out, the poachers from the Farm bar never saw the photos on the Internet, or, if they did, never identified the deer in the photos as the deer I had shown them.

Nevertheless, this put my stress levels over the top, so that I woke up about 2:00 A.M. on the second day of the season with my heart racing. This scared me so badly that I woke up my undercover partner, Shaun, who was sleeping in a separate bedroom, and asked him to check my heart rate. After taking my pulse for about a minute, he said, "Yeah, there's definitely something wrong, R.T. Your heart's beating faster than it should, maybe as fast as 120 beats per minute or more. We need to get you to a hospital."

The first thing they asked me at the local hospital emergency room was my name, and the first thing that came out of my mouth was my alias, Bill Stone. There I was, scared to death that my heart was racing out of control, but I couldn't tell the doctors and nurses my real name for fear of blowing my cover. As a result, they couldn't access my medical records. In the meantime, they began running tests and trying to get me stabilized. To be very honest I wasn't sure if I was going to live or die of what I suspected was a serious heart attack.

Shaun called Thompson, who arrived at the hospital as soon as he could. By that time the doctors and nurses had gotten my heart rate down, but now it had dropped too low, beating at a rate of only about forty beats per minute. With my heart bouncing from one extreme to the other, the doctors told me they were going to admit me to the hospital. They said they planned to keep me for two or three days to do more tests and stabilize my heart rate. Then they asked me what health insurance plan I had. In keeping with my cover story—remember, to them I'm Bill Stone—I told them I didn't have any insurance. The doctor frowned slightly upon hearing that, and walked out of the room. About half an hour later a nurse returned and started removing the tubes and other equipment attached to me. She told me I was now stable and the doctor was releasing me. Seeing what was happening, my supervisor got the emergency room doctor off to the side and told him who I really was.

To make a very long story short, the situation worked out for the best, at least in the long run. Most people experiencing the kind of symptoms that I was having are asked to spend at least three days in the hospital. But at that particular hospital, once the doctors discovered I was supposedly indigent, they discharged me immediately. I even had to beg them to give me a written statement saying I was indigent so I could qualify for a few four-dollar medications at Walmart.

The situation changed again when Thompson told the doctor who I really was. Once the hospital administrators learned my real identity, they panicked. Because I had first given them a false name, their response was to immediately contact their legal department. Meanwhile, since the hospital had already begun the paperwork to release me, they refused to re-admit me, even though they now knew my real identity. Instead, they discharged me to Thompson, who ended up driving me to my home hospital in southeast Ohio. The doctors there immediately asked for my records from the first hospital, and I had to tell them that the records were under my alias name. A few of the doctors at my home hospital knew what I did for a living, but it still caused confusion over my health records. From that day forward, getting copies of my health records has been a nightmare.

That entire hospital incident made me feel like less than a human being. I experienced total discrimination at the first hospital that treated me, something I had never felt before in my life. Before the doctors discovered that "Bill Stone" didn't have health insurance, the entire range of hospital facilities had been open to me. But once they thought "Bill Stone" was uninsured, their actions and attitudes changed completely. The hospital's policy stated that if an uninsured patient was stable, he or she was to be discharged immediately. The doctors and nurses followed that policy to the letter, clearly more concerned about their legal liabilities than my immediate health. It all made me feel close to worthless as a person. Having gone through that experience, I now have a much greater appreciation for indigent people and what they go through in their lives when it comes to health care.

As I was lying there on the gurney in the emergency room, I was feeling truly alone. My feelings must have been similar to those of a soldier wounded in battle in a foreign country, possibly dying with no family to comfort him, no mom, dad, or spouse at his bedside. "So this is how it feels to die," I thought. I didn't die, obviously, but at the time I didn't know that I wouldn't. All I knew for sure was that my heart was pounding out of control and I was truly scared.

The whole experience was very disturbing and unsettling. To this day, I still think about those hours I spent in the hospital that early morning, helpless and scared. I knew I was supposed to be the big, bad undercover wildlife officer, the guy who wasn't afraid of anything. But that morning, I wanted the company of someone close to me, someone from my family. Except for my undercover partner and my supervisor, I was alone, and I didn't want to die like that.

––––

My heart attack marked the beginning of the end of Operation Take 'Em and the end of my eighteen-year career as an undercover wildlife officer. As a result of my heart problems, my doctors strongly suggested that I retire from undercover work on a medical disability. They said if I continued working in the stressful environment of undercover operations, I would likely be back in their offices within a year—if my heart continued beating even that long. They said my heart was feeling the stress of having excessive amounts of adrenaline flowing through it for the past eighteen years, obviously not a good thing. I knew then that my undercover career was growing short. I eventually retired from the Ohio Department of Natural Resources, Division of Wildlife, on a medical disability in 2008.

My undercover partner, Shaun, told the poachers, including members of the DMC Club, about my heart attack. He also told them that I had gone back to convalesce with my extended family in West Virginia, which is where I had told them I was from. Members of the group would telephone me from time to time and ask how I was doing. As a result, during the course of that summer, I learned one last valuable lesson about undercover work.

My son and daughter in-law had just had a baby, born at a hospital in Huntington, West Virginia. A woman I was dating asked me the name of the hospital where my grandson had been born, and when I told her, she went online to look up the baby on the hospital's Web site. Since she knew me as Bill Stone, she searched for the baby as Tyson Stone, and what came back in the online search was, "Tyson S., child of Cliff S. and Tiffany S." Thankfully, the hospital Web site didn't give their full last name of Stewart, my real last name, but only the initial S. When I asked my woman friend how she had found that information, she said, "It's easy. I just went online to the hospital Web site and typed in the name of the baby." So I learned not to tell anyone I knew while working undercover what hospital I was in, for fear they might discover that my real last name was Stewart, not Stone. Instead, I told them I was staying with my daughter in West Virginia, and that she didn't have a landline telephone. "If you wanna call me," I told them, "just call my cell phone."

My heart attack had occurred early in the week of the Ohio season for hunting deer by gun, a time I should have been spending hunting with the poachers. Instead, Shaun and Mike had to pick up the slack for me. They spent some time hunting with the group of poachers that week, but weren't able to add much to the information and evidence we had already gathered on the group. As a result, the decision was made to wind down Operation Take 'Em.

About that same time, Myron Hamilton's father passed away unexpectedly. Hamilton called me, saying he was feeling pretty low about his father's death, and asked me if I felt well enough to drive to his house for a visit. He said he needed someone to talk to, a close friend. He even suggested coming to visit me if I didn't feel up to driving, a notion I didn't encourage. He also offered to pay for me to visit a heart specialist in Cincinnati, if I needed one. I was surprised. Apparently, he felt much closer to me than I'd realized. Toward the end of my career, I had built up a mental wall between me and the people I was investigating. I didn't let myself get as close to people psychologically as I had during my earlier cases. Now, though, I genuinely felt sad for Hamilton that his father had passed away. My dad had cancer at the time, so I could relate to some of what Hamilton was going through.

The need to confront my own problems helped me stay detached, however. I now had serious health issues of my own to deal with, leaving me little time to think about the bad guys. It also helped that I was living elsewhere, separated from them. This gave me space and time to reflect upon what had happened.

Had I still been involved with the investigation when Hamilton's dad died, I probably would have been asked to be a pallbearer at the funeral. I'm glad it worked out that I didn't have to do that. My involvement at the funeral would have been hurtful to Hamilton the rest of his life when he eventually learned that a person he thought was his friend was really an undercover wildlife officer.

In anticipating the takedown of Operation Take 'Em, we had uniformed wildlife officers gather at the headquarters of Wildlife District Five in Xenia, Ohio. There we set up our command center for ending the investigation. The next day, officers seized Hamilton's truck, duck-hunting boat, and anything else that had been used in the illegal taking of waterfowl, including firearms, blinds, decoys, and duck calls. Hamilton and all his fellow members of the DMC Club, as well as other suspected poachers, were arrested and convicted of multiple violations of the wildlife laws. All told, seven of the poachers in Hamilton's ring were arrested and convicted on sixty-three charges. We had a 100 percent conviction rate. All the poachers lost their hunting privileges in Ohio for ten years or more, and the courts also assessed stiff fines and courts costs. Our takedown also netted some of the second group of poachers that gathered at the Farm bar, including Chris Hill, the bar's owner. They too were charged with several wildlife law violations.

Remember the license plate on Hamilton's truck, the one that read "Duck Mag"? Well, he waited too long the previous year to renew his license tags, and someone else in the state requested that personalized plate. Shaun and I were at Hamilton's house when he was grudgingly swapping out his old plates for the new ones. Without Hamilton noticing, we took one of the old "Duck Mag" plates and hid it in my van. After the takedown of the case, we took a photo of me holding that license plate while standing in front of a Division of Wildlife truck—a truck that had Hamilton's duck-hunting boat and trailer attached to it. Several months after the takedown, Hamilton eventually realized what had happened and was heard to comment, "Those damn undercover game wardens even took my license plate!" All told, Operation Take 'Em had lasted nearly four years, the longest undercover case of my career. A career that was now officially over. Almost. . . .

# 10

# OPERATION ENOUGH

This last undercover investigation of my professional career took place in 2005 and 2006 almost literally in my own backyard—Meigs County, Ohio—and involved neighbors of mine living only a mile from my home. And I'm talking here about my true home, not a safe house used during one of my undercover investigations. Although I did not work as an undercover officer in this case, I was deeply involved in it as the coordinator of the investigation. You'll understand why as the story unfolds.

The case began with an extended family, the Cundiffs, living just down the road from me. They were notorious in my area, but since I was always working away from home, I never was able to personally address the many complaints the Division of Wildlife received concerning particular members of the family. They had a local reputation for poaching and other skulduggery.

On one occasion, I even found a patch of marijuana plants growing near their house. I spotted the patch one night when I was 'coon hunting. Although I was not hunting on the Cundiffs' property, I noticed the plants growing so close behind their house that it was obvious who had planted them and was tending them. I hesitated to alert local law enforcement about my discovery, however, for fear the Cundiffs might suspect me of turning them in and retaliate by trying to kill some of my 'coon hounds, or worse. Nevertheless, I did turn over the GPS coordinates of the patch to the police when they were scheduled to scout the area for illegal drugs by helicopter. But from what I later heard, nothing was spotted from the air.

My concern about retaliation was real, though. While the Cundiffs may not have known that I worked undercover, they did know that I worked as a state wildlife officer—or game warden, as they called it. In fact, given their activities, "game warden" probably was one of the more polite terms they used in describing me. The Cundiffs hadn't lived in the area very long before I began receiving complaints from neighbors saying they had seen a certain truck that belonged to the family sitting where it shouldn't be, or driving slowly along the back roads at night, possibly spotlighting and shooting deer. The head of the family, Hobert Cundiff, was known for disregarding wildlife laws, and two or three of his sons were just as bad, if not worse. Keith Wood (or "Woody" as described in Operation Ego), the local state wildlife officer then assigned to that county, was also receiving complaints about the Cundiffs.

My involvement began when a neighbor called me to complain that just seconds after he had seen Travis Cundiff (one of Hobert's sons) and another man drive slowly by his house, he heard a gun go off. Since this was Ohio's deer gun hunting season, the neighbor concluded that the young men had shot at a deer from the road, so he jumped into his vehicle and followed them. When he got to where he had heard the shot, however, the two young men immediately took off in their truck.

About a week later, the Cundiffs themselves contacted me, waving me down as I drove the road. They gave me their version of the road-shooting incident, insisted they were being blamed for something they didn't do, protesting their innocence, and saying that they were tired of hearing about it from others. "A lot of the neighbors have been complaining," I responded, adding sternly, "and you know what I do for a living. . . ." I also told them about finding the marijuana plants growing behind their house while 'coon hunting.

"The patch must be my dad's," said Hobert.

There was no way I believed that. Hobert was in his forties, and he was blaming his father, who was at least in his sixties. In short, I didn't trust Hobert or any of his family, and I was not alone. Their actions had made them strongly disliked in the community.

Three or four days later, I was in my basement, getting together some gear for an extended stint undercover—I was working Operation Take 'Em at the time—when I thought I heard someone walking around outside my house. Being in the basement, I wasn't sure, but since I live alone I decided to investigate. I was carrying a pair of cowboy boots, so I took a loaded handgun and slipped it inside one of the boots before walking upstairs. I looked out one of the windows without seeing anything, so I walked quietly out onto the back porch. Just as I did so, two bearded men stepped off my front porch. I had no idea who they were, but I knew they had to be strangers, since anyone who had been to my house before would know to come to the back door, not the front. I immediately snatched my handgun out of my boots and drew down on them, using some pretty strong language in asking them who they were and what they were doing. That's when one of the men identified himself as a member of the Cundiff family.

I lowered my handgun at that point, and the guy said, "Man, you really scared us . . . ," his eyes showing white all around.

"Same here," I said. "I thought I heard something, and when you came off the front porch and I had no idea who you were, what was I supposed to think?"

As our alarm subsided on both sides, the two men started talking about the incident the neighbor had recounted, concerning the gunshot he'd heard. The men again claimed their innocence, so I told them, "Look at it this way, guys. If you didn't do anything wrong, you don't have anything to worry about. But if you did, you'll probably be hearing from Woody before long."

One of the guys asked, "Well, what can we do about this?"

"There's nothing you can do," I said. Then I assured him yet again that if he hadn't done anything illegal, he had nothing to worry about. From this little visit and conversation, it was obvious to me that they or others of their family *had* been the ones shooting from the road that night and that they were worried about the repercussions.

————

Fast forward about a year. During the raccoon hunting season that fall, I was hunting close to the road near my home one night when I saw two pickup trucks drive slowly by, trucks I recognized as belonging to the Cundiffs. The trucks had no dog boxes in the back. What, I wondered, were they doing out in the wee hours of the morning, if they weren't 'coon hunting? When I finished hunting, I loaded my dogs into the back of my own truck and drove down the road toward home. Suddenly, I came across one of the Cundiffs' trucks, parked with no one around. I stopped, got out, and listened for a few minutes to see if I could hear 'coon hounds barking, but I heard nothing. This again aroused my suspicions. What was the group up to?

Within a few minutes, I saw about half a dozen lights coming down off a nearby hill. I always carry my handgun and state wildlife officer's badge when I 'coon hunt, just in case I run across a situation like this. I walked toward the lights and stood in the dark. It was bow-hunting season for deer, and I suspected that whoever was out there may have killed a deer, untagged or in some other way illegally, and was dragging it out to the road.

When the group of men got within a few yards of me, I turned on my flashlight and identified myself. "State wildlife officer!" I said. Then I asked them what they were doing, and the father, Hobert Cundiff, said, "We seen your truck parked down the road and didn't stop to ask you what the f___ you was doing! Why you askin' us?"

Needless to say, that kind of attitude immediately fired me up. Hobert was trying to intimidate me, as he did everyone else in the community, but I was having none of it. That's how this investigation eventually became known as Operation Enough. The entire neighborhood finally had had enough of this guy and his intimidating ways and wanted something done.

I told him, "I didn't know what you were up to, I'm just curious. . . ."

"We're trackin' a damn deer," he said.

"Did you find it?" I asked.

"No. I told you we was trackin' it," he said belligerently.

"Let me tell you something, Hobert," I said, pulling out my badge and showing it to him. "I'm a state wildlife officer, and therefore since you told me you're tracking a deer, I can ask you any question I like. And on top of that, you need to have a hunting license to track a deer. Now, who shot the deer?" I was ready to fight the guy, if need be, but also knew I had to remember my professionalism and try and keep my head.

"He shot the deer," Hobert finally said, pointing to one of his sons.

I turned to the young man and said, "Okay, if you shot the deer, I need to see your hunting license and deer permit."

"I don't have them with me," the young man stammered.

"Where are they then?" I asked.

"I must have left them in my hunting coat . . . up on the hill."

I asked him where he bought his hunting license and deer permit, and he hesitated in his answer. I knew right then he was lying, that he very probably had neither.

That's when Hobert cut in again, telling his son, "Just admit you don't have a f_____ hunting license, take the ticket, and let's get out of here."

I wrote down the young man's name, address, and other personal information, then told him that Woody would be back in touch with him to issue him a court citation for hunting deer without a license and deer permit. I then left, drove down the road, and was preparing my dogs to go hunting again when Hobert and the rest of the clan drove up beside my truck. He stopped, rolled down the window, and started complaining about his son being cited.

I listened to Hobert's rant for only a few seconds before cutting him off. "Hobert," I said, "I'm going to tell you something. You know who I am, where I live, and that we're practically next-door neighbors. You know what I do for a living, and up until now I've never bothered you. But I can either be your best neighbor or your worst nightmare. And you just made that decision!"

The next day, Hobert went to see Bob Crawford, another neighbor down the road, and complained to him about me giving his son a citation for no hunting license or deer permit. Like most of the locals, Crawford, a retired sheriff's deputy from another county, had his fill of the Cundiffs, so he telephoned me once Hobert had left and said that he had all kinds of information about the Cundiff family's illegal hunting activities, and that he was ready to tell me all he knew should I want to hear it. I was on light duty at the time because of my heart attack, but I talked to my supervisor and said, "Let's do something with this information. Let's begin an undercover investigation on the Cundiffs." So, we did, and my supervisor gave me free rein to coordinate the investigation.

My first move was to interview Bob Crawford to find out exactly what he knew about the Cundiffs' poaching activities. It turned out he had actually hunted with them several times—so often, in fact, that it was like having an undercover officer already inside the group. Crawford said that once he discovered how badly the group poached, he stopped hunting with them. "And when I heard you had cited one of them," he said, "I was willing to help stop the family's poaching once and for all."

As far as I was concerned, all of this was perfect timing. I asked Crawford if he was willing to testify against the Cundiffs in court, and he said yes, he was. He also said that he and others in the community were tired of all the poaching the Cundiffs did, and concerned about its effect on wildlife populations in the area.

While interviewing Crawford, I was able to identify so many charges against the Cundiffs that we decided to put two undercover officers on this case. The icing on the cake was that Bob Crawford owned the house the Cundiffs were living in; they were buying it from him on a land contract. He also owned a vacant house immediately across the road, a place he said we could use as a safe house for our undercover officers.

Knowing this would probably be a very short investigation, we asked a uniformed wildlife officer from northeastern Ohio to act as one of the undercover officers in this case. He was a relatively young man, so we paired him with a young female officer from central Ohio, asking them to pose as a boyfriend and girlfriend who liked to deer hunt together. Bob Crawford was instructed to tell the Cundiffs he had two friends coming to stay in the house across the road from them to hunt for a few days.

In orchestrating all of this, I was meeting the undercover officers at various locations and filling them in on what they needed to do and how to go about documenting evidence. The main objective of the investigation was to accumulate enough evidence to establish probable cause and obtain a search warrant from the local courts for the Cundiff residence. We wanted entry to the house because the Cundiffs reportedly had thirty to forty mounted deer heads hanging from the walls. When the male officer arrived and was introduced to the Cundiffs by Crawford, the Cundiffs bragged about every one of those heads, telling the officer, in detail, how each deer had been killed; not one of them had been taken legally. When the female undercover officer arrived a few days later, the Cundiffs repeated their descriptions of all the illegal deer for her, only this time the officer was wearing a body wire, and the Cundiffs' confessions were recorded on audio tape.

The two undercover officers hunted with the Cundiffs for a few days during the muzzle-loader deer-hunting season, accumulating charges against members of the family. Since we hadn't planned to run this investigation long, and since we had already identified multiple previous charges, we decided to take the case down.

Just as planned, we sought and obtained a search warrant for the Cundiffs' house and proceeded to search it. In addition to the many mounted deer heads seized, we took some forty guns from the residence, as well three ATVs, illegal narcotics, and eight thousand dollars in cash. During the court trial, only one of the many deer heads seized was eventually proven to have been taken legally. All of the other deer had been poached. This investigation also yielded evidence of illegal activity at a local deer check station, which was cited in turn. All told, nine poachers were charged with fifty-nine violations of wildlife laws.

————

Despite the success of Operation Enough, the Cundiffs have not changed their behavior. Since it was concluded, another member of the Cundiff family has been arrested for illegal deer hunting. He ran from wildlife officers when first spotted, and they had to bring in a helicopter to find him hiding in the woods. Moreover, the family still lives in the same house, minus the mounted deer heads. In fact, they now own the house, since Bob Crawford was not able to legally void the land contract he had signed with them.

Unfortunately, Bob Crawford paid a price for his involvement in the investigation. His house was shot multiple times with paint balls, and his hay field damaged by vehicles intentionally driving through it. Living so close to the Cundiffs, I also suffered some repercussions from my involvement in the case. Someone shot and killed three of my 'coon hounds. I can't prove it, but I have a good idea who shot them. In addition, my mailbox was knocked over.

If there is a hero in all of this, though, it's Bob Crawford. He was not going to tolerate the Cundiff family's poaching any longer, and he was willing to put himself on the line to see it stopped. For me, the case was a tough one on which to end my career. It hit pretty close to home, causing people living just down the road—practically my next-door neighbors—to hate me, but that's how things finished up. Still, I did warn Hobert that I could either be his best neighbor or his worst nightmare. Apparently, he didn't believe me.

# 11

# TRAINING DAY: PREPARING TO GO UNDER

When I first started working undercover in wildlife law enforcement, I had virtually no formal covert training; I had to rely instead on my instincts and abilities. One talent that helped me considerably was my ability to communicate with people and quickly get them to like me. Another was my gift for "reading" people. I also had skills that worked to my advantage. Having spent much of my life in the outdoors, I knew how to handle myself in the woods. I also had a good working knowledge of hunting and fishing, so that I just naturally fit the profile for an undercover officer sought by Ohio's Department of Natural Resources, Division of Wildlife. As far as specific, formal, undercover training, though, I had very little when I first began working in the field—in fact, practically none.

Before hiring on with the Division of Wildlife, I had worked some undercover projects with the Prosecutor's Office in Ohio's Athens County, buying illegal narcotics. I also had worked some with the Ohio Department of Liquor Control. In both jobs, I worked with experienced undercover officers, and although the work didn't constitute formal undercover training, it taught me a great deal. I picked up a lot just by being in various situations with veteran undercover officers and watching how they did things in the field.

Some of my life experiences also helped me. Earlier in my life, for example, I had spent time in various bars, so I was comfortable in that environment. I also benefited from the fact that I wasn't young when I became an undercover wildlife officer; I was thirty-five years old, which gave me a measure of maturity that helped me avoid certain kinds of mistakes.

Nevertheless, despite my age, experiences, skills, and abilities, the longer I was on the job, the more I saw that I would have benefited considerably from some basic training in undercover work before I started. Such training would have saved me a lot of time, trouble, and frustration. It would have helped me cope with all the paperwork involved in accurately and professionally documenting an investigation. It also would have given me a better understanding of legal predisposition and how to predispose a suspect during a case. For new officers starting their careers today, formal training is a valuable tool, but it was a luxury I was not granted at the beginning of my career. This changed as my career progressed, however. Beginning in the early 1990s, I began attending various training schools, about one per year.

———

One of the first courses I took was a two-week session in Savannah, Georgia, offered by the U.S. Fish and Wildlife Service. About sixty undercover wildlife law enforcement officers from around the world attended. What was surprising was that these officers were expected to do their jobs using tactics ranging from simple verbal warnings all the way to deadly force.

Officers from China, for example, gave only verbal warnings to poachers for wildlife law violations, while those from some African countries regularly used deadly force to dissuade poachers. A few African countries even hired mercenaries to track down and kill wildlife poachers on sight. The mercenaries would then post photos of the dead poachers in local African villages, so that relatives of the dead men could retrieve the bodies. Talk about a poaching deterrent!

I first attended this particular training course in 1993, the first year the U.S. Fish and Wildlife Service opened it to undercover wildlife officers from foreign countries. As a result, I got to rub shoulders and share war stories with undercover officers from around the world, an invaluable experience. I doubt there has ever been as large and diverse a gathering of undercover officers before or since. The international character of the class did pose some problems, though. One issue was language. Since several officers didn't speak English, they were accompanied by translators. Another issue was the cultural differences among those attending. For example, the African officers didn't think too highly of the Asian officers. One reason for this was that when the African officers passed around rhinoceros horn in class for demonstration purposes, the Asians broke off small pieces of the horn and chewed them. Apparently, they believed that the rhino horn was an aphrodisiac and a symbol of power, but their actions offended the African officers. In fact, the African officers suspected the Asians of attending the training school for devious purposes. They believed the Asians were there to learn how the African officers operated so that they, the Asian officers, could circumvent African game laws and deal in rhino horn and other illegal African animal parts.

During the two-week course, we studied various undercover topics, including the definition of *predisposition* and how to predispose a suspect, how to document an undercover case, how to determine an operation's short- and long-term goals, the differences between short-term undercover investigations and deep-cover projects, and the uses of surveillance. We also enacted various scenarios we might encounter in the field; in one, for example, we bought and sold illegal wild animal parts, such as black-market alligator hides or elephant ivory. By the end of the course, I not only was very impressed with the quality of training I'd received, but also felt much more confident as an undercover officer.

I attended that course immediately following Operation Clanbake, my first undercover wildlife law enforcement operation. Clanbake had been strictly a matter of learning by doing for me, and I was probably lucky the poachers didn't identify me early on, or even rough up or kill me. Looking back on it now, I believe the Division of Wildlife was just as ignorant about undercover wildlife law enforcement work at that time as I was. The agency knew that for certain cases it needed the kind of intelligence and evidence only an undercover officer could provide, so it turned me loose to see what I could do.

———

About a year later, I attended another training session, this time provided by the U.S. National Intelligence Academy in Fort Lauderdale, Florida. This weeklong course provided training on covert audio and video surveillance. We studied the basic techniques of wearing body wires and learned how to hook them up and how to build our own microphones. The school also taught us how to use infrared lights for surveillance. The Ohio Division of Wildlife didn't have much of this equipment at the time, so it helped me see what equipment was available to undercover officers.

The class also covered the legal issues surrounding covert surveillance. I learned that the laws in some states prohibit officers entirely from using hidden microphones or recording voices, while others, including Ohio, allow such tactics with one-party consent, meaning that as long as one person in the conversation knew the conversation was being recorded, it was legal to do so.

Out of the twenty-four officers attending the course, I was the only wildlife officer. As a joke, the instructors had me sit in the corner of the room with potted plants around my chair. I'd peer out from between the plants from time to time, to the great amusement of the other officers.

The next year, I returned to the same school to study audio and video installation and rolling surveillance—that is, following suspects in cars and other vehicles. Advanced classes taught us how to conduct undercover surveillance in motel rooms, houses, and other stationary locations. One of our assignments was to collect video evidence of counterfeiting. In one training scenario, we were told that suspects were believed to be counterfeiting by using an office copier, and our assignment was to collect video evidence of them doing so. To pass the class and graduate, we had to install a hidden video camera and capture the necessary video evidence.

I returned for a third time the following year, when I was again the only wildlife officer in attendance; everyone else worked for the Secret Service, the U. S. Marshals, or the Department of the Treasury. There was a certain unspoken dress code at these courses that I was unaware of when I first started attending. When I want to be comfortable, I normally wear shirts without sleeves, kind of looking like the popular, stand-up comedian Larry the Cable Guy. Such attire didn't go over too well with the school's administrators, however. One instructor even asked me one day, "Do they have sleeves on shirts in Ohio?"

"Not in my neck of the woods, they don't," I responded smartly. That's when I was relegated to the corner of the room amidst the potted plants.

Despite my minority status, the class did include a wildlife law enforcement scenario among those we enacted. In this scenario, our objective was to obtain video surveillance of illegal fishing taking place along a river, so we went out and set up our hidden cameras on one side of the river, then ran a microfiber cable underwater to the recording equipment set up on the other side of the river. That had never been done before during this class, and the other students and instructors wondered how we managed to get the cable across the river. I simply took a fishing rod, cast the line across the river, then attached the microfiber cable to the fishing line and pulled it across. It was a simple solution to the problem, but it worked really well. After my demonstration, I like to think that the other students and the instructors were impressed with my ingenuity. Maybe they no longer thought of me as quite the ignorant country hick they may have previously.

————

Another training session I attended was the Midwest Covert Seminar, a three-day class held for undercover wildlife officers in the midwestern states every two years. Most of the undercover courses I had attended until then emphasized illegal narcotics. They included very little training specifically for wildlife law enforcement, so I had to adapt what I learned to my kind of work. This course, however, focused strictly on wildlife violations, which was, of course, right down my alley. This made it especially valuable.

I also attended a few undercover classes in Ohio, at the Ohio Police Officer Training Academy, but eventually I stopped attending because of who my fellow classmates from the police might know. I was afraid I might become too well known in Ohio, making my job even more difficult and dangerous than it already was.

———

When I first began attending these various training classes, I was amazed at the amount of technology available to undercover officers. In my early undercover operations, I used very little surveillance equipment, mainly because I didn't have any such equipment and wouldn't have known how to use it if I had. In Operation Clanbake, for example, I didn't use any audio or video surveillance equipment or techniques, while in Operation Redbud, my second undercover operation, I used only a small tape recorder, the kind anyone could buy at a typical electronics store. This changed after I learned what was available. The classes showed me the many ways I could use this technology in a variety of undercover situations.

My first video surveillance camera was large, almost the size of those used today by TV news crews. Not surprisingly, that didn't work too well, so I switched to a twelve-volt VCR recorder hooked up to a couple of pinhole cameras in my undercover van. That equipment was so primitive that I had to get out of the van and go around to the back of the vehicle to turn the machine on—not exactly ideal for undercover work!

As surveillance technology evolved, my equipment improved. My next step in this process was the purchase of a High-Eight recorder, using something called Z-Boxes on which to record. It was a self-contained unit, recording both audio and video, turned on by the flip of a switch. I usually mounted the switch on the steering column of my undercover van. Today, with the advent of microchips, it's unbelievable how small undercover surveillance equipment has become, literally the size of a cell phone or even smaller. The lens of a pinhole camera is now exactly that, the size of a pinhole.

Over the course of my career, the audio and video surveillance equipment used by the Division of Wildlife advanced light years, from simple still cameras and large, unwieldy video recorders to the minute high-tech equipment employed today. It would take a very well-trained eye to detect any of this new, state-of-the-art surveillance equipment, even if a poacher suspected its presence.

———

Another topic covered in the formal training I received was the handling of informants, witting, unwitting, and confidential. Most informants in wildlife law enforcement cases are motivated by revenge; they've been involved with a group of poachers, have for some reason fallen out with the group, and want to get even. A *witting* or *knowing informant* is someone who knows the identity of the undercover officer. An *unwitting informant* does not know, but provides information to an undercover officer through a third party. A *confidential informant* provides information about a case anonymously.

The advantage of using an informant (especially a witting or knowing informant) to help crack a case is that the informant can save you time and money. It may take you a year or more to infiltrate a group of poachers on your own, but a knowing informant can get you inside a group within days or weeks. The disadvantage of using a knowing informant is that since he is playing both sides of the fence, he could turn on you at any time. Over my career, I used a knowing informant twice: once during Operation Clanbake and again during Operation Stir-fry. I used unwitting informants—people who fed information to my supervisor, who then relayed the information to me—many times. The advantage of using an unwitting informant is that his ignorance of your identity provides one more layer of protection between you and the bad guys. Not surprisingly, I preferred working with unwitting informants.

———

I also attended training classes on firearms, edged weapons (mainly knives), and the use of deadly force by hand. The use of deadly force in hand-to-hand fighting is rarely taught to uniformed law enforcement officers, because they usually have some sort of weapon with them: chemical mace, a baton, a stun gun, or a sidearm, for example. Because of the nature of their job, however, undercover officers often carry no weapons, a condition known as "going sterile."

When one undercover officer asks another, "Are you sterile?" it has nothing to do with the ability to reproduce sexually. The question means, "Are you carrying a gun or any other weapon?" If you aren't, you have to know how to defend yourself if a gun or other weapon is pulled on you. Can you take the gun away from the person pointing it at you? If not, can you incapacitate or even kill that individual, using only your hands, arms, legs, and feet as weapons? Training in unarmed combat is *very* intense. It taught me that it was possible, almost easy, to kill someone using only my body. The trick is to regularly practice these techniques, so that if you ever need them you perform them quickly and instinctively, the moves becoming second nature.

Using natural pressure points on the body to control a person can be very effective, for example. If you need to incapacitate a person, one effective technique is to hit him on both ears simultaneously with the flat of your hands, breaking his ear drums. This involves a violent strike on both sides of his head. Popping out an eyeball out with your thumb will likewise incapacitate an opponent. Other moves are potentially lethal. Striking the front of a person's throat, for example, can collapse his windpipe, while an upward thrust with the heel of your hand to someone's nose, if done correctly, can drive the bones of his nose up into his brain, killing him instantly. And when I talk about such techniques, I'm talking about doing them with all the force you have in your body. You can't employ these techniques half-heartedly and get the expected results. In class, we practiced on mannequins that registered the force used against them. This allowed us to administer a violent strike and learn firsthand what it took to incapacitate or kill someone.

Again, these techniques are not in the force continuum (that is, the range of force you can apply, from minimal to maximum) usually taught to uniformed law enforcement officers. Uniformed officers use only the force necessary to stop an aggressive person. Undercover officers, however, may not have the option of merely stopping an opponent; it may be a matter of kill or be killed. If you are "going sterile"—that is, carrying no weapons—you may have to make a life-and-death decision within seconds to save your own life.

Thanks to my edged-weapons training, I always carried at least one boot knife and knew how to use it—how to cut in a knife fight. To incapacitate an attacker, we were trained to cut his Achilles tendon at the back of the foot, making it difficult for him to walk or run. If we needed deadly force, we learned to cut the vital areas of a person's body, such as the arteries under the arms, in the inside of the legs, or in the throat. Another technique is to drive the knife blade down into the top of a person's shoulder, piercing the heart.

Again, you wouldn't use these techniques in normal law enforcement work, but a person working undercover, often isolated with several bad guys, needs to be ready for anything. Our instructors in these classes were careful to warn us not to share this potentially deadly information with uniformed officers, though, since they aren't part of their force continuum. Not surprisingly, many of our instructors for this type of lethal training were retired military personnel.

Since I always felt I could handle myself in a fight, I was comfortable learning these techniques. Thankfully, I never had to use any of them during my career. I'm not a small man, so my size probably worked in my favor many times, intimidating some poachers and helping me to avoid fights. My confidence and the way I carried myself no doubt helped, too—and my knowledge of these techniques and readiness to use them if necessary was part of the basis for that assurance. Since I constantly practiced the self-defense techniques just described, I had the mental and physical confidence that if someone pulled a gun on me I could take it away from him without getting shot.

I often demonstrated this as a student in our own Division of Wildlife law enforcement training scenarios. The first thing I'd do was take the gun from the bad guy, a strategy that won me occasional compliments from our training officers but could also frustrate them. In one scenario, for instance, I was asked to stand before a closed curtain in a room and respond to the threatening situation presented when the curtain opened. The only people present were the actors portraying the bad guys, me, and the critiquing officer. I had no backup officer. On one occasion, the curtain opened to reveal a bad guy standing in front of me and pointing a handgun at me. I immediately hit him in the chin with my fist, then wrestled him to the ground and took the gun away from him. At that point the training officer blew his whistle, stopping the scenario.

"I'm glad to see someone who would finally actually fight," the actor said, rubbing his chin. I helped him up and brushed him off.

But the training officer made me repeat the scenario, as apparently there was more to the situation that I never got to because I had simply disarmed the guy. In fact, my reaction demonstrates the difference between the way an undercover officer is trained to respond to a situation and the way a uniformed officer might react. When I repeated the scenario, I again responded by applying techniques from the high end of the force continuum. I went straight for my gun, bypassing using the baton and chemical mace hanging from my belt, and put the bad guy on the ground. I chose to go for my gun because I didn't carry the other equipment in the field. These reactions didn't win me points with that particular training officer, who again blew his whistle to stop the scenario, saying I couldn't do that. "You have to repeat the scenario again, R.T.," he said, "only this time use the various steps in the force continuum."

The third time, I used my baton as I was supposed to, but the actor then pulled a handgun on me. This made me mad. I took the gun from him, put the actor on the ground, and was about ready to "shoot" him when the training officer blew his whistle yet again.

"Man, you undercover guys are different," he finally said, shaking his head. "We forgot about that when we designed these scenarios. . . ."

As I said, uniformed officers and undercover officers are trained to react very differently to the same threat. After all, uniformed officers are more likely to have backup available; their uniforms themselves may provide some protection, by causing the bad guy to hesitate. As I have already explained, it's different for undercover officers. They are more likely to be alone and unarmed, perhaps facing more than one bad guy.

In each scenario just described, the bottom line in those training scenarios is that I won. Had it been a real-life situation, I would have survived the threat. Law enforcement officers have a saying that I've always remembered: "It's better to be tried by twelve than carried by six." I always told myself that if I ever found myself in a life-threatening situation, I was going to win. It was my mindset to do whatever I had to do to survive.

Here's another example. If a man is sitting at a table with me or beside me at a bar and he pulls a gun, I have two choices: either he's going to shoot me or I'm going to take the gun away from him. Even if I'm armed, I don't have time to pull my gun and shoot since he's already got the drop on me. My best option at that point is to take the gun from him, and being able to do that requires knowing the proper technique and applying it with perfect timing. To succeed, an officer must practice constantly, so that his body reacts instantly in a real crisis. I always had that aggressive mindset. I'd practice taking a handgun from an assailant at least one or twice per month. And knowing that I could take a weapon away from an aggressor—and do it with relative ease—built my confidence and kept me thinking aggressively.

Different situations require different responses, however. If a guy is pointing a gun at you from a distance, your only option is to run or take cover. If it comes to that, and you're not armed with a gun yourself, it can get ugly. In actual life-and-death situations, you will react the way you were trained, so I always took my training very seriously, believing that the techniques I learned and the hours of practice I logged might someday save my life. I was determined that should I ever get into a physical confrontation, I would use the law enforcement techniques I'd been taught rather than revert to street fighting, since those techniques are much more effective in controlling an assailant and winning a fight.

———

Ohio's Division of Wildlife eventually became one of the forerunners in under-cover wildlife law enforcement work and training across the country, mainly because of the longevity of the agency's undercover program and because of my own experience as the Division's first undercover officer. Around the year 2000, I began teaching undercover techniques to officers from other states. Since by then I had accrued expertise and experience in nearly all phases of undercover wildlife law enforcement work, I was asked to pass on my knowledge to new officers just beginning covert work.

Officers attending our weeklong, Ohio undercover schools had their choice of basic, intermediate, or advanced classes, all of which were very intensive training. We packed a lot into the few days we had. Our training scenarios were based on actual wildlife undercover cases that had taken place throughout the United States. Sometimes we would invite undercover officers from other states to assist us as instructors in the intermediate and advanced classes.

One scenario we used in our basic undercover class grew out of a situation that I experienced in the field. While working an undercover case, I signed up for a dating service. To join, I had to fill out a fairly detailed application. I also had to pass a background check.

One of the questions on the application was, "Are you single, married, sepa-rated, divorced, or widowed?" Depending on your answer to that question, subsequent questions asked for more detailed information—information that could be searched and verified through public records. You had to answer the questions with an ink pen, so changes to an answer were obvious, and might raise a red flag to the person reviewing the questionnaire. Most people answer questions on a questionnaire in order, not bothering to look farther down the page before marking an answer. But, fortunately, I *did* look down the page before I answered, and left the question about my marriage status blank.

When the person reviewing my questionnaire asked me why I had not an-swered that question, I told her that I needed some clarification. I told her that I had had a live-in girlfriend for several years, but we were never legally mar-ried. Hearing my explanation, she said, "No problem," and marked the question "single," which meant I didn't have to answer the other questions requiring more detail. As a result, I was accepted by the dating service, answering only the few questions requiring general background information.

When we held our basic Ohio undercover training classes, each officer taking the class was expected to arrive with a solid background story supporting his or her alias, together with full, personal identification. We used many of the same questions from the dating service questionnaire I had filled out in making up our own questionnaire and then added a few of our own. When the officers arrived for the first day of class, we gave each of them an ink pen and told them to begin filling out the questionnaire. What this exercise taught them was to read the entire application first, *before* beginning to fill it out. By doing so, they could avoid providing any information that might blow their cover. Many of the students in the basic class got trapped by the questionnaire but learned from their mistake.

Once they successfully completed the questionnaire in such a way as to preserve their covers, the officers were informed of "poachers" selling illegal yellow perch and walleyes and given a scenario to infiltrate the ring. The officers were then told how they could meet the contact bad guy, played by me. We put them in this situation to see what they'd do, how they'd react. Some officers hesitated, remembering what we had taught them concerning predisposition and entrapment and wouldn't make the buy of illegal fish when first offered.

Later in the week, we taught them to always make a buy of illegal wildlife if and when one was offered. Some officers thought they had to predispose the poacher first, before making a buy, but that is not necessary. We instructed them to make the buy whenever they could and handle the predisposition later. Since our students had not placed the thought of doing anything illegal in the bad guy's mind, the defense of entrapment was not an issue; as the bad guy in this scenario, I had been the initiator, by offering to sell illegal wildlife to the undercover officers. In short, we taught our students to make the buy anytime and anyplace, without hesitation.

I enjoyed playing the bad guy in those scenarios and would always use actual bars during open business hours for setting up the initial meetings with the officers. The bar owners and patrons had no idea what we were doing. I wanted it that way, to keep the scenarios as realistic as possible.

When the officers arrived at the bar, all they had was a description of me. Since they'd never met or seen me before, they would first have to identify me, and then approach me, introduce themselves, and start to build a rapport. If they passed that part of the scenario—that is, if I thought they were believable—that's when I'd set up a time for them to meet me again and buy the illegal fish. We would also assign a surveillance team to watch the undercover officers' interactions with me. Then, later in the week, we'd critique the entire scenario in front of the class.

The officers' ultimate goal for the week was to infiltrate my group of poachers and buy as many illegal fish as possible. However, they had other duties as well. For one thing, they were required to prepare a written report of their undercover investigation, to be handed in it at the end of the week's training. We told the officers when they first arrived on Sunday that they could drink or party as much as they wanted during the week, but that their investigation report was due first thing Friday morning, no exceptions. Another thing we expected was that the officers accomplish certain tasks to earn points over the week. Each officer had to earn a certain number of points to pass the class and graduate.

———

The point-earning activities we devised for the students were designed to be difficult in different ways. One of the ways to earn points was for a small group of officers to go into a bar and keep the attention of the bar patrons for fifteen minutes—and the officers weren't allowed to just sing Happy Birthday. We did this to force the officers outside their normal comfort zones, so that by handling an uncomfortable assignment in an unfamiliar setting ultimately they would gain confidence in their own abilities. Usually, we assigned four or five officers to each team, and it was up to the team to keep the bar's attention for fifteen minutes.

Some of the teams were pretty ingenious in handling this assignment. One team sent a guy or two into the bar ahead of the rest, and these advance members told the bar patrons that they had buddies who would be arriving shortly for a bachelor party, and asked them each to make a toast to the new husband-to-be. Another ploy was to stage an argument. If there was a woman undercover officer in the group, sometimes she and a male officer would arrange to fake a quarrel in the bar, while the other officers tried to calm them down and break up the fight. Still another group tried to bum money from the bar patrons to get "bus fare home."

Another way officers could earn points was by spending a night in a homeless shelter. Again, our purpose was to put them in an unfamiliar, uncomfortable setting. To push our students into approaching strangers, we sometimes would drive down a street in a large city, choose an apartment building at random, and tell an officer that he or she had exactly fifteen minutes to talk the people living in one of the apartments into allowing the officer to come into their home and wave at us from the balcony. This helped the officers learn to talk to anyone, anywhere, and be convincing.

We had another exercise we often used to increase someone's ability to be convincing. We would pass a hat filled with notes describing different situations or topics, asking each officer to pick one. The officer then had three minutes to consider how to present the topic to the class so convincingly that class members wouldn't know whether the officer was lying or telling the truth. Only the instructors knew beforehand.

The topics offered in the hat were all intended to be embarrassing, and some were off color. We did this to get officers to think on their feet and be convincing—in other words, to lie well. A sample topic was: "What's the worst thing you've ever done on the job that your boss doesn't know about?" Usually, four or five students per class of fifteen were so convincing that the class was split as to whether they were lying or telling the truth.

There were many possible ways our students could earn points, but nearly all of them were intended to force them out of their comfort zones into new situations where they had to deal confidently or even assertively with strangers. Relatively easy ways to get points included getting up and singing a song in a karaoke bar, obtaining an autograph from a public official, or returning to the training facility after being dropped off in a large city with no money or identification. Other tasks were more challenging. One student might be asked to go to a gay bar and dance with someone of the same sex. Another might be told to go into a bar and talk someone of the opposite sex out of their underwear. We weren't asking the officer to have sex with his or her target, just to get the target to give up the underwear he or she was wearing at the time. A male officer would have to talk a woman out of her panties or bra; a female officer would have to talk a guy into giving her his boxers or briefs. Obviously, this is not something most people would do in the real world, but it did place the officer in an uncomfortable, unfamiliar situation and allow us to assess how he or she would react and perform. The officers had to be convincing to pull this one off, so to speak.

————

The classes and the various tasks for earning points were keeping our students plenty busy, yet they still had to document their activities and write their final reports. Some still tried to drink and party on their own time for the first night or two, as we had told them they were free to do, but they quickly learned that if they partied too hardy they wouldn't have time to complete their work, earn their required points, and pass the course. All of the officers were running on adrenaline from Sunday through Thursday, and by Friday they were beat and ready to go home. One of the most frequent comments we heard at the end of the weeklong course was, "I've never been through training so intense in my life, even in the military. But it was worth it. . . ."

For students in our intermediate undercover classes, we held scenarios at outpost camps. The undercover officers were assigned to live with a suspected group of poachers for several days in a wilderness setting. I would usually pose as a poacher, along with experienced officers from various states, while other instructors portrayed illegal hunting guides and outfitters.

Our students would be instructed to infiltrate our camps, gain our trust, and gather information on any illegal hunting or fishing activities they observed. And they had to do all of this, of course, without tipping their hand. Meanwhile, we training officers were trying to break their cover or provoke them into screwing up in any number of ways. At the end of the week, each group of students was required to explain, in front of the class, how they had infiltrated their ring of poachers and to present any evidence they had gathered.

Some groups were very good, gathering information from me so cleverly that I had no idea how they obtained it. One group of trainees, for example, quietly got up in the middle of the night, while we "poachers" were asleep, and found illegal bear carcasses we had hidden. They also memorized hunting license numbers and serial numbers on guns they saw only once. Very impressive.

One day, I took my students across state lines. We had already discussed in class the differences in the laws of various states, identifying which states allow undercover officers to record conversations and which don't. So, posing as a poacher, I took them across the Ohio-Pennsylvania border, knowing all the time that they probably had a hidden tape recorder running, but also knowing that they wouldn't be able to use what I said in Pennsylvania in a court of law.

For students in our advanced training course, we offered classes in the technical aspects of audio and video surveillance. These were basically electronics nerd classes, but our students woud need the information they offered in order to handle the technical aspects of their job.

―――

Out of each basic training class we held, two or three students would discover that undercover work was not for them. "It wasn't what I expected . . . ," most of these would say. Some of them said they weren't raised to lie. Others couldn't bring themselves to perform actions that bordered on the unethical. "Undercover work is just not for me," they'd say and simply pack up their belongings and go home.

We didn't regard such outcomes as failures, though. Our courses deliberately put the students in situations they found uncomfortable in order to stretch them mentally. After all, I knew from years of personal experience that these officers would often encounter such situations in the field; we were trying to prepare them for that eventuality. Given these aims, it was good that the training weeded people out. It was much better that they discovered the realities of undercover wildlife work during training rather than in the field, when their discomfort or unwillingness to do what was necessary could get them or their partners hurt or killed.

For instance, if I had to go into a gay bar and dance with someone of the same sex, I wouldn't have a bit of trouble doing that. It would be no big deal for me. But some people just can't handle that kind of thing mentally. They freak out at the very thought of it. I tried to explain to the officers that going into a gay bar didn't make them gay, any more than going into McDonalds made them a hamburger. But some people's personalities or beliefs just wouldn't allow them to do such things.

One year we had a cowboy from North Dakota attend one of our classes, and initially I thought he would not do well in such a situation. In reality, though, he surprised and impressed us all. He not only danced with someone of the same sex at a gay bar, he actually took the guy in his arms at one point and dipped him. I would never have dreamed that this officer could pull that off, but he did. It just goes to show that you don't know how people will react until they are actually confronted with a specific situation.

When an undercover officer encounters a stressful situation, he has to be able to play the part. He has to be an actor. He has to be able to separate his actions on the job from his preferences as a private person. He has to be willing and able to do things professionally that he wouldn't do on his own time—and do them convincingly. He has to be able to mentally change into his poacher persona, whoever that might be.

Personally, I never found that transition difficult, but some officers do, and those people usually aren't cut out to be undercover officers. I had no trouble talking to strangers. Charming people I didn't really like into liking me became second nature. I even found I could shoot animals illegally if that was what it took to get the evidence I needed. The only thing that I really had trouble doing was singing or playing music in front of a group. I couldn't play a tune on the radio if my life depended on it, let along carry a tune with my voice.

On the final day of all of our Ohio undercover courses, we always ended by playing a certain country song for the officers, popular at the time. It was "Whiskey for My Men, Beer for My Horses," sung by Toby Keith and Willie

Nelson. I was always the instructor who played that song for the officers on a CD player. I'd then tell them the following:

"Ladies and gentlemen, at some point in the future, when you're working an undercover operation and things aren't going well or you're feeling down or alone for some reason, play that song. And whenever you do, remember your fellow undercover officers, knowing that somewhere, sometime there is likely another officer feeling the same way you are. And that song will help you persevere and make it through another day on the job."

I told the officers they could even play the song while sitting around with their suspects. The poachers would have no idea of the hidden meaning behind it, while hearing the song just might help the undercover officers make it through one more tough day undercover.

———

Later in my career, another of my responsibilities was breaking in new field officers assigned to Ohio's Covert Investigations Unit. For those officers that I knew lacked previous undercover training, the first thing I did was take them somewhere they would find uncomfortable, such as a bar or a strip club, to see how they handled themselves in a stressful, possibly unfamiliar situation.

The new officer's reactions told me how much I would have to worry about him or her in the field, or, in other words, how much veteran officers would have to "babysit" the new recruit. Those first few experiences I gave the new officers told me a lot about them. Some people can adjust to almost any situation and some cannot, and their reactions very quickly helped me separate the one kind from the other. Time after time, I found that officers who were uncomfortable in a controlled stressful situation were usually very uncomfortable in a similarly stressful situation with actual bad guys and probably would make a mistake or screw up while undercover.

I remember taking one of our new male undercover officers to his first strip club, and he was very unnerved by the experience. In fact, what he saw going on inside that establishment nearly blew his mind. Not only did he encounter the expected nudity and hard drinking, but some of the patrons were snorting cocaine and using other illegal drugs. The new officer was worried about the crimes he was witnessing and questioned if we should even be in such a place while "on duty."

"Just relax and enjoy the show," I told him, but he couldn't. Once he was in the field, I wasn't surprised to learn that this officer did screw up a time or two.

Moreover, after about a year of undercover work, he finally decided it wasn't for him.

By contrast, I took a new female undercover officer to the same strip club, and she handled the experience very well. What she witnessed inside the club didn't faze her in the least.

Sometimes an officer is able to overcome initial discomfort. One particular new male officer I worked with on his first case seemed so uncomfortable that his eyeballs always looked as if they were about to pop out of his head. The stress and anxiety of being undercover were obviously affecting him. He even admitted to me there were times during the investigation when he had to walk up the hill behind our safe house and have a serious talk with himself just to stay in the right frame of mind to continue the covert project. He was so unsure of himself and his abilities that it constantly worked on him. Eventually, though, he attended an intense, formal undercover training class in Canada and returned to his job in Ohio with much more confidence.

Developing a level of comfort and confidence aren't the only skills an under-cover investigator needs for success; he or she also has to learn how to fit in with the suspects. Back in the seventies and eighties, you could often identify an undercover narcotics officer because he usually wore an olive-green, military field jacket from the Vietnam era. And you could usually spot an undercover liquor agent because he generally wore a Carhartt work coat. Conforming to stereotypes can be disastrous for someone working undercover. Those officers thought they were blending in with the group of bad guys they were trying to infiltrate, but instead they stood out as cops. If you really want to blend in, you must be observant and flexible.

The first time I'd walk into a bar when I was working undercover, I'd quickly look to see what most of the patrons were drinking, and then order the same myself. What you didn't want to do first thing through the door was order something radically different. If most of the guys were drinking Miller Lite or Coors beer, for instance, and you ordered an Amber, the bar regulars would know you weren't one of them.

Dressing for undercover work requires similar flexibility, and it helps to have good intelligence about a case before you make your approach. Such intelligence will probably tell you the caliber or class of people you'll be dealing with and give you a sense of the community in which they operate. Obviously, you should dress like your targets do. If you're trying to connect with a group of poachers that have beards and long hair, you're not going to try and infiltrate the group wearing a military style, high-and-tight haircut. If, however, you're going after upper-middle-class poachers who are usually well groomed, a high-and-tight hairstyle might not be too far off the mark.

Similarly, if you plan to portray a dealer or seller of illegal wildlife, you need to dress as if you have money. In my eighteen-year career, I dealt with nearly all classes of people, from the lowest of the lowlifes to affluent, upper-middle-class poachers. And in each case, I had to adjust my dress and demeanor to blend in with that particular group. You must convince the people you're rubbing shoulders with—both consciously and subconsciously—that you are on the same economic level they are, neither below them nor above them.

Another thing I always told new undercover officers was to avoid wearing much jewelry, since jewelry can reveal too much information about an officer. It is better not to reveal any of your real affiliations, even ones that might not seem important. "Just don't do it," I'd tell new officers. "It will make your life as an undercover officer much easier if you don't." And since jewelry can symbolize affiliations, officers should be careful about what jewelry they wear. If you are a Mason and wear a Masonic ring, for example, its significance might be recognized by one of the suspects. If even one of them was also a Mason, he might try to use that link between you to seek certain favors. Likewise, wearing a cross might identify you as Catholic, or wearing a wedding ring might reveal that you are married.

I would also advise the new officers to have a ready explanation for any jewelry they *did* wear. To return to the example of the wedding ring, if a married officer feels he should continue to wear his wedding ring during an investigation, he needs to keep in mind that the suspects he is targeting may be curious about his wife, and he might have to produce a "spouse" for them to see. "If you have to wear your wedding ring," I would tell new officers, "wear it on a chain around your neck, out of sight under your shirt." That way, if a suspect does see the ring, the officer can claim to be a widower or widow who is wearing the ring as a memorial. Undercover officers must always be thinking ahead about how to answer even the smallest question from a suspect. Slipping up on even the smallest of details can raise suspicion.

All that said, every undercover officer eventually develops his own style of dress, a style he feels comfortable wearing. My own trademark was wearing a white cowboy hat. That came to be my signature look and seemed adaptable to most of the groups I was trying to infiltrate. But wearing a cowboy hat was nothing new or unusual for me. I'd worn one most of my adult life, even before becoming a wildlife officer. Although some officers may not be able to pull off such a trademark look, my hat worked for me and the persona I was trying to project.

Was I ever underdressed for a particular undercover investigation? The short answer is yes. I believe that I showed up underdressed at the beginning of Operation Cornerstone, the investigation into the poaching of yellow perch in northeastern Ohio. There were two types of poachers operating in that area. The first type consisted of young guys who didn't have much money and so didn't dress too well. But the second type consisted of older men who had money and dressed accordingly. I showed up for that operation straight from working other cases in which I was dealing with low-class poachers, and my clothes just didn't fit in with those of the new group. To do my job effectively, I had to quickly elevate my clothes—and my mindset, as well. I don't think I've ever shown up to begin a case overdressed.

Most officers undertake an extreme makeover when they first begin to work undercover, trying to change their outward appearance as dramatically as possible, although the extent of the change depends in part on how long the officer has worked in uniform or as a civilian. A dramatic change in outward appearance often helps the new officer adopt the mindset of his new persona more quickly and completely. Once an officer has accomplished that transition—and it may take years—he gains a certain self-confidence, and outward appearance is no longer all that critical. At that point, it's how he handles himself while with the bad guys that really sells the lie. There are all kinds of people, especially in America, and they all dress somewhat differently, even within their own social or cultural group. So an officer needs to be aware of his outward appearance and how he dresses without obsessing over it.

Especially at the beginning, details can be important. When a new undercover officer would first arrive to work with me, I'd always ask him to slowly turn around so that I could take a look at his clothing. This may have seemed an odd request to the newbie, but I was looking for details in his dress that might tip his hand to the bad guys and flag him as a wildlife officer.

Wearing green boots, for instance, was always a no-no: only wildlife officers wear green boots. A wide, black uniform belt was also a giveaway and needed to be replaced. Many uniformed wildlife officers like wearing green boots and a black uniform belt with their street clothes on their days off. They think they are out of uniform. But to the average citizen, and even more to a seasoned poacher, those small details shout, "Cop! Cop!"

I once had a group of poachers challenge my identity over a pair of binoculars. They were expensive Steiner binoculars, coated with green rubber to help make them waterproof. They were my own personal binoculars, which I had purchased years before coming to work for the Division of Wildlife. But the bad guys saw them and said, "All game wardens have them green binoculars . . . You ain't a game warden, are ya?" I talked my way out of the situation, but it was a close call. That episode made me pay closer attention to the details of my dress and of the personal equipment I brought along on investigations. You just never know what kinds of things people are going to notice, so the more you can distance yourself from *anything* that could tip someone off as to your real identity as an undercover officer, the better. An undercover officer should scrutinize even small items, such as pens, key chains, and refrigerator magnets, to make sure they don't say Division of Wildlife, Fraternal Order of Police, or something similar. If I was working an undercover case and left to spend a few days at home, for instance, I'd tell my undercover partner when I came back, "Hey, go sterilize my truck, will you?" That meant he was to look over my truck from top to bottom, removing anything that might identify me as a law enforcement officer. And despite my experience, sometimes my partner would find items that I'd missed. It might be something I'd left by mistake or a small item my spouse or kids had inadvertently put there. My partner and I would search each other's vehicles, as you are more likely to spot something out of context in someone else's vehicle than in your own.

Here's an example of how a small thing can trip up an undercover officer. During one of the undercover training courses I attended with the U. S. Fish and Wildlife Service, I was put on a team with two officers from Africa. During the first part of the class, we were given some paperwork to fill out and handed an ink pen that said U. S. Fish and Wildlife Service on it. After completing the paperwork, one of the African officers put his pen in his front shirt pocket. During the mock undercover investigation scenario that followed later in the week, a "bad guy" actor noticed the pen and pulled it from the officer's shirt pocket.

"What's this?" he asked, reading the writing on the pen. "Are you guys cops?"

Thinking quickly, I said, "Cops? Hell, no, we ain't cops. They gave my friend here that pen when he came through customs at the airport."

I had no idea where that lie came from, but it seemed I was able to come up with them in an instant, time and again during my career. The instructors were so impressed that they even commented on my quick thinking later in the week, in front of the class. The point is that when you're undercover, little things—details—can generate suspicion, possibly blow your cover, and maybe even get you killed. The key is to have a logical explanation for everything you have and everything you do. And don't hesitate to tell your cover story if questioned. You don't want to seem to be trying to cover up something by hesitating to speak or by being evasive.

But I better stop now. I've most likely already given away too many trade secrets as it is.

# 12

# LIVING THE LIE: SOME FINAL THOUGHTS

The ultimate goal of any wildlife law enforcement program is to deter poaching, but some hardened poachers are not deterred by the presence of a uniformed officer. If they are commercializing wildlife—selling the illegally taken wild animals for profit—they regard the occasional conviction for a minor violation as just the cost of doing business. It is to catch poachers of this kind that undercover wildlife conservation officers are unleashed.

Several preliminary steps must be completed before an undercover investigation is authorized. After a state or federal wildlife agency receives a formal request for an investigation—usually generated by a uniformed field officer or complaints from members of the public—the agency reviews the request, asking the following questions:

- What effects are these law violations having on wildlife populations?
- Is commercialization of wildlife taking place, and if so, to what extent?
- How long will this particular undercover investigation take and what will it cost?
- What will be the objectives and goals of the investigation?

Once these four questions are answered, the agency then decides whether or not to place one or more officers undercover.

Undercover wildlife investigations vary in duration from a few months to several years, and may involve anything from simple surveillance to gather intelligence to the deep-cover penetration of poaching rings. Since any undercover operation can be dangerous, though, officer protection and safety is always the number one priority and concern.

Did I ever believe I was in danger of exposure, of being "made," while working undercover? Certainly I did. In fact, I was questioned by poachers during every undercover operation I was involved with. I think it's only human nature for people breaking the law to be suspicious of strangers.

More than once, when I was asking too many questions, poachers would ask me directly, "What are you, some kinda game warden or something?" One time, I deflected the question by leaning forward and saying, "Yeah, and speak right into this microphone under my shirt, will you? I'm taping this conversation." Well, all the other poachers sitting at the table with us laughed at that, but the joke was on them. I really *was* taping their conversation.

As you'll recall, when I was working Operation Redbud, a young man identified me the very first day I met the poachers, yet I convinced them the young man was mistaken. He kept insisting he knew my real identity, but the group of poachers wouldn't believe him. That was their downfall. During Operation Clanbake, I joked regularly with the poachers about being a game warden.

Undercover officers need a range of personal qualities and skills to work effectively. In addition to being convincing, an undercover officer has to be "hungry," meaning he or she must have a strong desire—almost a compulsion—to work undercover. The job is so demanding that it takes total commitment; a halfhearted effort just won't cut it. An officer also must be able to think on his feet and possess the ability to read people. He must be able to talk to most anyone about most anything. And he has to have a little knowledge of just about everything, so that he can blend in and adapt to nearly any situation or setting.

An effective undercover wildlife officer also needs good woods sense—that is, experience in the natural world and skill at hunting and fishing. If a suspect has been poaching for years, he has this quality, and he can tell pretty quickly if you do, too. Officers also must be self-sufficient. Most of the time you're working on your own, and if you get into trouble, you cannot expect backup anytime soon.

As far as penetrating poaching rings, time and patience are the two keys to undercover work. Each group of poachers is different, and getting inside depends on the nature of that group and how it operates. Sometimes I used a confidential informant to introduce me to the gang, since a good informant can do for you in just a few days what you might need months to accomplish on your own. As I stated earlier, though, this can be dangerous because the informant knows you're an officer and may change his mind at any time and blow your cover.

If you don't have a confidential informant, you must "go cold turkey"—that is, work your way into a ring of poachers on your own. In this situation, you do whatever you have to do to get inside. You might remember that in Operation River Sweep, for example, I joined the local YMCA because two of the poachers worked there, while in Operation Redbud, since the hub of that poaching ring was a local bar, all I had to do was show up regularly at the bar and get to know my fellow patrons. In Operation Clanbake, the poachers liked to socialize amongst themselves, so I got myself invited to their weekend parties.

Once you have infiltrated a group of poachers, the way you conduct the investigation and collect evidence is vital to your chance of success. If you're posing as a poacher, you've got to make it look like you poach. When I could, I'd try and do so without actually killing wildlife, although this can get tricky. For instance, if I was out with a group of poachers at night spotlighting and shooting deer from a vehicle and my turn came to shoot, I'd often intentionally miss the deer. Sooner or later, though, I'd have to show up with some illegal game, so that's when we'd stage events. We would put in a request to our uniformed officers to supply a deer or other wild animal, and when they showed up with game that had been legally killed, I'd take the animals to the poachers and brag that I'd killed them illegally the night before. That kind of act is very convincing, and quickly builds credibility with poachers. Of course, they have no idea they are being set up.

Although undercover officers often use special equipment, such as hidden tape recorders, video cameras, and still cameras, to collect evidence, sometimes they have to improvise, and things can get very low-tech. I've had to write the serial numbers of guns in the mud along the side of a road because I didn't have a pencil and paper handy, returning later to record the numbers. I've also used my finger to write such firearm serial numbers in the dust on my vehicle's dashboard.

Stress, loneliness, and isolation are the enemies of the undercover officer. I've often been asked how to handle the constant pressure of long stints undercover. My answer is that occasionally you have to get away from your suspects and find a way to relieve the stress. In my case, 'coon hunting was my escape. Being alone in the woods with my dogs allowed me to relax.

How each officer does this varies, but all need to find such a safety valve. If you don't relieve the accumulating stress from time to time, you can actually forget the real world and start to become the fictitious personality you are portraying. There is such a thing as getting too far under. I've experienced it. Many an undercover officer has fallen into the life of crime he or she was supposed to be fighting.

Undercover work presents special challenges if an officer is married. A short trip home during a long undercover operation can be tough on both the officer and that officer's spouse. My ex-wife could testify to that. It's difficult for an undercover officer to switch gears overnight. For a time when I'd first arrive home, I'd be moody, irritable, and just plain hard to live with. Unfortunately, undercover work put so much stress on my marriage that my wife and I eventually divorced, and such an outcome is not uncommon; my supervisor, Kevin O'Dell, likewise lost his wife to divorce. In fact, statistics confirm that a very high proportion of married officers working in all types of covert law enforcement work—wildlife or otherwise—eventually end up divorced. Undercover work is tough on a marriage because you're forced to live a double life, a life of lies when you're working and a normal life when you're at home.

Imagine living every day telling and living lies, always being worried that someone will discover the truth about you. Then imagine going home and being expected to instantly turn all of that off and resume ordinary life. Psychologically, it just doesn't work that way—or at least, it doesn't work that way quickly. A person can't change his demeanor that fast. It takes time. An officer breaking cover is very much like a soldier returning from combat and being expected to resume a normal life as soon as he arrives home. Undercover officers experience great stress, both short-term and long-term, which is why the average undercover career is so short. Today, most law enforcement agencies place officers undercover for no longer than three to five years. Unfortunately, though, they still do very little, if anything, to prepare the spouses of undercover officers for what to expect from their husband or wife.

I worked undercover for eighteen years, so the stress of the job just kept accumulating. As my career progressed, I found myself spending more and more time away from home. I simply didn't want to return to reality. I was having a good time working, basically living my life with no constraints. As I said, you can't turn off how you've been living in a matter of minutes or even hours. It takes days, weeks, or even months to deprogram and relax your mind. So I found myself staying away from home for longer and longer periods of time. Ultimately, it cost me my marriage.

Let me describe one incident that demonstrates the problems undercover work can cause in a marriage. I remember coming home for a few days during one undercover investigation, looking and feeling pretty rough. I had grown a full beard and long hair, and my wife wanted me to go with her to her office Christmas party that evening. I really didn't want to go because I didn't know any of the people who would be at the party, and I was in no frame of mind to meet anyone new. In short, I didn't want to socialize. I just wanted to relax for a few days, kick back and decompress. At that time, my wife worked in the medical field, meeting daily with doctors, nurses, and other professional medical staff, and was well respected by these people.

I walked into that Christmas party wearing my signature white cowboy hat, and sat down at a table with my wife and several other medical professionals. One of the doctors looked at me and jokingly asked, just trying to make conversation, "Where'd you park your horse?" I was in no mood for such a comment, so I looked him square in the eye and replied in a loud voice, for all at the table to hear, "F___ you!" Everyone went quiet for several moments, and needless to say my wife was terribly embarrassed.

Things already had not been going well between my wife and me, and soon after that incident we divorced. She told me later that people at the hospital couldn't believe I'd said what I had to that doctor. But that incident shows how difficult it is to make the transition from living with bad guys to functioning in normal, everyday society. It is clear to me now that my response to the doctor was out of proportion to his comment and unfair to my wife, but it would have been perfectly appropriate in the undercover situation I had just left. Often an undercover officer doesn't realize he has failed to make the transition until it's too late.

The stresses of undercover work can have an equally harmful effect on an officer's children. For example, I didn't go to either my son's or my daughter's high-school graduation ceremonies for fear of being seen and recognized by the wrong person and jeopardizing the case I was working at the time. If you are dedicated to your work and believe in what you are doing—and you really want to catch the bad guys—you don't take chances. But can this be tough on your kids? You bet. That's why this book is dedicated to my two children.

Knowing all that is necessary to make an effective undercover wildlife officer, and all the personal problems the work can cause, makes it critical to recruit the right person for the job. State and federal agencies need to hire the best-qualified, most ethical men and women they can find, because the officers not only must endure extreme stress for long periods of time but will also face extreme temptation. Money, illicit sex, illegal drugs, and almost any other vice you can think of will be offered to them. An undercover officer is constantly rubbing elbows with the devil, and the devil may rub off if he or she isn't careful.

In my own case, given all the pressure, danger, and personal sacrifice, why did I do it? Why did I choose undercover wildlife law enforcement as my life's work? Everyone has to earn a living somehow in this world, and I chose a profession that I truly enjoyed. I loved being a wildlife officer. I was determined to help protect our wildlife resources and I believed I could do so more effectively undercover than in uniform. In looking back, I guess I did it for self-satisfaction.

My choice did have its downside, though. It cost me my marriage and hurt my children. I also saw a seamy side of life that was disturbing, to say the least. I saw so much wildlife slaughtered illegally that it sickened me. It's hard to believe what goes on in the woods and fields if you don't see it for yourself, firsthand. Some poachers seem determined to kill any animal that walks, flies, swims, or crawls. The hardcore poacher has no respect at all for wild animals or the wildlife laws enacted to protect them. To that kind of person, an animal is simply something with a dollar sign on its head, or even worse, just a temporary boost for the poacher's ego.

Much more wildlife poaching goes on than most people realize or can even imagine. Most of the poachers caught are the ones who can't keep their mouths shut, who have to brag about what they do to their buddies. Others are caught because someone they pissed off turns them in. The poachers who stay quiet about their illegal hunting are extremely difficult to catch. Fortunately, those poachers are few and far between.

Once the objectives of a covert investigation are met, the job of an undercover wildlife officer is done and he or she simply drops out of sight. It then becomes the responsibility of the uniformed officers to serve the search warrants and make the actual arrests. Later, after some well-deserved rest and relaxation, the undercover officer moves on to the next covert operation.

It takes both undercover and uniformed officers to protect North America's wildlife. Each officer plays a very specific and important role in wildlife conservation efforts. These men and women daily risk their lives to protect our natural resources and are to be commended for it. The bottom line is that when an undercover wildlife operation is successfully concluded—the bad guys having been caught, fined, and serving jail time—it feels good. Real good.

So if you ever consider stepping across the line when it comes to wildlife laws, just remember, we're out there. Catch ya later. . . .

# INDEX